The Saint Vincent Basilica
Latrobe, Pennsylvania
One Hundred Years

Edited by Kimberley A. Opatka-Metzgar

Principal Authors

Brian D. Boosel, O.S.B.
Nathan M. Cochran, O.S.B.
Philip M. Kanfush, O.S.B.
Omer U. Kline, O.S.B.

Louis G. Haas, O.S.B. (1855-1936)
Melvin C. Rupprecht, O.S.B. (1915-1974)
Quentin Schaut, O.S.B. (1899-1986)

Principal Photographers

Emil Kuhar
Charles Martin
Bill Metzger
Kimberley A. Opatka-Metzgar

Saint Vincent Archabbey Publications
Latrobe, Pennsylvania
2005

Acknowledgements

The assistance of Rev. Brian D. Boosel, O.S.B., Br. Matthias Martinez, O.S.B., and Rev. Omer U. Kline of the Saint Vincent Archabbey Archives; Sarah Yaple and Katie Hughes, Archabbey Public Relations Assistants; Dr. Holly Rine of the Saint Vincent College Department of History, and Saint Vincent College history majors Amanda Cox, Mary Hines, Douglas McIndoe, Jack Miniotis and Elizabeth Walters in researching various aspects of the Basilica's history and searching through the Archabbey's glass plate and print photograph collection has been invaluable. Thanks also to Dr. Kevin Decker of the Department of History, State University of New York College at Plattsburgh, for providing resources on architect William Schickel, as well as to Kenneth E. Anderson of Olean, New York, the architect's great-grandson for providing biographical information and the photograph of the architect. Providing valuable editorial suggestions were retired Archabbot Paul Maher, O.S.B., Rev. Omer U. Kline, O.S.B., Rev. Warren Murrman, O.S.B., Brother Nathan Cochran, O.S.B., and Bill Malloy.

Scripture texts in this work are taken from the *New American Bible with Revised New Testament and Revised Psalms* © 1991, 1986, 1970 Confraternity of Christian Doctrine, Washington, D.C., and are used by permission of the copyright owner. All rights reserved. No part of the New American Bible may be reproduced in any form without permission in writing from the copyright owner.

The Crypt, by Quentin Schaut, O.S.B., Saint Vincent Archabbey Press, 1949. © Saint Vincent Archabbey.

Saint Vincent Archabbey Church, by Melvin Clarence Rupprecht, O.S.B., was originally written in partial fulfillment of the requirements for the degree Bachelor of Arts, Saint Vincent College, Department of History, June 3, 1938. © Saint Vincent Archabbey.

St. Vincent's. Souvenir of the Consecration of the New Abbey Church, August 24, 1905, on the Fiftieth Anniversary of the elevation of St. Vincent's to an Abbey, by Louis G. Haas, O.S.B., St. Vincent's Print, 1905. © Saint Vincent Archabbey.

The Sportsman's Hall Parish, Later Named Saint Vincent, 1790-1846, by Omer U. Kline, O.S.B., was originally published by Saint Vincent Archabbey Press, Latrobe, Pennsylvania, in 1990. © Saint Vincent Archabbey.

Images © by Emil Kuhar, Rita Malloy, Chuck Martin, Bill Metzger, Kimberley A. Opatka-Metzgar, Jonathan Nakles and the Saint Vincent Archabbey Archives. Used with permission.

Text not taken from the publications listed above was written by Brian D. Boosel, O.S.B., Nathan M. Cochran, O.S.B., Philip M. Kanfush, O.S.B., and Kim Metzgar © 2005 Saint Vincent Archabbey.

Cover photo by Bill Metzger and Chuck Martin

Book design by Kimberley A. Opatka-Metzgar

All rights reserved. No part of this book may be reproduced or transmitted in any form or by any means, electronic or mechanical, including photocopying, recording, scanning or by any information storage and retrieval system without permission in writing from the publisher.

ISBN 0-9708216-6-2

Printed by Laurel Valley Graphics, Inc., Latrobe, Pennsylvania

His Holiness Pope Benedict XVI

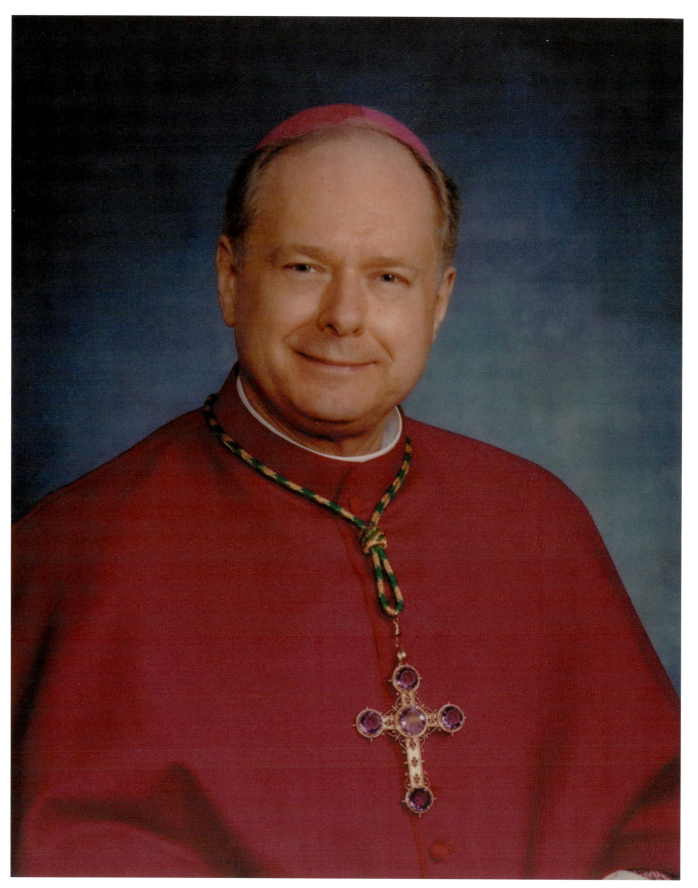

Most Reverend Lawrence E. Brandt

Introduction

What a delight to read the story of Saint Vincent Basilica and to see many the photographs that accompany the story from its beginning a hundred years ago! On behalf of all the people who love this beautiful church, I extend heartfelt gratitude to Kim Metzgar, the designer and editor of the book, and to all who contributed to its production. I was particularly pleased to learn that a number of Saint Vincent College history majors were involved in the research on various aspects of the Basilica's history.

A church building or temple is one of the richest images used in the Bible to illuminate the deepest mysteries of faith. A church is not simply a building: it possesses a sacramental character whereby it becomes the visible means of personal faith—encounters with the Divine Presence. In the liturgy for the dedication of a church, we read: "We thank you now for this house of prayer in which you bless your family as we come to you on pilgrimage."

As you read this book and when you come to the Basilica for liturgy or quiet prayer, I hope you are reminded of the biblical images that open our hearts to the reality of the Divine Presence. St. Paul tells us: "You are like a building with the apostles and prophets as the foundation and with Christ as the most important stone. Christ is the one who holds the building together and makes it grow into a holy temple for the Lord. And you are part of that building Christ has built as a place for God's own Spirit to dwell." (Ephesians 2:20-22). Perhaps the most dramatic use of the temple imagery in the entire Bible is found in the Book of Revelation: "I saw no temple in the city, for its temple is the Lord God almighty and the Lamb." (21:22). We are the "temples of the Holy Spirit who lives in us" (1Cor 6:19) and the Lord God is a temple in whom we live.

May our celebration of the hundredth anniversary of the construction and dedication of Saint Vincent Basilica deepen our faith so that in "all things God may be glorified."

+Douglas R. Nowicki, O.S.B.
Archabbot

The Basilica History Book

The Basilica has served as a symbol of the evangelization efforts of Saint Vincent founder, Benedictine Father Boniface Wimmer, for one hundred years. Although construction was begun in 1891, four years after Wimmer's death, it had been his dream to someday build a magnificent church for the monks of the Archabbey, students at the College, Seminary and Prep School, as well as parishioners of Saint Vincent Parish. Many of the events in the Basilica's history have marked the anniversary of other dates of significance in the history of Saint Vincent.

• April 16, 1890, was the centenary of the transference of the tract of land called Sportsman's Hall to Father Theodore Brouwers. He was the first resident pastor of the parish centered at Sportsman's Hall (which later became Saint Vincent) and the first Catholic priest to establish a permanent residence in western Pennsylvania. Archabbot Andrew Hintenach, Wimmer's successor, took this occasion to propose that work begin on the erection of a new church.

• Construction began in 1891 and took fourteen years. The dedication date was scheduled for August 24, 1905, the 50th anniversary of the elevation of Saint Vincent to the dignity of an abbey.

• Fifty years later, on August 22, 1955, Pope Pius XII designated the Archabbey Church a minor Basilica, to honor the spiritual and educational contributions of the Saint Vincent Benedictine Community and to commemorate the one hundredth anniversary of the elevation of the monastery to an Abbey.

Thus, it is only fitting that the centenary of the consecration of the Basilica be marked in a special way with this publication. This book pulls together much of the published history of the Basilica and the words of those who witnessed many of the significant periods in its history, including the construction and consecration.

This publication features the work of Bill Metzger and Chuck Martin, who, over a period of two years, began the painstaking process of capturing many of the elements of the Basilica's interior and exterior in richly-detailed large format photography. Their photos are accompanied by captions written by Rev. Brian D. Boosel, O.S.B., Br. Nathan Cochran, O.S.B., Rev. Philip M. Kanfush, O.S.B., and Kim Metzgar. The book follows the construction efforts from the laying of the cornerstone in 1891 to continuing renovations in 2005, in a pictorial history of the Basilica. Several works of import in the history of the Parish and the Basilica have been reprinted, including articles describing the consecration and Rev. Omer U. Kline's history of the early years of the parish, done in honor of the parish bicentennial in 1990 and long out of print. Hundreds of photographs and postcards from the Archabbey Archives were sorted through in an attempt to portray the various aspects of the Basilica through its history.

With the assistance of students from the Saint Vincent College Department of History, the uncatalogued glass plate collection in the Archabbey Archives was searched for anything relevant to the Basilica. Several unique plates were discovered, including a scale model of what the interior of the Basilica was to look like. Many of these photographs have been digitized and retouched for this publication.

Accompanying this book is a color fold-out brochure of the Basilica, which features a map by Bill Metzger. The book coordinates many of the elements in this photographic tour of the Basilica with Metzger's map, so that even from the comfort of a cozy chair miles from Latrobe, readers can be visually transported to the prayerful quietude of this sacred space.

It has been a pleasure working with the many contributors to this publication, which would not have been possible without the support of Archabbot Douglas R. Nowicki, O.S.B., and members of the Saint Vincent monastic community.

Kim Metzgar, Editor

The Basilica

On the one hundredth anniversary of the establishment of Saint Vincent Parish, April 16, 1890, Archabbot Andrew Hintenach proposed a fitting tribute to honor Saint Vincent founder Archabbot Boniface Wimmer — that work begin on construction of a new church. Plans for a new church had been discussed as much as twenty years prior to this initiative. Archabbot Boniface, who died on December 8, 1887, had always dreamed of a magnificent church. But, during Wimmer's time, his efforts were focused on establishing schools, missions and daughter abbeys to serve Roman Catholics throughout the United States.

Once the determination was made to proceed with plans for the church, Archabbot Andrew and parishioners began searching for

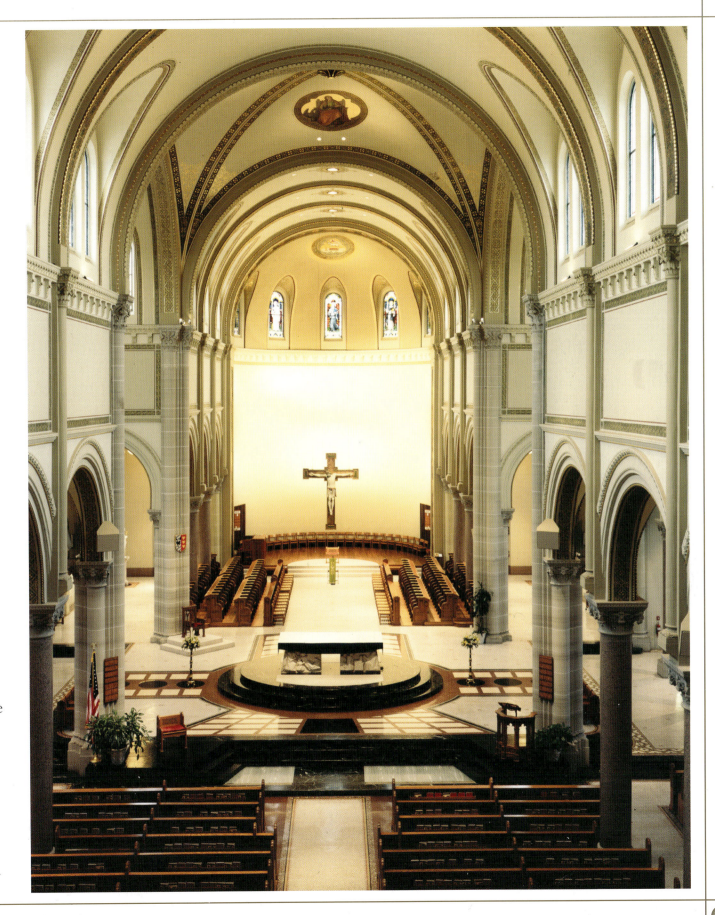

an architect. They selected J. William Schickel (1850-1907), a German immigrant who had formed William Schickel and Company in 1885. He was one of six children of Johannes and Gertruda Newman Schickel. His parents, devout Catholics, greatly influenced his work.

Schickel studied architecture at the "Ecole des Beaux Arts" in Paris. In 1870, on the day of his arrival in the United States, family lore says he found a job with Richard Morris Hunt, a prominent New York City architect. After six months he went on to work for a German architect, Henry Fernbach, until he founded his own firm in 1883, in partnership with Isaac E. Ditmars and Hugo Katka. In the mid-1890s, after the Saint Vincent project had begun, the firm changed its name to Schickel & Ditmars. The firm continued under Ditmars' name following Schickel's death in 1907.

Ecclesiastical projects made up a large part of the firm's commissions, many for religious orders and parishes of German ethnicity. Among the more than twenty churches Schickel designed were Saint Boniface Roman Catholic Church in Rochester, New York (subsequently destroyed by fire) the Church of Saint Ignatius Loyola in Manhattan; and Boston's Our Lady of Perpetual Help Parish, which is now a historical landmark. Additionally, he was commissioned to design a number of Catholic convents, seminaries and schools.

Schickel designed commercial buildings for many of the well known entrepreneurs of the time including Constable, Macy, Stern Bros., Woolworth, Astor, Ottendorfer and others, many of whom also commissioned him to design their residences. He also was considered an expert in hospital design and was responsible for designing a number of New York City area hospitals and for consulting on others.

It is estimated that William Schickel completed about 300 projects during his lifetime.

His funeral at Saint Ignatius Loyola Church, which he had designed, was attended by numerous dignitaries. He is buried in Calvary Cemetery on Long Island.

J. William Schickel

The illustration at left shows William Schickel's initial design for the Basilica, with two imposing front steeples. A lack of funds prevented the steeples' completion when construction was "finished" in 1905. In 1999, however, two spires, fifty-five feet high, topped by ten foot high crosses, were constructed in time for the celebration of the new millennium. Although these were not as intricate or lofty as Schickel's original design, the new steeples finally fulfilled the architect's original plans for the Basilica. William Schickel's signature appears in the lower right-hand corner of this illustration.

Once the decision was made to proceed with the church, but before actual construction began, the monks of the Archabbey started making bricks. A vibrant red-orange color, each brick used in the church was made on the Archabbey grounds by the monks. During the peak period of brick manufacture, they were producing between 12,000 and 15,000 bricks daily. By the time ground was finally broken for the project, the monks had already stockpiled over one million bricks.

Two local construction companies, Brown Brothers and John Kirchner, were hired to quarry stone at Donohoe Station and the Kuhn's farm, located nearby. The Marble-Hill Quarry Company of Pittsburgh did the facing on the foundation stone. Stone was hauled to the building site by men from the parish.

Actual work on the church began on December 21, 1891, with a Solemn High Mass. Father Edward Andelfinger, O.S.B., the pastor, invited the children of the parochial schools to remove the first sod for the excavation. Following Mass, about one hundred and forty boys and girls, dressed in their holiday best, marched outside, and with their elders watching, began digging. The children represented some of the region's earliest Catholic families, and reflected the close

relationship the monks had established with the community. Once the children had filled all of the available carts, stronger arms took over and excavation began in earnest.

In April of 1892, a little over four months later, to celebrate the twenty-fifth anniversary of Archabbot Andrew's ordination to the priesthood, the first stone of the foundation was laid by Pittsburgh Bishop Richard Phelan, Archabbot Andrew, and visiting abbots and guests on hand for the silver jubilee celebration. While the foundation stones, many of which are over six feet wide, are of pink Indiana limestone, the cornerstone is from the local Kuhn's farm, which provided much of the sandstone used in the church.

Although Archabbot Boniface Wimmer, O.S.B., never lived to see his dream of a magnificent church carried out, the Wimmer family still had a hand in the Basilica's construction through Wimmer's nephew, Sebastian. Born in Thalmassing, Bavaria, January 5, 1831, he was a son of George and Theresa Wimmer. He attended the Technical and Polytechnic schools and pursued an engineering course. Following graduation, he emigrated to the United States on June 2, 1851, and accompanied his uncle, Boniface, to Saint Vincent, where he studied for a short time. He began his engineering work in 1860 with Hastings and Preisser of Pittsburgh and spent most of his professional career doing survey and engineering work for various railroads throughout the country. When the time came for construction of the Archabbey Church, he returned to Latrobe, where he helped engineer and supervise the foundation work. Following his retirement he lived for a short time in Minnesota, then spent the last four years of his life at the Archabbey, where he died on December 1, 1921. In the photo are: standing, Sebastian Wimmer, son of George, (seated, from left) Sebastian Wimmer, Anthony Wimmer, and Anthony's daughter Sister Beatrice, O.S.B.

Lay craftsmen and members of the monastic community worked side by side during the construction of the church. While no photograph of the actual groundbreaking ceremony has been found in the Archabbey Archives, this print, made from a glass plate negative, is one of the earliest photos of the excavation work on the foundation. Sebastian Wimmer, who engineered and supervised the laying out of the foundation, is second from left in the front row. Note the steam line, which pre-existed the construction, is already present. The doorway to the monastery was removed during construction and re-used as the main entrance to the present carpenter shop/press building.

This photo was taken in April of 1892 at the time of the silver jubilee of the priesthood of Archabbot Andrew Hintenach, O.S.B. (pictured at left), when the foundations were officially begun and the first stones were laid. Pictured in the second row are: Sebastian Wimmer, left; Abbot Benedict Menges of Alabama, second from left; Bishop Richard Phelan of Pittsburgh, fourth from left; Archabbot Andrew, fifth from left; Abbot Fintan Mundwiler of Saint Meinrad's Abbey in Indiana, seventh from left; Abbot Innocent Wolf of Kansas, eighth from left; and Abbot Bernard Locnikar of Minnesota, ninth from left.

Archabbot Andrew Hintenach, O.S.B., was Boniface Wimmer's successor. Born May 12, 1844 in Schollbrunn, Baden, Germany, his family moved to Maryland when he was young. He entered the novitiate at Saint Vincent in 1860 and was ordained a priest in 1867. He was elected Archabbot on February 8, 1888, a position he held until he resigned on June 14, 1892. A major achievement of his tenure as archabbot was to begin the long-awaited building of the new archabbey church. Andrew Hall (monastic library and choir chapel) was also begun at this time.

Workmen were presented with a set of rules governing their behavior—a decidedly monastic set. The melting pot of immigrants to western Pennsylvania was reflected in these rules, which were presented in four languages: German, English, Polish and Slovak.

"Rules to be observed by the workmen.

"1. All must attend Convent Mass daily, the Sermon on Sundays and Holidays, and Benediction on Saturdays.

"2. All are required to be peaceful, polite and gentlemanly at all times.

"3. Order and cleanliness in the rooms must be insisted upon.

"4. No one is allowed to bring intoxicating drink to the premises or have same brought by others.

"5. No one must leave the premises without permission.

"6. In the corridors and refectory of the Monastery silence must be observed.

"7. No one must enter any apartment of the Monastery, such as the kitchen, cellar, &c., unless he is sent there.

"8. After nine o'clock P.M. all must be in their rooms and silence must be observed."

Progress continues to be made on excavation for the site, and the foundation walls are beginning to take shape. This view is taken looking toward the west, at the monastery tract of buildings (Gregory Hall to the right, Anselm Hall to the left), where the sacristy and the apse of the church are located. The photo was taken before Andrew Hall was constructed.

There are twenty-four workmen and one horse pictured in this print. (One man is barely distinguishable in a doorway in the building on the right.) Some of the men, or parts of the men, appear blurry due to the long exposures required with early photographic techniques. Unless a person was standing perfectly still during the photo, the motion was captured on the glass plate negative. In addition to horse-drawn carts, a track was installed around the perimeter of the foundation in order to move the heavy foundation stones into position. In the center of this photo a large foundation stone sits on a cart, ready to be put into place. To the left of where the cart with the stone on it waits is a mason at work on one of the stones. Along the right side of the photo are piles of rock shavings from the cut stone. The carpenter shop is seen in the distance. To the right is the old school building of one and a half stories where Father Boniface Wimmer and his companions found quarters when they first arrived at Saint Vincent in 1846.

This print shows the progress made on the foundation walls of the structure. Note the steam line running down the center of the construction site, as well as the Victorian-style fashions of the men and women in the picture. This photo is taken during the laying of the cornerstone, October 1892, which was also the day of blessing of the new Archabbot, Leander Schnerr, O.S.B. (right).

The east side of the monastery quadrangle was chosen as the site of the new church. The six-foot wide Indiana Limestone foundation stones were laid in early 1892, to a depth of ten feet. The completed foundation work appears to be decked by flooring as a temporary roof over the crypt. Because of other pressing construction needs at Saint Vincent, and a period of national economic depression, work on the Basilica was suspended from 1893-1895. Work recommenced in 1895 and the shell of the whole structure was completed in 1896. This view, taken from the northeast corner of the church foundation, shows the two-story choir chapel, which was connected to the church during construction. The choir chapel, Andrew Hall, was built in 1892. The majestic bell tower (1871) is shown in the distance. The choir chapel was destroyed in the fire of January 28, 1963, and only the quick thinking of the pastor, Father Marcian Kornides, O.S.B., and the heroic efforts of local firefighters, prevented the Basilica from being consumed by the flames. This photo has been retouched from the original glass plate negative.

The beginnings of the complex scaffolding for the church can be seen to the left. Along the walls about midway on either side of the picture are two frames for the doorways, and in the foreground are the beginnings of some of the massive support pillars for the structure. The view is looking east, toward the carpenter shop.

This view, looking west toward Andrew Hall, shows significant progress made on the walls of the Basilica crypt and completion of the support pillars on the lower floor. The door at the center (east side) of Andrew Hall currently connects the sacristy of the Basilica with the "work sacristy," which is actually in Andrew Hall.

This photo, retouched from the original glass plate negative, shows another view of the crowd congregated for the laying of the cornerstone in October of 1892, which was also the day of the blessing of Archabbot Leander Schnerr, O.S.B. The lower right-hand corner shows an area used to mix mortar. The building in the background is the carpenter shop. It was situated where the current memorial statue to Archabbot Boniface Wimmer stands. The woodwork for the church was fashioned on-site in the shop. The carpenter shop was not razed until after the church was completed.

The choir chapel, once begun, received attention until it was completed. Note the progress made on the chapel in comparison with its status on page 19. At the same time comparison of the two phases indicates little progress on the foundations of the Basilica. Note also the high library windows and the second floor choir chapel windows in Andrew Hall. At the bottom, left of the photo is the south ambulatory with windows and door. The photo was taken in 1891 or 1892.

The enormous roofing structure and ceiling are supported by 18 columns. These columns, made of rose-colored Peterhead Granite, were quarried in 1893 in Aberdeen, Scotland, then known as the "Granite City." The columns were finished and sent by steamship to New York City, and then by railroad to Latrobe. The columns are unique in that they are solid from base to capital. Most large buildings that have granite columns have them cut and cemented together. The capitals are barrel-vault, later carved in place by Ladislaus Vitalis. Two workmen, both blurred from motion, can be seen, one on either side of the image.

 It is partially cropped on the bottom, but the October 25, 1896, date on this photograph indicates that it was taken within the same time period as the Basilica builders (see following pages), which has been frequently reproduced. Printed on very thin, delicate fiber paper, it shows Brother Wolfgang Traxler, O.S.B., (1854-1931, also pictured at left) the monk who supervised the building's construction. The monks and parishioners expected the church to be completed by 1896, the fiftieth anniversary of the Benedictines' arrival at Saint Vincent. However, a nationwide economic depression or "panic" contributed to financial uncertainties which delayed its completion for another nine years.

A complex scaffolding arose gradually, much as the walls did. Monks working on property the Benedictines owned on Chestnut Ridge sawed down the trees, made hand-hewn beams and assembled the framing. Each part specifically cut for the actual structure of the church was numbered—the monks used Roman numerals—and then brought down the mountain by horse and carriage, where it was fitted into the design. These workmen are the same ones pictured in the more famous Basilica builders photo, reproduced on the following page, the only difference being that this photo was taken from the present-day choir area looking toward the rose window above the main entrance. The next photo was taken from the main entrance area looking toward the choir area. This photo was taken two days after the photo of Brother Wolfgang Traxler on page 28.

This frequently-reproduced photo of the Basilica Builders shows many of the men holding a specific tool of their trade or attribute of their role in the project. The eighth man from the left in the second row, dressed in white and holding a trowel, is Giles Andrew Brandt, grandfather of Most Rev. Lawrence E. Brandt, Bishop of Greensburg. Giles Brandt was a bricklayer who helped build the Basilica. Other surnames of the builders include Thomas, Schaeffer, Ransil, Reilly and Smith. Photo retouched from original glass plate negative.

Two different views show the walls going up. The top view is from the south. The bottom view, from the east, in addition to showing the church under construction, also captures the Saint Vincent Gristmill on the right side, and someone traveling along the road by horse and buggy.

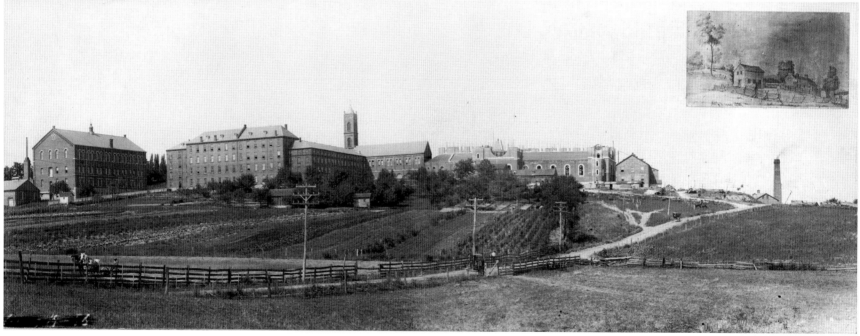

More views of the wall construction from the south. The bottom photos shows the beginnings of the roof framing. Additionally, like many panoramic photos taken of the church during this time period, an old illustration of the Sportsman's Hall Parish is printed in the upper right hand corner. Note the horse-drawn mower in the lower left corner, a parked horse and buggy in the lower center, and a horse and buggy traveling up the hill in the right corner.

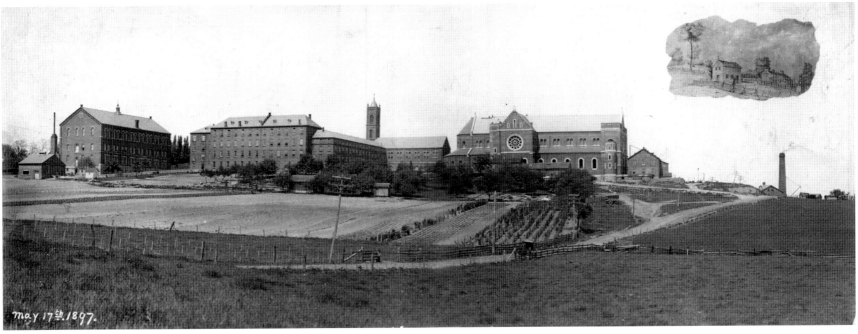

May 17th 1897.

The top view, taken in the year 1896, saw good progress made toward getting the structure under roof. Taken from the south side of the church, it shows the proximity of the carpenter shop at the front of the building. Many of the early views of the Basilica were taken from the Route 30-side of the structure. Once Aurelius Hall was completed in 1923, adding segments outside of the "quadrangle" which was the early Saint Vincent campus, this particular view was no longer possible. Later views were taken more from the east, until the Parish Center, which is attached to the south side of the Basilica, was completed in 1997.

A photo of the nearly-completed church taken from the southeast following the razing of the carpenter shop. Some of the rubble which has yet to be removed can be seen in the foreground.

Also on this page is a postcard of the church, of note due to the mode of transportation pictured at the foot of the stairs.

On page 35 is a view of the completed Basilica taken in 1911.

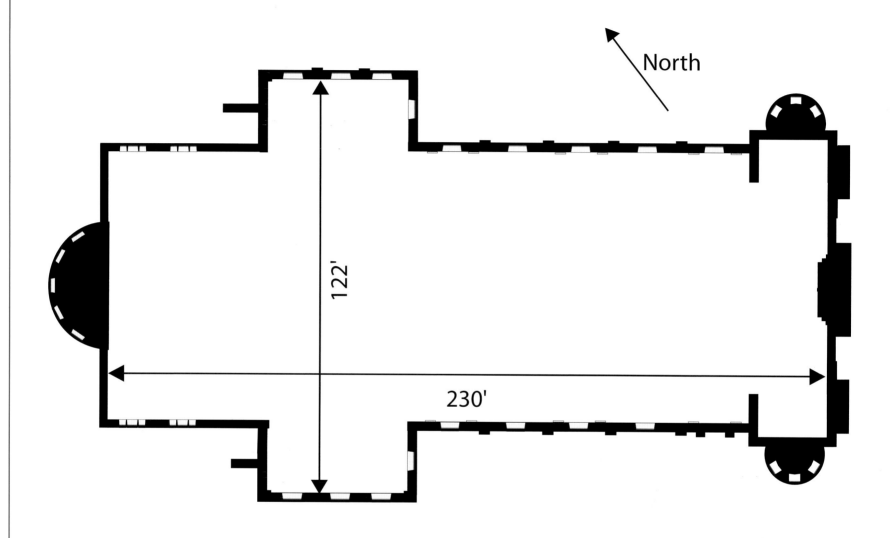

The finished church is 230 feet long from the front doors in the east to the apse wall in the west. At the crossing or transept (from the current Blessed Sacrament Chapel wall to the Resurrection Chapel wall) the church is 122 feet wide. The height of the nave and choir ceiling is 62 feet. The sanctuary and transept ceilings are 68 feet high. The back towers are 150 feet high and the front towers were 195 feet high before the addition of the 55-foot high spires in 1999. The Basilica is made in a cross or *Cruciform* shape.

Once the outside structure was completed, work began on the inside of the church. The high altar, situated at the meeting of the choir and nave crossing, was one of the most striking features. It was one of nine altars in the church. There were three on each side of the choir, and one in each of the transepts.

The High Altar was fitted with eighteen candlesticks specially designed for it. The crucifix, center, was crafted from bronze with Sterling silver accents. Note the early lamps in the background.

The high altar was constructed of brick and covered with white Carrara marble and accented with Siena marble. Note the intricate inlaid marble of the cupola. The altar table frontispiece depicts the classical *Agnus Dei* (Lamb of God). It was inlaid with Siena marble to accent the white, "wedding cake" style. The altar was removed in 1955 to make room for a new altar, which is still in use.

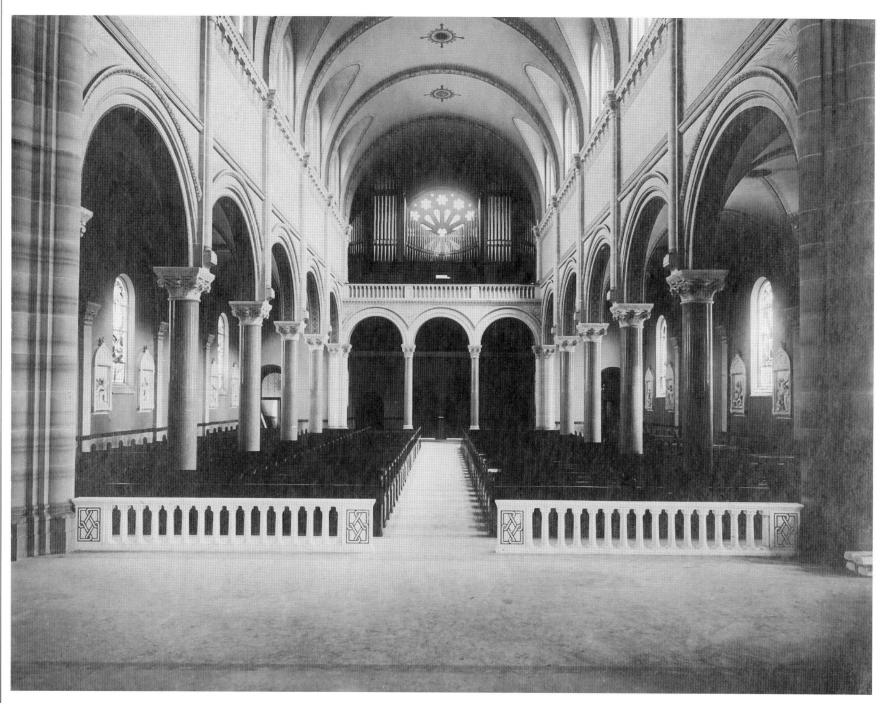

View from the altar looking toward the rose window over the entrance doors of the church. Note the pipe organ at the rose window. This photo was taken prior to the addition of the confessionals and pulpit.

This wineglass shaped pulpit was made by R. Geissler of New York City. Carved from white oak, the pulpit was stained or semi-antiqued to match the other wood furnishings. The pulpit contained elaborate carvings of the Four Evangelists' symbols. J.J. Holwell and Son of Brooklyn, New York, crafted an oval sounding board, with a representation of the Holy Spirit depicted as a white dove in a blue sky. The sounding board was mounted above the puplit to project sound into the cavernous church. In the background, note the ornate framing around the Stations of the Cross.

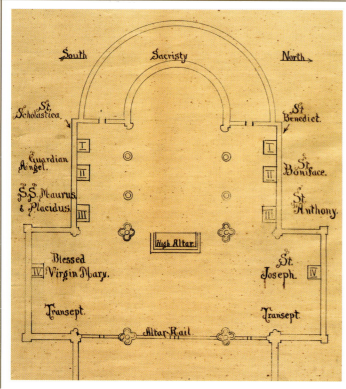

Map for the original designations of the altars — the additions of the statues changed all that in 1930.

The minor altars were named and consecrated in honor of the Blessed Virgin, with the relics of Saint Callistus and Saint Crispin, by the Most Rev. Sebastian Gebhart Messmer, Archbishop of Milwaukee; in honor of Saint Joseph, with the relics of Saint Melithon and Saint Urban, by the Most Rev. Francis Albinus Symon, Archbishop of Attalia; in honor of Saint Anthony of Padua, with the relics of Saint Theopistus and Saint Aurelia, by the Most Rev. Henry Joseph Richter, Bishop of Grand Rapids, Mich.; in honor of Saint Boniface, with the relics of Saint Flavia Domitilla and Saint Apollonia, by the Most Rev. Camillus Paul Maes, Bishop of Covington, Ky.; in honor of Saint Maurus and Saint Placidus, with the relics of Saint Dennis and Saint Crescentius, by the Most Rev. Leo Haid, O.S.B., Bishop of Messene, Vicar Apostolic of North Carolina and Abbot of Maryhelp Abbey.

Above the altar of repose in the north transept on Good Friday.

Additional altars were consecrated in honor of the Guardian Angels, with the relics of Saint Candidus and Saint Columba, by the Most Rev. John E. Fitzmaurice, Bishop of Erie; in honor of Saint Benedict, with the relics of Saint Victor and Saint Donatus, by the Most Rev. Eugene A. Garvey, Bishop of Altoona; in honor of Saint Scholastica, with the relics of Saint Zephyrinus and Saint Ignatius, by the Most Rev. John W. Shanahan, Bishop of Harrisburg.

This photo was taken after the installation of the statues of Saint Maurus and Saint Scholastica, which changed the original designation of the altars.

These side altars on the south side of the choir incorporated the statues of Saint Maurus and Saint Scholastica. During subsequent renovations, the statues were placed on new pedestals and remain essentially where they were installed a century ago. Saint Scholastica's statue is underneath the window depicting the "last Meeting of Saint Benedict and Saint Scholastica."

These side altars on the north side of the choir incorporated the statues of Saint Benedict, left, and Saint Placidus. Saint Benedict's statue is located underneath the window depicting the *transitus* (passing into heaven) of Saint Benedict.

View from the apse above the organ's pipes looking at the choir area. The lectern in the center of the photo is currently used as the ambo facing the nave. The drape in the upper right-hand corner of the photo is part of the canopy for the portable abbatial and episcopal throne. Some of the material has been utilized to provide a festive covering used on the new altar during the Easter season.

A glass plate negative discovered during research for this project features a scale model of the interior of the Basilica. This model indicates much more frescoed artwork in the Beuronese style had been planned for the apse and above the arches on the sides. The interior scale model, in the photo above, was quite large, judging by the light fixtures shown in the background of the room where it was on display.

Procession, with the relics, on the dedication day, August 24, 1905.

Finally, after fourteen years and millions of bricks, construction was completed and the church was ready to be consecrated. Two dates were suggested: July 19, 1905, the seventieth anniversary of the dedication of the old church; or, August 24, 1905, the fiftieth anniversary of the elevation of Saint Vincent to an abbey. The latter date was chosen to ensure the artisans enough time to finish last-minute tasks. Guests began arriving days before the consecration — archbishops, bishops, abbots and monsignors, priests and laymen. Many were graduates of Saint Vincent. Most Rev. Diomede Falconio, the Apostolic Delegate, represented the Holy Father at the celebration.

On the vigil of the consecration, the relics of the holy Martyrs that were to be enclosed in the altars of the new church were examined by the consecrator, Bishop J.F. Regis Canevin, fifth Bishop of Pittsburgh, then *matins* and *lauds* of the Martyrs were chanted by the monastic choir. An opening recital was given on the grand organ by Caspar P. Koch, organist of Carnegie Hall.

On consecration day, promptly at seven a.m., Bishop Canevin was escorted in procession to the front of the new church and began the ceremony with the blessing of the foundation and walls, while the monastic Schola Cantorum chanted the liturgy, using the grand and time-honored Benedictine melodies of *Solesmes*. Amid chanting of psalms and the peal of the church bells, the sacred relics were borne to the new house of worship, accompanied in solemn procession by the members of the community and all the visiting dignitaries and priests. After the procession entered the church, the relics were deposited in the sanctuary and the consecration of the altars took place.

The High Altar, in honor of St. Vincent de Paul, was consecrated by Bishop Regis Canevin, and received the relics of Saint Vincent, Martyr, and Saint Cyprian. After the consecration of the altar, the Apostolic Delegate celebrated Solemn Pontifical High Mass. Others present were: Bishop James A. McFaul of Trenton, who gave the homily; and Bishop Patrick J. Donahue of Wheeling. Benedictine Abbots were: Peter Engel, Saint John's Abbey, Minnesota, President of the American Cassinese Congregation; Frowin Conrad, Conception Abbey, Missouri, President of the Swiss American Congregation; Archabbots Leander Schnerr and Andrew Hintenach, Saint Vincent; Abbots Athanasius Schmitt, Saint Meinrad, Indiana; Innocent Wolf, Atchison, Kansas; Hilary Pfraengle, Newark, New Jersey; Nepomucene Jaeger, Chicago, Illinois; Charles Mohr, Saint Leo, Florida; and Bernard Menges, Saint Bernard, Alabama. Monsignors Michael J. Decker of Erie and Peter Dauffenbach of Brooklyn, N.Y., and more than two hundred priests also participated.

The frontispiece of the old high altar (right) is currently incorporated into the altar of the Mary Mother of Wisdom Student Chapel.

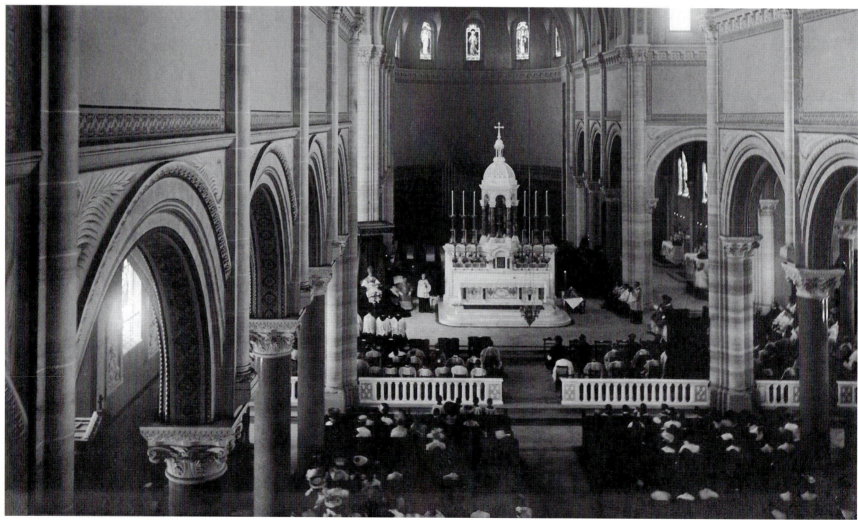

This photo shows minor additions which were made in the altar area, including the statue of the Blessed Virgin Mary and the statue of the Sacred Heart of Jesus, carved by Giovanni Sugari. The statue of the Sacred Heart of Jesus, at the time of this publication, is located on the second floor of the Parish Center. The statue of the Blessed Virgin Mary is currently in the Immaculate Conception Chapel, formerly the Baptistry.

DESIGN FOR CHOIR ORGAN AND MURAL DECORATION OF THE APSE
ST. VINCENT ARCHABBEY CHURCH, BEATTY, PA.

This delicate drawing by P. Raphael, O.S.B., shows another version of planned artwork for the apse. Extensive decoration of the fourteen panels above the side arches was also considered in 1924, with a number of drawings and proposals presented. None, however, was ever undertaken. Father Raphael Pfisterer (1877-1942) was a priest working at the Studio of Christian Art, Saint Anselm's College, Manchester, New Hampshire, which was an offshoot of the Catholic Altar Building Stock Company of Saint Vincent Archabbey. The Altar Building Company moved to New Hampshire after the death of Brother Cosmas Wolf, O.S.B.

Another drawing of artwork considered for the apse. Boniface Wimmer is pictured in the ship along with other early abbots.

In 1931, the statue honoring Archabbot Boniface Wimmer, founder of Saint Vincent and of Benedictine monasticism in North America, was installed. Its sculptor, Ferdinand Seeboeck, was born in Vienna, Austria, May 27, 1864. He spent most of his life working in Italy, four years in Florence and forty-one in Rome. Seeboeck was originally commissioned by Saint Vincent Archabbot Aurelius Stehle, O.S.B. (1877-1930) to carve the statues of Saint Maurus and Saint Placid. Later, he was hired to carve the statues of Saint Benedict and Saint Scholastica (pictured with Seeboeck in his studio). But on the Saint Vincent campus, he is best known for his artistry in creating the bronze Wimmer Memorial Statue that stands before the Basilica. With these five statues, Saint Vincent can boast of the world's largest collection of sculptures by Seeboeck. The Vatican has two busts of Pope Saint Pius X, and the Salvatorians in Rome have three statues, one each of Jesus. Saint Peter and Saint Paul.

Seeboeck maintained a warm friendship with Father Blase Strittmatter, O.S.B., a monk of the Archabbey who studied in Rome at the time the Wimmer statue was being created. They remained lifelong correspondents, the last letter from the sculptor to Father Blase written eight hours before Seeboeck died on December 18, 1952.

For more information on Seeboeck's work at Saint Vincent, see, *Forward, Always Forward, The History and Construction of the Wimmer Memorial Statue,* written by Father Blase and published posthumously by Archabbey Publications in 2004.

In conjunction with the 1946 centennial of the arrival of Boniface Wimmer, the crypt of the Archabbey church was redesigned to commemorate the contributions of the Benedictine Order to the religious, artistic and intellectual development of Western civilization. Father Quentin Schaut, O.S.B., headed the project and commissioned liturgical artists Emil Frei of Saint Louis, and Jan Henryk de Rosen of Warsaw, Poland, for the artwork. Emil Frei's well-known works are located in the Shrine of the Immaculate Conception in Washington, D.C., and at Saint Meinrad Archabbey in Indiana. Jan Henryk de Rosen's work graces the papal chapel at Castelgandolfo, Italy, and the National Cathedral (Episcopal) in Washington, D.C. He painted the triptych above the Basilica crypt's main altar. The altars were consecrated on September 3, 1946.

The original locations of the altars and the dates of foundation of filial abbeys and of their elevation to abbatial rank are listed below. Note that when a ramp was installed to make the Crypt accessible to those with disabilities, some of the altars on the south side were removed. At the time the altars were installed, each contained relics of several saints.

MONTECASSINO
Dedicated to Saint Martin of Tours
Relics of Saint Justin and Saint Blase
Consecrated by Archabbot Alfred Koch

Saint Michael
Metten, Bavaria
Relics of Saint Barnabas and Saint Luke
Consecrated by Abbot Cuthbert Goeb

Holy Cross
Cañon City, Colorado
1886; 1925
Relics of Saint Valerian and Saint Aloysius
Consecrated by Abbot Leonard Schwinn

Saint Peter
Muenster, Saskatchewan
1892; 1911
Relics of Saint Meinrad, Saint Anthony, Saint Albert
Consecrated by Abbot Severin Gertgen

Saint Bede
Peru, Illinois
1910
Relics of Saint Justin and Saint Benedict Labre
Consecrated by Abbot Lawrence Vohs

Saint Leo
Saint Leo, Florida
1889; 1902
Relics of Saint Gregory I, Saints Epiphanius, Ursula and companions; Consecrated by Abbot Bertrand Dolan

Saint Procopius
Lisle, Illinois
1885; 1894
Relics of Saint Andrew and Saint John of God; Consecrated by Abbot Theodore Kojis

Saint Boniface
Relics of Saint Aurelius and
an unknown martyr
Consecrated by Abbot Mark Braun

Saint John
Collegeville, Minnesota
1856; 1866
Relics of Saint Basil and Saint Erhard
Consecrated by Abbot Alcuin Deutsch

Saint Benedict
Atchison, Kansas
1857; 1876
Relics of Saint Pancratius and Saint Valerius
Consecrated by Abbot Cuthbert McDonald

Saint Mary Immaculate
Newark, New Jersey
1857; 1884
Relics of Saint Euricus and Saint Pancratius
Consecrated by Abbot Patrick O'Brien

Maryhelp
Belmont, North Carolina
1884; 1910
Relics of Saint Lucidus and Saint Emeran
Consecrated by Abbot Vincent Taylor

Saint Bernard
Saint Bernard, Alabama
1891; 1891
Relics of Saint Bernard and Saint Valerius
Consecrated by Abbot Boniface Seng

The ten side altars, of Indiana Limestone, were dedicated to the ten abbeys which owed their beginnings to Saint Vincent and its founder, Boniface Wimmer. The Saint Leo, Saint Bede and Saint Peter altars were taken out in 1995 when the ramp was installed, making the crypt handicapped-accessible.

The original plans called for a triptych to be placed above each altar. Thus, the windows were meant to be subdued in tonality to act as a foil for the altar paintings.

The three steps to the main altar and the continuous predella for the other altars are black.

The following text on the crypt and its artwork is taken from *The Crypt*, a booklet published by Archabbey Press in 1949 and written by Rev. Quentin Schaut, O.S.B. His manuscript follows:

"The Archabbey Crypt is the result of a practical need and a significant idea. The practical need was the demand for more altars to accommodate the growing number of priests in the community as well as to provide facilities for diocesan priests to offer Mass during their annual retreats. The significant idea was that the Crypt should stand as a permanent memorial to the efforts of the monks laboring for the first hundred years on American soil.

"A tribute to these pioneers as well as an inspiration to Benedictines of the future, the Crypt was developed as part of the program commemorating the centenary of the founding of Saint Vincent Archabbey and the Benedictine Order in America. The limestone altars, of marked simplicity and stability in design, were consecrated in a most unusual joint ceremony on September

3, 1946, by thirteen abbots representing American and European abbeys.

"During the first century of its existence Saint Vincent Archabbey founded ten daughter abbeys. An altar was dedicated to the patron of each of these abbeys. The idea of filiation was carried backward also to indicate the ancestry of the Archabbey. The main altar memorializes Montecassino, the cradle of Western monasticism, where Saint Benedict wrote his *Rule*. This altar is dedicated, not to Saint Benedict, since he is represented in the altar of one of the daughter abbeys, but to Saint Martin of Tours, in whose honor Saint Benedict dedicated his first chapel at Montecassino. It was in the chapel of Saint Martin that Benedictines began the chanting of the Divine Office, and it was in this chapel that Saint Benedict died.

"A second altar represents Saint Michael's Abbey, Metten, Bavaria, where the Founder of Saint Vincent came from. A third is dedicated to Saint Boniface, patron of Boniface Wimmer, the Founder of Saint Vincent Archabbey and of Benedictinism in America.

The five crosses are the places that are anointed with Sacred Chrism by the Bishop during an altar's consecration. They represent the five wounds of Christ.

Polish-American artist Jan Henryk de Rosen (1891-1982) of Arlington, Virginia, painted The Montecassino Triptych in 1946. The painting illuminates the main altar in the Crypt.

"Succisa virescit ("Cut down, it grows again"), the motto of Montecassino, serves as the theme of the triptych over the main altar, which memorializes Montecassino as a cradle of Western civilization and of the perpetual renewal of that civilization. The motto has been realized in the periodic destructions and restorations experienced in the life of the abbey at Montecassino. The artist has developed his theme by selecting famous abbots of Montecassino, particularly those associated with periods of greatest revitalization. As the basis of his work he took the celebrated chronicle of Leo, eleventh-century monk of Montecassino, who became Cardinal Bishop of Ostia. The names of the persons represented are in the beautiful Beneventan script, at the height of perfection when Leo was writing, and used by him.

"Beginning at the spectator's left, the first figure is that of Leo of Ostia writing his *Chronicle*. Behind him stands Pope Stephen X (d. 1058), who was abbot of Montecassino when Leo became a monk there. The next figure is Desiderius (d. 1087), builder of the great basilica and most celebrated of the abbots after Saint Benedict himself. He became Pope Victor III. The central figure is Saint Benedict. To his left is Petronax (d. 750), a native of Brescia who found Montecassino lying in ruins since its destruction by the Lombards. He became a monk and abbot and restored the abbey. The kneeling figure is Boniface Krug, a monk of Saint Vincent Archabbey, who went to Montecassino in the 1860s and became one of the great modern abbots of that monastery. The last figure is Aligernus (d. 986), who restored the abbey after its destruction by the Lombards.

"In the background are depicted the building of the great basilica of Desiderius, the visit of Charlemagne, the meeting of Eastern and Western monasticism, suggested by the visit of St. Nilus the Younger. Finally there is Montecassino destroyed — as it was in 1946, the

year this triptych was painted. But over the ruins of the bombed monastery a new Montecassino has arisen. *Succisa virescit!*

"The painter of this triptych was Jan Henryk de Rosen, recognized as one of the great church painters of the twentieth century. He was chosen personally by Pope Pius XI to paint the papal private chapter at Castelgandolfo. Many important buildings in Europe and America contain work by him, among them the Armenian Cathedral in Lwow, Poland, and the chapel of Joseph of Arimathea in the Cathedral of Saints Peter and Paul (Episcopal) in Washington, D.C. He also created the apse mosaic of Christ the Judge in the National Shrine of the Immaculate Conception in Washington, D.C.; and, what is believed to be the largest mosaic in the world on the dome of the Saint Louis Cathedral in Saint Louis.

"St. Benedict's *Holy Rule* threads the sixteen stained glass windows of the Crypt into a unified composition, just as it is the source of vitality and permanence in Benedictine life and work. Beginning with the writing of the Rule and concluding with the glorified Benedict the windows depict virtues and accomplishments, the *Ora et Labora,* of monks and nuns through fourteen centuries of Benedictine history.

"For each century an eminent Benedictine is chosen, together with some typical virtue or activity exemplified by his life or work. These ideas are represented symbolically. Instead of drawing a picture the artist has employed symbols, a feature of Christian art as old as the catacombs.

"The windows are the work of Emil Frei, of St. Louis, Missouri, under whose supervision the Crypt has been developed.

I
The Holy Rule

"The hand of Saint Benedict writing the *Holy Rule* predominates in the first of the windows. Two descending lines begin at the *Chi Rho,* a symbol for Christ (the first two letters of the name in Greek), and at the triangle representing the Blessed Trinity at the top of the composition. The lines descend in waves of inspiration — one to the pen in the hand of Saint Benedict, and the other traced by the Holy Ghost in the form of the Dove to the words 'Holy Rule.' Across the window is the declaration, 'This is the Law.'

"When a candidate seeks admission into the monastery, the Rule is to be read to him, says Saint Benedict. And then he is to be told, 'This is the Law' under which he will have to live if he chooses to remain in the monastery.

II
Saint Gregory the Great — Plain Chant
(6th century)

"The name of the first great Pope given to the Church by the Benedictine Order is permanently associated with her official music, Gregorian chant, which the monks sing day after day. In the lower part of the window are inscribed a few musical notes, the first phrase of the *Gaudeamus*, the introit of the Mass used on certain feasts, among them that of Saint Benedict. The words, 'Let us all rejoice in the Lord,' accent the gladness that is a recognized characteristic of religious life.

"In the upper part of the window is a triangle, representing the Triune God. Within this triangle is an ear. From the choir on earth sacred melodies rise to please the ear of God.

III
Saint Benet Biscop — Building
(7th century)

"Benedictines are builders, not transients. They sink their roots into the soil and become a permanent part of the community where they establish themselves. This characteristic is well exemplified by Saint Benet Biscop, abbot of the great twin monasteries of Wearmouth and Jarrow. The story of how he brought masons from the continent to build his church in stone and glaziers to teach the English their craft comes to us from the pen of Saint Bede. It is still regarded as an epic of the early church in England. Benet Biscop built well and beautifully.

"These ideas are suggested by the trowel in the lower part of the window, the bricks, and the wall in process of construction. At the top of the window the cross is placed at the apex of the finished structure as seen in the mind of the builder, thus realizing the Benedictine motto, 'That God may be glorified in all things.' The inspiration and guidance received by Biscop is again designated by the Dove proceeding from the triangle of God.

IV
Blessed Alcuin — Education
(8th century)

"Blessed Alcuin, the distinguished scholar and prolific writer and, later, abbot of Tours, may well represent the work of educating the young. Through his superintendence of the educational reforms of Charlemagne (who himself became Alcuin's pupil) he exerted enormous influence in the restoration of learning in Europe.

"The theme is portrayed in the window on the basis of the parable of the Sowing of the Seed. The seed comes from the hand of God emerging from the Trinity. Some falls on stony ground and issues into a weak scraggly growth. Some is choked by thorns. The birds of the air get some. But some falls on good ground and yields a flourishing stock of wheat. This is Christian education, identified by the cross.

V
Blessed Rhabanus Maurus — Scripture Study (9th century)

"Among monastic studies Holy Scripture holds first place. Rhabanus Maurus, distinguished pupil of Blessed Alcuin and glory of the historic German monastery of Fulda founded by St. Boniface, is famous, among other things, for his scholarly commentaries on Holy Scripture.

"In this window the eye of Rhabanus Maurus studies the open book of Holy Scripture. Symbols suggest events in the Old and New Testaments: the serpent and the apple, Noah's Ark, the Ten Commandments, the pomegranate, symbol of fertility, for Ann, the mother of Samuel as well as for Ann the mother of the Blessed Virgin; the Incarnation (Christ—the *Chi Rho*—born of the Virgin, who is represented by a lily), Christ on the cross, in the sepulchre, and ascending to heaven. The Holy Spirit in the guise of a dove issuing from cloudlike forms points to the divine inspiration of the Sacred Scriptures.

VI
Roswitha — Drama
(10th century)

"Roswitha is an excellent example of how the Church transforms pagan materials or techniques for Christian purposes. This remarkable nun of Saxony, called the 'Nightingale of Gandersheim,' tells us that she saw many Catholics risking contamination by their addiction to the works of pagan authors, particularly the plays of Terence. To offset this danger she composed Latin plays in the style of Terence, but on elevated themes.

"The last of her plays was *Sapientia*. It dramatizes the martyrdom of Faith, Hope, and Charity, three daughters of Wisdom, who gave their lives for the Faith during the reign of Hadrian. In the window Faith is symbolized by a cross; her sister Hope, by an anchor forming a cross, one of the oldest Christian symbols of hope. The third daughter, Charity, is represented by the flame of love. Lines rise from these martyrs to unite them with the Trinity.

VII
St. Anselm — Dogmatic Theology
(11th century)

"Saint Anselm enjoys the distinction, almost unique for a Catholic saint, of winning the praise of both German philosophers and English historians. He appears here in his role of dogmatic theologian. It was by his writings in this field and that of speculative theology that he earned the title of 'Father of Monasticism.' One of his most celebrated works was *Cur Deus Homo — Why God Became Man*, a profound study of the Atonement.

"'I believe in God ... and in Jesus Christ, His only Son, Our Lord; who was conceived by the Holy Ghost, born of the Virgin Mary.' Coming forth from the hand of God, the Holy Spirit descends into the Immaculate Lily. The triangle of the upper section of the window, embracing the Father, Son, and Holy Spirit, converging at the mystery of the Incarnation, overshadows the earth with a second triangle which casts the image of the Triune God upon the world. The redemption of mankind is symbolically completed with the union of heaven and earth through the crucified Son of the Father ascending heavenward.

VIII
Peter the Venerable — Discipline
(12th century)

"The idea exemplified in this window is monastic discipline, and it would be difficult to find a better instance of it than Peter the Venerable, celebrated reforming abbot of Cluny. From the natural we rise to the supernatural. Here the natural order is suggested by the day and night alternating with unfailing regularity. The Christian, much more the religious, must introduce this harmonious regularity into his life on the supernatural level. He does so under the light and grace of Christ. In the light emanating from Christ (the *Chi Rho*) are seen three monks in exactly the same position — perfect discipline.

IX
Pope Saint Peter Celestine V — Renunciation
(13th century)

"Renunciation is an essential element in the life of a monk. At the lower left the young monk Peter Celestine is praying. Two lines lead upward, the more regular and direct symbolizing Celestine's desire for the life of a recluse; it is marked by hands folded in prayer. The other line indicates the life he actually led — the honors and authority forced upon him. This line is marked by the stole of the priesthood and the tiara of the papacy.

"Elected Pope on July 5, 1294, he renounced the papal throne on December 13 of the same year. His successor Pope Boniface VIII imprisoned him in order to safeguard him from those who threatened his life. After nine months of prayer and fasting in a narrow cell in the tower of Fumone near Anagni his soul was led by the Holy Spirit to its eternal home.

X
St. Gertrude — Mysticism
(14th century)

"In the thirteenth and fouteenth centuries there was a remarkable flowering of mystics. Among the greatest of these is Saint Gertrude, nun of Helfta, Saxony. She is pictured in the lower part of the window with hands raised above her head in prayer to God. The *Chi Rho* symbolically rises from these hands uniting her with Love Itself. Along a path flames of love soar heavenward and encircle the Triune God. By another path flames descend to Gertrude, revealing the intimate union with God which is experienced by the mystic. Saint Gertrude's spirituality is marked particularly by a tender devotion to the Sacred Heart and to the Humanity of Christ.

XI
John Lydgate — Poetry
(15th century)

"Creative writing is typified by John Lydgate, voluminous poet, monk of Bury St. Edmunds, England. In the window the eye of God looks down, approving what Lydgate has written. The scansion on the page is for the lines quoted from Lydgate's *Te Deum*:

> '<u>*Te Deum laudamus!*</u> *to the lord sovereyne*
> *we creaturys knowlch the as creatoure.*'

"God is glorified when man properly employs the talent given him. Lydgate's talent was for versification. His reputation in fifteenth-century England was very high. Caxton, the first English printer, ranked him above Chaucer.

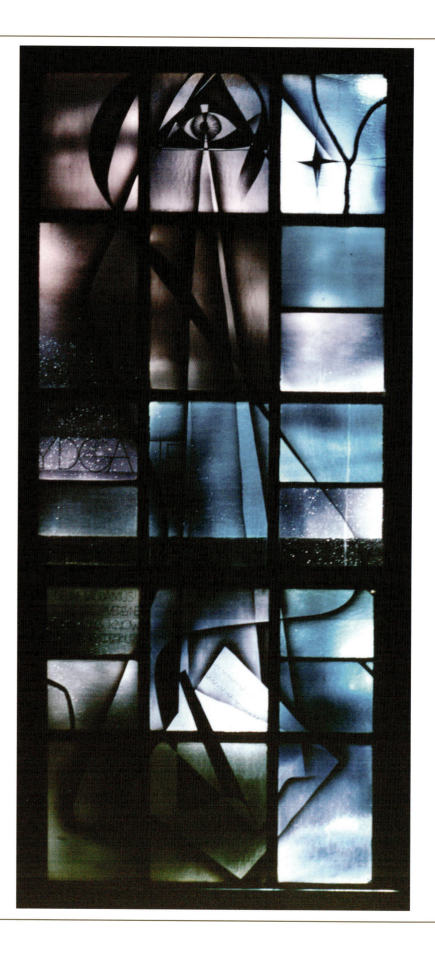

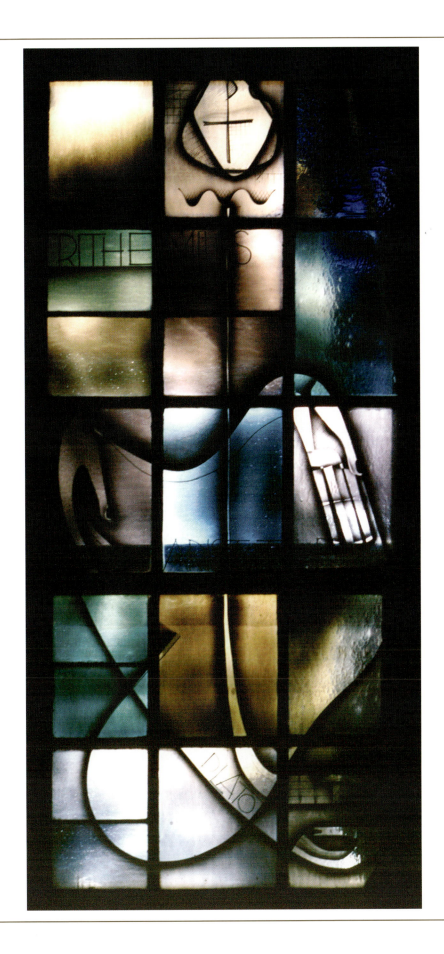

XII
John Trithemius — Humanism
(16th century)

"The part played by the Benedictine Order in the preservation of the classics of ancient Greece and Rome is one of the commonplaces of history. The monks not only preserved books; they developed scholars, with stress on the humanities. Humanists are of various kinds — pagan humanists, Christian humanists, and devout humanists. The place of Trithemius is in the last group, among distinguished names like those of Saint Thomas More and Saint Francis de Sales.

"Classical knowledge, represented in the window by the names of Aristotle and Plato, is handed down to the pupil by Christian teachers like Trithemius. From the right hand of the student a line rises to the *Chi Rho*. What the student receives from his Christian teacher he gives back to Christ.

XIII
Haeften — Asceticism
(17th century)

"The conception of asceticism intended in this window is that of Saint Paul — self-denial and cultivation of virtue, not for the sake of torturing oneself, but to keep in athletic condition for the race each Christian must run.

"The life and writings of Benedict van Haeften, prior of Afflighem in Belgium, made him a model for the monk. Filled with the monastic spirit, his commentaries have scarcely any superior in the opinion of the learned Marténe.

"In the most famous chapter of his *Rule* Saint Benedict tells us that there are twelve degrees of humility. If we climb them all and pass beyond them we will be united in the perfect love of God. Haeften has done this, rising from the earth pictured by the circle at the bottom of the window, and passing beyond the twelve steps to heaven where he is united with the Trinity.

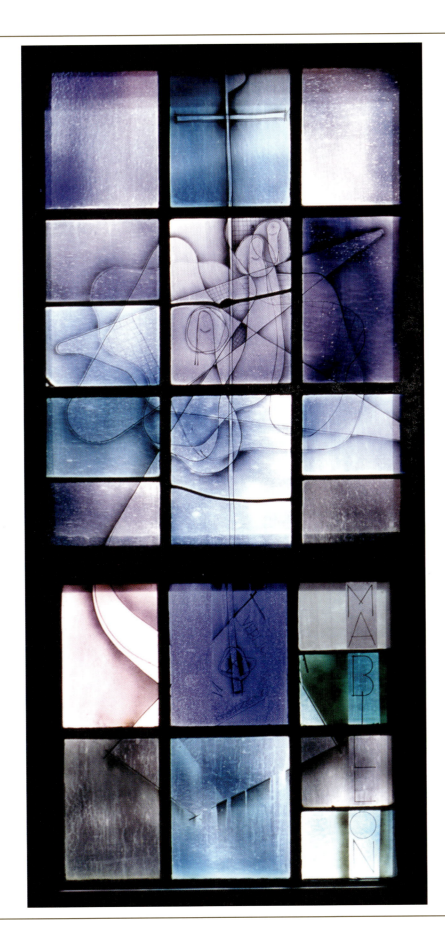

XIV
Mabillon — Scholarship
(18th century)

"Through the mass of false and forged documents suggested by the confused lines at the center of the window the conscientious and critical methods of Jean Mabillon, monk of the Congregation of Saint Maur, pierce through to the truth, symbolized by the *Chi Rho*, Christ. The motto, 'Knowledge is the vindicator of truth and justice,' appears upon the title page of *Re De Deplomatica*, the fundamental work for the science of diplomatics, in which Mabillon set forth the rules for testing the authenticity of documents. A scholar's greatest asset is his ability to penetrate to the truth. When he does so, it reflects itself in his work, as the *Chi Rho* does on the page written by Mabillon.

XI
Boniface Wimmer — Leadership
(19th century)

"Setting out from his mother abbey, St. Michael's at Metten, Bavaria, Father Boniface Wimmer looked forward to the New World while sailing across the Atlantic Ocean. Guided by the Holy Spirit the great leader planted the Cross of Christ upon the knoll where the huge Archabbey now stands. From the Archabbey Benedictine life and work spread out in many directions. One line leads to wheat and grapes, signifying agriculture. Others lead to the painter's brush and sculptor's chisel and mallet. Cultivation of the sciences is represented by a graph. Crosses indicate missionary and parochial work. The building and tower point to abbeys and colleges established throughout the country. The work was richly blessed, and one after another the passing years rise in witness to the wisdom and inspiring leadership of the Founder of Benedictinism in America, Boniface Wimmer.

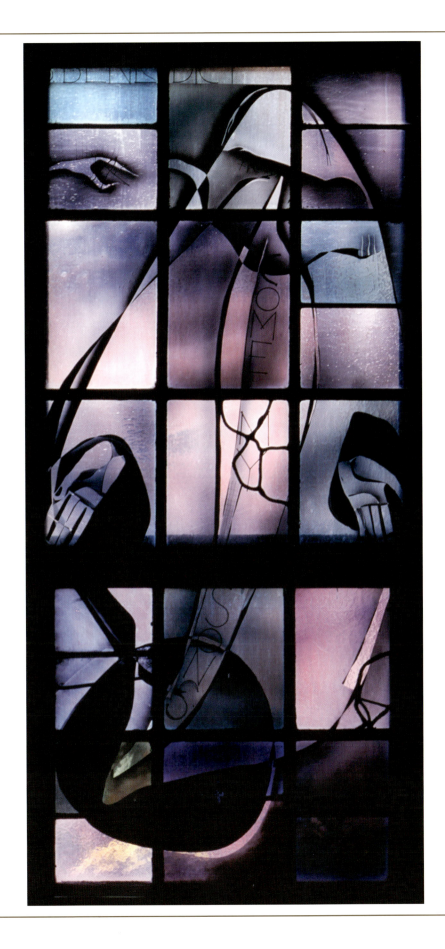

XVI
Saint Benedict

"A spirit-like form of Saint Benedict, clad in the cowl, the choir garb of the monk, fills the window. Hovering over the world this form welcomes into heaven the souls of his faithful followers, not only those of this procession of Benedictine centuries, but also those of all time. Just as the abbot invites the novices on the day of their profession to approach the altar to offer their vows, so Saint Benedict awaits them in heaven, inviting them with the same words they heard at profession. 'Come, my sons,' he says — not to take up the yoke, but to receive the crown."

Andre Girard's triptych in oil is hung above the Saint Bernard Altar, illustrating Saint Bernard's sermons on the *Canticle of Canticles*. The saint, Girard wrote in the August 1950 issue of *Liturgical Arts* magazine, "tackles the most provocative phrases, strips them of their sensual envelope and makes of the bride a church enamored of the divine spirit, the latter, according to Saint Bernard, being represented as the spouse. Understood after this fashion, the poem takes on its full meaning for one who believes and seeks to find behind its images the spirit which gives them life." The artist painted four versions of the triptych, more than seven portraits and fourteen drawings of the saint, twelve scenes illustrating the "song of songs" and six of "our lady's life," and illustrated twenty-four scenes of Saint Bernard's life, before arriving at the final version of the crypt triptych.

Girard was a French painter of religious subjects and a professor of art at Queensborough Community College in Bayside, Queens, at the time of his death at age 67 in 1968. He was noted for his technique of painting on film, not in separate pictures but in a continuous sequence. He was a native of Chinon, France. While a student at the Ecole des Beaux-Arts in Paris, he met Georges Rouault, the celebrated artist, and studied under him from 1918 until Rouault died in 1952. His work is represented in the permanent collections of the French State Museum and other museums in Europe.

The outer panels of the Saint Bernard Triptych depict scenes from the saint's life. The three panels on the left are from the Song of Songs—the bride is the Church and her garments are Church steeples. The three panels on the right are from the life of the Blessed Mother, to whom Bernard had a great devotion. The main panel shows Saint Bernard in prayer.

The outer left-hand panels, from top to bottom are:

1) Aleth, mother of Saint Bernard, reared her children in an austere discipline.
2) Hombeline, sister of the saint, visits him at Clairvaux.
3) Saint Bernard composes the statutes of the Knights Templars.
4) At Saint Benoit-sur-Loire Saint Bernard introduces the King of France to the exiled Pope, Innocent II.
5) Crowds acclaim the saint when he arrives at Genoa to settle the peace between that city and Pisa.
6) In the church of Saint Ambrose, in Milan, Saint Bernard cures an epileptic girl with a few drops of the eucharistic wine.

The next three panels, on the left side, from top to bottom, are:

7) The bride: "I sat down under his shadow, whom I desired: and his fruit was sweet to my palate."
8) The bridegroom: "Thy cheeks are beautiful as the turtle-dove's, thy neck as jewels."
9) The bride: "In the streets and the broad ways I will seek him whom my soul loves."

The inner panels on the right side are, from top to bottom:

10) The Annunciation.
11) Jesus meets his mother.
12) The Assumption.

The outer panels on the right side from top to bottom:

13) The monastery at Clairvaux increases in numbers and new buildings are erected.
14) Interview between Saint Bernard and Louis le Gros, King of France.
15) Death of Gerard, brother of Saint Bernard.
16) Saint Bernard preaches against the heretics in southern France.
17) Saint Bernard preaches the crusade at Vezelay, in the presence of the King of France.
18) Death of Saint Bernard in his cell.

Father Quentin Schaut, O.S.B., President of Saint Vincent College, said of Girard, "when he approaches a subject he immerses himself in it through reading and meditation until he becomes saturated with the idea. He then works with a lavish expenditure of energy and effort, restless until he comes as close as possible to the realization in line and color of the living thing that is in his mind. A master of his materials and techniques, he is a dedicated artist at work."

Behind the altar is a *bas relief* in walnut by Jean de Marco. Saint Boniface, Apostle to Germany, brought Benedictinism to Germany. He is standing with hand raised in blessing and holding the axe used to cut down the sacred tree of the Frisians. Below him, kneeling, is the monk Boniface Wimmer, Apostle from Germany, who brought the Order of Saint Benedict to North America. Wimmer is about to set forth on his apostolate under the aegis of his patron, Saint Boniface. Jean de Marco spent three years in making this large plaque, which shows the faith and courage of Father Boniface, who was once a Bavarian peasant. The artist was born in Paris and first came to America in 1928, later becoming an American citizen. His work has been exhibited in the Brooklyn Museum, the Art Institute of Chicago, the National Academy of Design in New York, and many other museums and galleries in the United States and Europe.

A crucifix by Eugene N. Rutkowski hangs above the side altar dedicated in honor of Saint Procopius and uses wood and enameled metal to depict Christ as King and High Priest. A network of colorful, abstract shapes forms both Christ's body and another cross, terminating at each end with figurative portrayals of his head, hands and feet.

Rutkowski, of Mount Lebanon, Pennsylvania, was only 37 years old when he died in 1973. An accomplished artist, sculptor and designer renowned for his contemporary work in liturgical art that at times created some controversy, he was well-known for his oil paintings, metal sculptures, ceramics and stained glass windows. Rutkowski designed the interiors, artwork and windows for many Western Pennsylvania and Northern West Virginia Catholic and Orthodox churches as well. He was a member of the Guild for Religious Architecture, an affiliate of the American Institute of Architects.

This crucifix, carved by Rene van Seumeren of Holland, is over the altar consecrated to Saint Benedict. It shows a living Christ just before death. The artist used wood and stone found on the grounds of Saint Vincent to create this unique work.

Above the altar consecrated to Saint Michael is a carving of Saint Michael the Archangel by Gleb Derujinsky, honoring Saint Michael's Abbey, Metten, Bavaria, Boniface Wimmer's native abbey. Gleb Vladimirovich Deruizhinskii (the Russian variation of his name) was born in Smolensk, Russia, in 1888. He entered the University of Saint Petersburg in 1904 and received his law degree in 1912. Also in 1904 he entered the School for the Encouragement of Art, which was directed by the well-known painter Nicholas Roerich. In 1911, he studied with Verlet in Paris and the following year with Injalbert at the Colarossi School. He received encouragement to continue his studies from Rodin and in 1913 entered the Russian Imperial Academy of Art where he studied under Hugo Zaleman. He went to New York in 1919 and became an American citizen in 1932. He exhibited widely in the 1920s and 1930s, winning numerous awards. During the 1940s he increasingly turned to executing commissioned work for religious institutions. He worked in bronze, marble, clay, terra cotta and wood. His works in wood were among his most famous and it was the material he liked the best. He died in 1975.

A statue of Saint Benedict, carved by Janet de Coux of Gibsonia, Pennsylvania, was placed at the entrance of the crypt during the 1946 renovation to indicate one is entering a Benedictine space.

The work is a life-sized depiction of the founder of the Benedictine Order, and is carved from limestone. It is highly stylized, which links it to archaic Greek sculpture, medieval sculpture, art deco and modern sensibilities.

Born in Niles, Michigan, de Coux (1904-1999) studied at the Carnegie Institute of Technology from 1925-1927; the Industrial School in New York; the Rhode Island School of Design and the Art Institute in Chicago.

An enlarged photograph of this statue was shown in an exhibit at the Columbus Gallery of Fine Arts in 1949 as part of a show from the Liturgical Arts Society's "Statue Project."

The Crucifix of the Montecassino altar was executed by M.F. Holland. The cross is of walnut; the corpus is of quarter inch brass with incised lines. It is so arranged that this crucifix can be detached from its base and used as a processional cross.

The chapel in the crypt was not used until 1907, when it was fitted with pews and altar to serve Slovak parishioners, with a special curate assigned to preach to them in their native language. Pittsburgh sculptor Francis Aretz later constructed the Lourdes Grotto, which was blessed on May 23, 1920, as a wedding chapel. Aretz, a well-known Pittsburgh sculptor, spent seven years carving the tympanum above The Cathedral of the Madeleine in Salt Lake City, Utah.

He carved the statue of the Blessed Virgin out of Carrara marble. The rest of the chapel, including the altar and figure of Saint Bernadette, is done in cement stone. The Blessed Virgin appeared to Bernadette Soubirous 18 times between February 11 and July 16, 1858. On March 25 of that year she told Bernadette, "I am the Immaculate Conception." (The Dogma of Mary's Immaculate Conception was proclaimed by Pope Pius IX on December 8, 1854).

The floor in the crypt is bluestone from a quarry in Saugerties, New York. The pews were designed by John T. Comes and fashioned in the Saint Vincent carpenter shop.

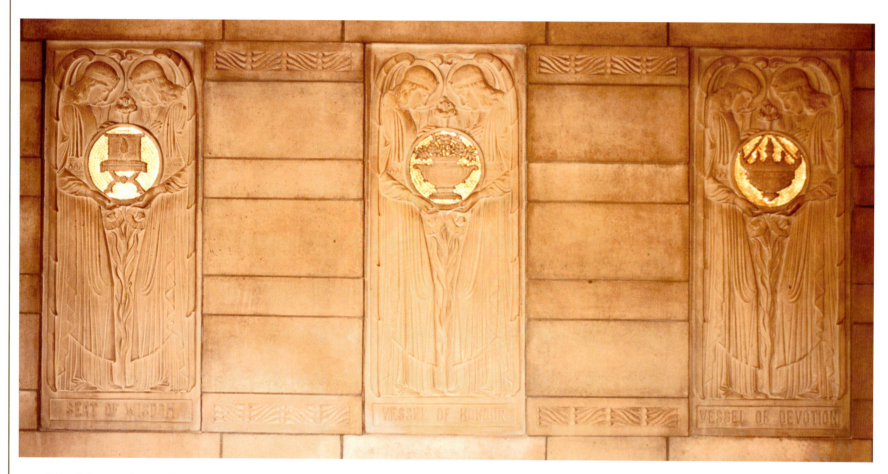

All of the works in this chapel are also the work of Francis Aretz, including the six panels on the side walls and decorative frieze. The six panels each have carvings of two angels holding rondels representing six titles of the Blessed Virgin Mary. To the left of the entrance, the artwork reads, from left to right, Ark of the Covenant, Gate of Heaven, Health of the Sick. To the right of the entrance, the artwork reads Seat of Wisdom, Vessel of Honour and Vessel of Devotion.

Both the original and current altars were consecrated altars. In order to be consecrated the altar must touch the ground. The foundation of the altar can be seen here. Note that the steam line from the power plant to the rest of the campus pre-existed the construction of the Basilica and the builders used the Roman arch so the line would not have to be relocated.

The Crypt of the Archabbey Church was originally intended to be a place of burial for individuals who had been influential in the foundation of the Parish and the Archabbey, College and Seminary.

Red doors mark the entrances into the area that was designed to be the Mausoleum in the Crypt.

The Crypt was designed in such a way that it had alcoves along the side walls under the choir and apse which were to serve as individual tombs. By the time of the Basilica's consecration in 1905, however, the legislature of Pennsylvania had passed laws which forbade the burial of individuals within buildings. Today, the area is used for storage. Above, a marble slab in the ambulatory on the north side of Andrew Hall fills the space intended to be a lowering place for coffins into the Crypt.

August of 1955 marked the centennial of the elevation of Saint Vincent to the rank of an abbey; and, in preparation for the event, extensive renovations of the church were undertaken. The lighting and sound systems were redone, the church was cleaned and painted, and a new main altar was planned. The photo at right shows a scale model of the planned renovation, parts of which were executed and parts which were not.

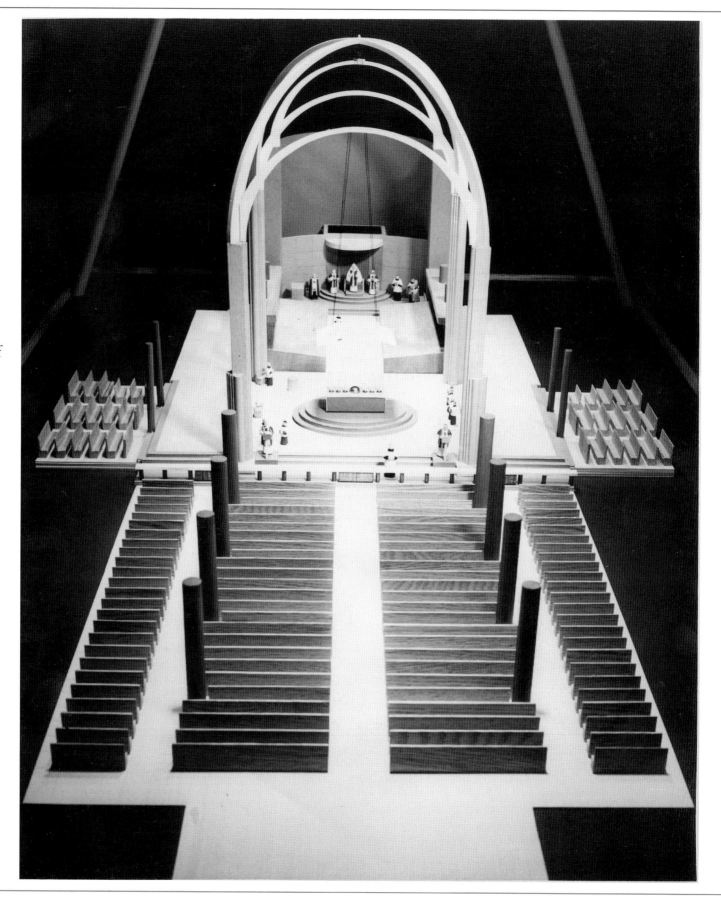

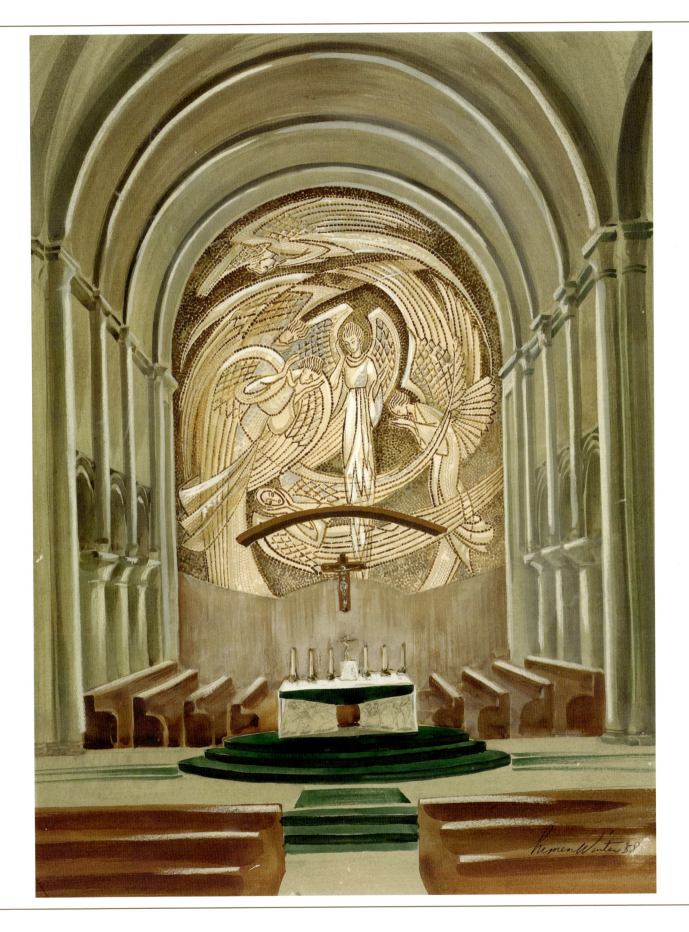

Renovation was meant to be an ongoing process in the Basilica, and in the 1950s, the idea of elaborate artwork in the apse was once more presented. This painting and the one on the following page show two different proposals for the apse.

A different variation of a large angel on the walls of the apse.

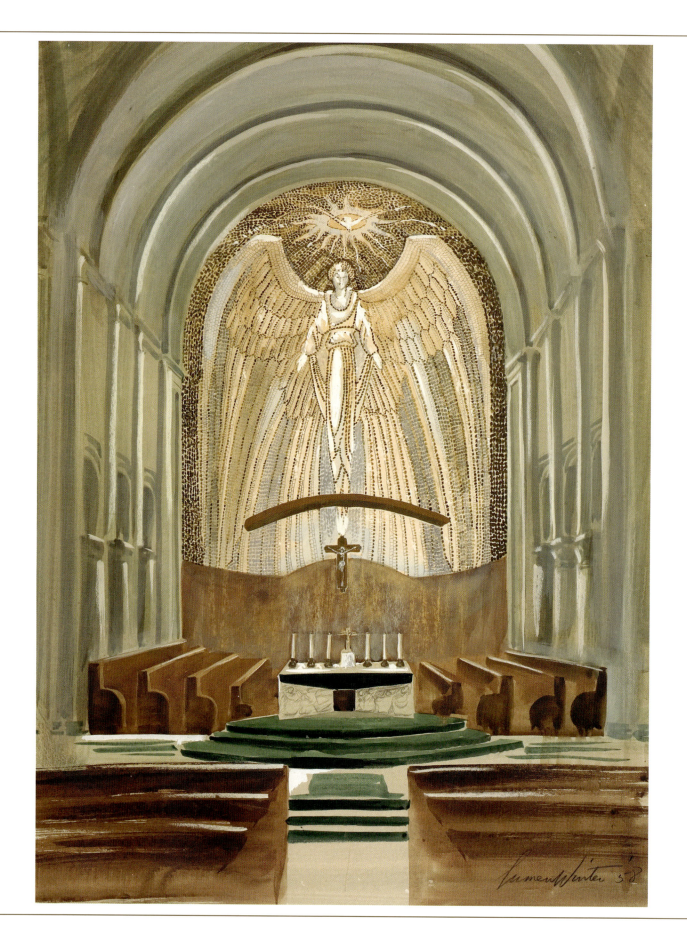

The church as it looked during the renovations in the mid-1950s. Note the slender steel scaffolding, in contrast to the round wooden poles and thick planks used during the original construction.

A view from the apse after the original high altar, altar rails and gates were removed.

Workmen removing the altar railing, a view of the wineglass pulpit, and an appropriate warning sign for men working in the church were a part of the early 1950s renovations. The baptismal font shown in this photograph is incorporated into an ornamental fountain and garden outside of Saint Gregory the Great Chapel.

A tester of aluminum and wood was hung above the new altar. Like a canopy or baldichino, the tester marks and protects a sacred space. The aluminum corpus was designed to reflect a Lucan Christ, that is, one without a crown of thorns. Unlike the present-day crucifix, one side of the cross was a mirror image of the other, so that Christ crucified was in full view to parishioners in the nave and monks in the choir. One corpus now hangs at the west end of the north ambulatory.

A new main altar was designed by Brother Rene Gracida, O.S.B., a monk at Saint Vincent Archabbey, who was also an architect. A native of New Orleans, he was ordained to the priesthood in 1959. He went on to become a diocesan priest in Florida, eventually becoming the first Bishop of Pensacola-Tallahassee, from 1975 to 1983. He moved to the Diocese of Corpus Christi, where he served as Bishop from 1983 until his retirement in 1997. The altar has two base blocks of Botticino marble, each weighing five thousand pounds. The mensa, or table-top, is five by ten feet and weighs ten tons. It is Verde Scuro Fraye marble.

Dr. Leo Ravazzi of Pietrosanto, Italy, carved the four panels on the base blocks of the altar. The table-like altar was designed to reflect contemporary theological emphasis on the Eucharist as both a sacrifice and a meal.

The altar is a free-standing altar, which makes it possible to say Mass from either side. When later liturgical changes had priests face the people during Mass in the Basilica the priest merely had to move to the other side of the altar.

Prior to the main altar's consecration, temporary altars were set up, one for the monks' choir stalls and the other for the parishioners in the nave.

A final stage of the 1950s renovations included rebuilding of the organ. That decade saw a great deal of construction on campus, including completion of the activities building (named Sportsman's Hall), Wimmer Hall, which was a seminary residence at the time, the library, and new athletic fields.

The renovations were completed by August of 1955, which was the centennial of the elevation of Saint Vincent to the rank of an abbey. In honor of the occasion, which was also the fiftieth anniversary of the consecration of the church, the Holy See raised the church to the rank of a minor Basilica.

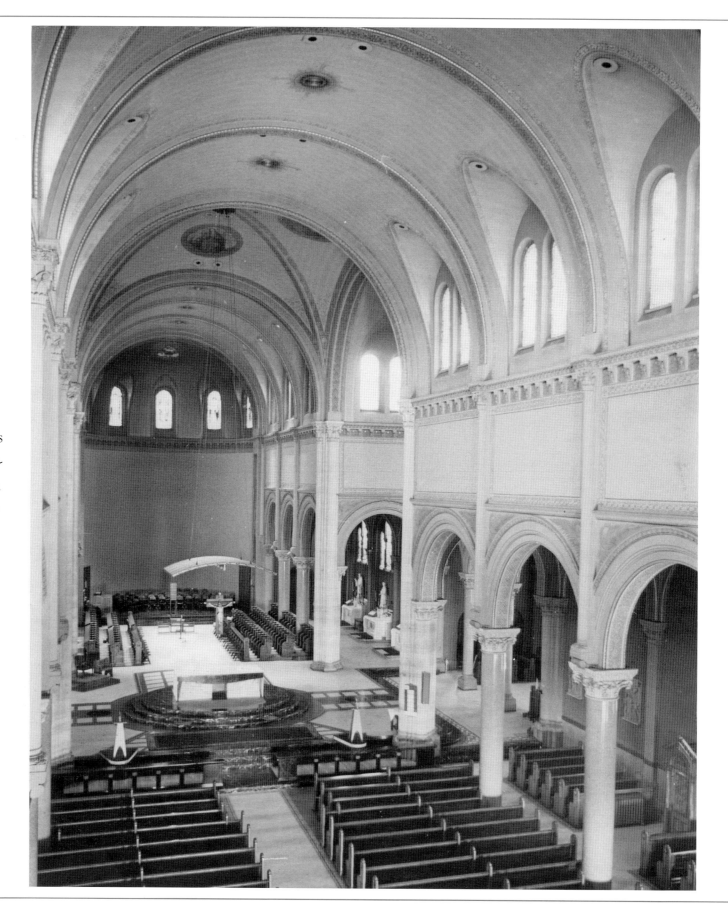

The statues of the Sacred Heart of Jesus and the Blessed Virgin Mary were moved from the altar area to the narthex of the Basilica, during the 1955 renovation.

This photo clearly shows how Andrew Hall and the choir chapel were connected to the Sacristy of the Basilica, and, as the account on the following pages indicates, how the Basilica was saved during the fire of 1963.

On Monday, January 28, 1963, the Basilica was nearly lost in the tragic fire which destroyed many of the old quadrangle buildings at Saint Vincent. The blaze started in the biology laboratory where Old Main (Benedict Hall) met Father James Stillinger's 1835 parish church, which later became the Students' Chapel. College students were on semester break, although seminarians and prep school students were on campus.

Ronald Palenski of Virginia, reported to Brother Colman McFadden, a prefect in the scholasticate, that he saw smoke coming from the biology building, and the alarm was raised. Firemen arrived, but it was so cold outside the brass nozzles of the fire hoses froze. Buildings were evacuated and students and monks joined firemen attempting to douse the blaze. In just over an hour, fire had destroyed the Students' Chapel and had spread to the top floor of the monastery.

Aerial view showing fire damage to the buildings in the quadrangle on campus, and how close the fire came to the Basilica.

Brother Philip Hurley, O.S.B., sacristan, was setting out vestments for the next day's Masses. As the inferno developed in the Students' Chapel, Brother Philip feared it would spread to the Basilica. He and several seminarians began moving vestments from the sacristy. As Brother Philip and students continued to move vestments and sacred vessels to the seminary, the lights went out all over campus. They lit candles and continued their work, as Brother Philip realized that even if the fire didn't reach the sacristy and storage rooms, the water would.

Uncertain whether the Basilica could be saved, Archabbot Denis Strittmatter approved a suggestion to remove the Blessed Sacrament from the church, and Prior Leopold Krul and several other priests and clerics formed a tiny impromptu procession, taking two ciboria from the tabernacle and transferring the Blessed Sacrament to the library chapel.

Father Marcian Kornides, O.S.B., pastor of Saint Vincent Parish, began directing the firemen entering the Basilica, who were intent upon dousing the fire in the choir chapel, which was behind and above the Basilica sacristy. Father Marcian showed the men a door high in the back wall of the sacristy, through which they could enter the rear of the choir chapel to fight the blaze. Fifteen men faced almost unbearable temperatures as they battled the blaze for more than an hour. They were under orders not to advance more than halfway through the chapel as it was feared the bell tower would collapse onto the chapel roof. Later accounts attributed the efforts of these men with saving both the chapel and the Basilica, a turning point in the battle. The choir chapel was scorched and the flames halted before they reached the Basilica. Father Marcian's quick thinking in directing the firemen to the sacristy door helped save the Basilica, with one of the firemen noting that had there been even a fifteen-minute delay, it might have been too late.

Shortly after noon, the fire was under control and firemen began chopping holes in the floors of some of the buildings to allow accumulated water to drain. Monks and seminarians formed bucket brigades to clear out the water that had flooded the Basilica.

More than one hundred monks were burned out of their rooms, but classes resumed within a week of the fire, which had caused nearly $2 million in damages. Father Stillinger's old church, the Students' Chapel, was gone, as were the biology building and the bell tower. Large sections of the monastery and prep school were also destroyed. The Basilica had sustained extensive water damage and the choir chapel and monastic refectory in Andrew Hall were also damaged. While the losses were extensive, it was more important that no lives had been lost.

Page 109: Cleanup efforts were begun.

Parishioners and visitors to the Basilica through the mid-1990s saw a church in need of restoration. Years of soot and smoke from the region's industrial heritage accumulated on the once vibrant orange-red brick, and exposure to the elements naturally caused additional deterioration. Keystone Waterproofing Co., Inc., of Greensburg, headed by President Ron Raimondo, a parishioner, undertook the masonry restoration. The above photo was taken by the late Fred Rogers, "Mister Rogers" of the famous children's television program, who was a frequent visitor to the Saint Vincent campus.

Scaffolding surrounded the Basilica as renovations started. First, workmen used electric grinders, hand chisels and rakes to remove vertical and horizontal joints. All of this was done with great care so as not to destroy the surface of the brick and stone.

Then came a thorough washing, scrubbing and low pressure application of a mild restorative cleaner.

| New Restoration Brick | Deteriorated Exterior Wall Brick | Damaged Interior Wall Brick |

Brick Size: 8.5" x 2.5" x 4.125"

In addition to cleaning and repointing, some bricks were so badly damaged that several areas needed to be completely rebuilt. The parapet walls on the north and south gable ends were completely rebuilt with special-sized matching brick, which were custom-made from Cushwa Brick Company of Maryland. Ninety percent of the brick underneath the gutter areas had to be replaced or relaid.

A crew of experienced tuckpointers applied a premixed mortar and sand (with high lime content) into the joint cavities in layers, and tooled to match the previously tooled joints. After the repointing, all previously caulked areas were recaulked with a polyurethane sealant.

The four terra cotta turrets were completely deteriorated, and in some cases, pieces could be removed by workers with their bare hands. The stone bases and crosses were cracked on the top portion of the gables. Edwards Stone Company of Iowa was contracted to recast all of the pieces.

In several areas stone door and window trims were broken, cracked, delaminated or missing. Special patching material from Europe was used for some of these repairs.

Before and after restoration photos of the Tympanum above The Great Portal, or main entrance, to the Basilica.

While the cornerstone on the northeast corner of the Basilica is dated 1892, identical monuments with the dates 1896 are at the high points on both the north and south walls. These signify the year the walls of the church were completed. Before and after photos show the restoration of these monuments.

Ornate stonework restored.

The deteriorated old slate steps were replaced, and a Parish Center built adjacent to the south side of the Basilica.

These photos show the work in progress of the step replacement.

The new steps are of pink granite.

Before the restoration.

After the restoration, which included a new roof installed by Kalkreuth Roofing Co.

At the same time exterior renovations were underway, scaffolding was erected for interior renovations, which included cleaning and repainting.

Father Vincent Crosby, O.S.B., coordinated the renovation and designed many of the new elements, such as the Shrine of the Holy Oils and the Shrine of the Benefactors, the reconciliation rooms, the sacristy and clerestory windows, and the candle stands and design of the Chapel of the Immaculate Conception. He designed and worked with Norbert and Victoria Koehn on the crucifix over the main altar, the Blessed Sacrament Tower and Tabernacle as well as the Chapel of the Resurrection.

The stained glass restoration was executed by Phillips Stain Glass, now known as Renaissance Glass. A.J. Vater & Co., Inc., of McKees Rocks, painted the church. Replacement tiles in the marble mosaic floor were designed by Father Vincent. The tiles were produced by Favret Mosaics, Pietrasanta, Italy, and the flooring was installed by Fantin Flooring, Inc., Pittsburgh.

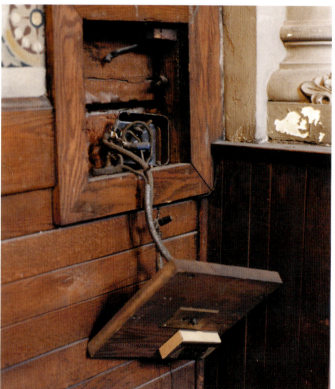

In addition to infrastructure improvements such as electrical work, the Stations of the Cross and stained glass windows were restored. The Baptistry became the Chapel of the Immaculate Conception.

The font depicting Jesus' baptism in the River Jordan by John the Baptist is presently located in the Mary Mother of Wisdom Student Chapel.

The statues of the Sacred Heart of Jesus and the Blessed Virgin Mary, which once graced the two sides of the sanctuary, facing the body of the church, had been moved during the renovation of the mid-1950s to the narthex. During the 1990s restoration they were moved again. The Blessed Virgin Mary statue was placed in the former Baptistry, which was redecorated as a Marian chapel, and the statue of the Sacred Heart of Jesus is on the second floor of the Parish Center, outside of the Assembly Room.

This statue of the Sacred Heart of Jesus and the statue of the Blessed Virgin Mary, were done in white Carrara marble, executed in 1913-1914 by Giovanni Sugari.

Phillips Stained Glass Studio cleaned and repaired the windows in the Basilica, including the rose windows.

The old clerestory windows were removed and replaced.

The side altars were also removed, circa 1995-1996, leaving only the four statues of Saint Maurus, Saint Placidus, Saint Benedict and Saint Scholastica, now mounted on new pedestals by Norbert Koehn in the same locations.

View of one of the side altars. Note the deep rose-colored paint on the walls, which gave a darker appearance to the interior of the church. The statue is that of Saint Placidus.

Following the exterior restoration, construction began on the Parish Center, located on the south side of the Basilica (1995-1996).

Prior to construction of the Parish Center, parish offices had been housed on the ground floor of Leander Hall, to the north of the Basilica.

In addition to the parish offices, the Parish Center also houses the Basilica Gift Shop, restroom facilities and a large multi-purpose assembly room on the second floor. An elevator provides handicapped access to the Basilica.

When William Schickel drew up his original design in 1891, two imposing spires were to have topped the towers at the front of the building. When the Basilica was finally "completed" in 1905, after 14 years of construction, a lack of funds prevented that from happening.

Capping the renovations of the Basilica, in time for the new millennium, spires were added to the front towers.

The pre-fabricated 55-foot spires were assembled in the parking lot in front of the Basilica in three sections, then lifted by crane to the towers.

The base of the south tower spire is lifted into place.

The top section of the south tower spire is about to be hoisted into place.

The top section of the south tower spire is completed.

The middle section of the north tower spire is lifted skyward.

The north tower is nearing completion. The new spires match the Basilica's tern-coated stainless steel roof in style and color.

Each front spire is topped by ten foot high crosses.

Cross being lifted into place.

The north tower houses three bells, weighing nearly two tons. The bells are programmed to ring throughout the day by automated controls equipped with state-of-the-art electronics.

The bells are named Jesus, Mary and Joseph. They were initially manufactured by the R. W. Vanduzen Company of Cincinnati for Blessed Sacrament Church, April 12, 1914, as the inscription states.

In 1999, then-Monsignor Lawrence Brandt, who was named the Bishop of Greensburg in 2004, was attending a Seminary Board of Regents meeting on the day the bells were placed in the north tower. His grandfather was a bricklayer pictured in one of the photos of the workmen building the Basilica.

Archabbot Douglas R. Nowicki, O.S.B., prepares to ascend via crane to bless the steeples and crosses following completion of the construction.

Archabbot Douglas R. Nowicki, O.S.B., prepares to bless the bells in the north tower.

His Eminence Francis Cardinal Arinze, who in 2005 was the prefect for the Congregation for Divine Worship and the Discipline of the Sacraments, blessed the new baptismal font and bell towers on April 29, 2000.

A winter view of the completed Basilica, with new spires.

Among the many carved stone inserts on the exterior walls of the Basilica are depictions of angels representing the meeting of heaven and earth, and reminding those who are entering that this is the "House of God."

These figures are also a sign that Saint Vincent Archabbey and the whole American-Cassinese monastic congregation was placed under the patronage of the Holy Guardian Angels by the apostolic brief of Pope Pius IX, on August 24, 1855.

View of the Basilica from a courtyard behind the sacristy. The garden is affectionately known as "Sebastian's Garden," after Father Sebastian Samay, O.S.B., who has tended to its blooms for many years. Note the ornate stonework that is present throughout the design of the church.

Rose window in the north wall of the Basilica.

Located near the northeast corner of the Basilica (see above), is a "boot scraper," which early parishioners—many of whom were farmers—used to scrape the mud from their boots prior to attending church services.

Since ancient times, Christian churches were seen as microcosms—little versions—of the Kingdom of God. The facade of the Basilica has three portals. The Great Portal is the largest and most ornate. Following Romanesque traditions it is comprised of a large Roman arch, which is divided by archivolts with foliage and geometric patterns. The archivolts are supported by four jamb columns on each side. Over the double set of double doors is the tympanum depicting Christ giving the keys of the Kingdom to Saint Peter.

The oversized doors have special, ornate hinges designed by William Schickel. All of these works of art join together to create a fitting entrance to the House of God.

In the center above the door is the Tympanum or half-moon shaped piece of stone. The Tympanum depicts Christ giving the keys of the Kingdom to Saint Peter (see Matthew 16). Medieval tympanums most often depict the Last Judgment of Christ. After the Protestant Reformation, Catholic churches frequently placed this depiction above their portals to show their solidarity with the Holy See. Peter is kneeling before Jesus. Jesus asks him, "Who do you say that I am?" Peter responds, "You are the Christ, the Son of God." Jesus replies, "No mortal has told you this ... you are Rock, and upon this Rock I will build my church ... I will give you the keys to the Kingdom of Heaven." Above the central column of the door is an angel.

The sculptor was Polish artist Ladislaus Vitalis. The Polish variation of his name is Wladyslaw Witalis, with Witalis pronounced as "Vitalis." Other than the artist's nationality, no information on him is available in the Archabbey archives. He also carved the capitals atop the columns inside the church, while perched on a platform erected around the pillars. (See page 27 for a view of the capitals prior to carving.)

There are angels above the two side doors on the exterior, and angels appear sporadically in the stonework on the second tier of the Basilica around the Church. Angels are the messengers of God, who continually sing his praise. They announce good news to mankind, and serve as guardians and guides. Their presence in stone throughout the Basilica represents their spiritual presence. These side door tympana are also the work of Ladislaus Vitalis. In this photo, of the angel above the door to the left of the Great Portal, the Latin is *Super Hanc Petram Aedificabo Ecclesia Meam*, or "On this rock I will build my church." Carved below the angel on the door to the right of the Great Portal is *Tibi Dabo Claves Regni Coelorum*, or "To you I give the keys of the kingdom of heaven." Both verses are from the Gospel of Matthew.

The Saint Vincent Archabbey coat of arms hangs from the back balcony. It is composed of a field of white and blue lozenges taken from the coat of arms of the Royal House of Bavaria—the Wittelsbach family—whose scion, King Ludwig I, became the royal patron of Archabbot Boniface Wimmer's missionary vision. The chevron with three silver roundels is borrowed from the coat of arms of William Penn, the founding father of Pennsylvania, but it has been reversed to form a "V," standing for Saint Vincent. Three black crosses were added to the silver roundels to symbolize the three-fold Benedictine monastic vows of Obedience, Conversion of Life and Stability.

The Basilica is designed in the Romanesque style. This type of architecture hearkens back nearly 2,500 years to ancient Rome. The name "Basilica" derives from ancient Greek: *Basiloikos*. This word is composed of two Greek words: *Basileus,* which means "king," and *Oikos*, which means "house." Hence, *Basilikos* or Basilica, literally means royal or kingly house.

Eighteen columns of dark red Peterhead granite are employed in the Basilica. Those in the Nave are 14 feet high, two feet wide and weigh four and a half tons each.

The black spots on the columns are natural imperfections in the stone. The monks faced them away from the doors so that people would not notice them when they entered the church. Procured through the firm of Batterson and Eisele of New York City, the columns come from Aberdeen, Scotland.

The sculptural work was done by a Polish artist named Ladislaus Vitalis, the same man who carved the Tympanum above the Great Portal and the angels above the two side doors. Perched on a platform erected around the pillars, he chiseled intricate designs on the rough Indiana sandstone once they were in place.

The pilasters are decorative and are made from plaster molds.

The flooring is composed of three-quarters of an inch square Cararra marble pieces, sized, cut and hand placed by Italian craftsmen in 1901. The cube-like blocks are set in mosaic fashion in such a way that the predominant gray field is checkered at regular intervals by block-like formations of light brown marble. The same kind of stone of various colors also forms a border around the whole. Every free floor space is composed of these mosaics, all of which were imported from Italy by the contractors, Pellarin and Co. of New York City.

The choir stalls, pews, main ambo (lectern) and benches were carved in the carpenter shop, adjacent to the Basilica, out of native oak and pre-blight American chestnut by the lay brothers. The woodwork is based on designs by William Schickel.

A craftsman named H.J. Engbert from New Baltimore, Pennsylvania executed the pews.

From the back organ loft one has a view down through the nave, to the crossing where the main altar stands, to the choir where the monks sing the divine office, and the apse.

The main ambo or lectern is hand-carved, and on the book rest is inscribed "*In omnibus glorificetur Deus*" (May God be Glorified in All Things). Brother Mark Floreanini, O.S.B., created the stained glass windows in the doors leading into the Chapel of the Immaculate Conception.

Charles McKenry of Pittsburgh built the confessionals. McKenry carved the red oak by hand to match those furnishings made by the monks. During the renovation in the 1990s, the original confessionals were enlarged and redesigned to allow for face-to-face confession. Glass removed from the borders of the Nave windows was used in new doors for the confessionals.

The sacristy is in the classical shape of an arc that bends around the exterior apse wall. It is furnished with solid wood cabinetry that serves to house the liturgical vestiture and sacred vessels used for Mass and sacramental celebrations in the Basilica. The flooring is done entirely in white Carrara marble tiles to match those of the main body of the church.

The woodwork was refinished in 2005.

The sacristy, located behind the curved wall of the apse, is lined with cupboards, shelves, and drawers of ornately carved oak which matches the woodwork in the Basilica.

Handcarved and worked wood retains its strength and beauty after a century of use. This cabinetry is in the "work sacristy."

The entrance way into the "work sacristy" is actually a passage through the exterior wall of the Basilica into the monastic refectory in Andrew Hall.

Two hallways form "arms" that architecturally embrace the Basilica from the external north and south sides of the apse and choir. These hallways serve to provide a peaceful transition from the main part of the campus to the Basilica. They are called "ambulatories" — from the Latin *ambulare,* which literally means "to walk." The ambulatories have also been used as places of procession and places to form the *statio* line for solemn events in the Basilica. With their unique acoustics, college students have dubbed them "whispering hallways" due to the way in which the human voice carries down the hallways.

The sacristy is used for vesting and preparations for the various liturgical celebrations in the Basilica. It was completed in 1904 and renovated in 1955 and again in 2005.

The Benedictine Cross is reflected in much of the Basilica's artwork, from the woodwork to stone sculpture in the walls. These fixtures are called the "Consecration Candles." They were originally lit on August 24, 1905, as the Basilica was being consecrated. There are twelve of them, representing the 12 apostles, who are the foundation of the Church. Each Benedictine Cross signifies where the church was anointed with Sacred Chrism by the Bishop.

At right, is the "elevation bell." It is rung to announce the entrance of the ministers into the church from the sacristy at the beginning of a liturgical service.

Below is a piece of monastic ingenuity. This thin slit in the northern sacristy door, (visible from inside the sacristy) allowed for the sacristan to monitor liturgies without being conspicuous.

Two frescoes adorn the sacristy walls, both executed by Joseph Reiter. The first, below, the Sorrowful Mother (*Mater Dolorosa* in Latin) is a depiction taken from the prophecy of Simeon in the Gospel of Luke, Chapter 2:34-35:

"Behold, this child is destined for the fall and rise of many in Israel, and to be a sign that will be contradicted (and you yourself a sword will pierce) so that the thoughts of many hearts may be revealed."

The second, above, is *Ecce Homo* (Behold the Man). Pontius Pilate presents Jesus to the gathered crowd in John 19:5, "Behold, the man!" Jesus has been scourged, and crowned with thorns.

Seating capacity is approximately 800. The sanctuary and monks' choir occupy nearly half the space of the building.

The monks and lay brothers of Saint Vincent made many of the wood furnishings for the Basilica, such as the choir stalls behind the altar (opposite page).

The Baptismal Font is the first element encountered once visitors pass through the climate controlled doors at the main entrance to the Basilica. It is the work of Norbert and Victoria Koehn of Cleveland, Ohio. Carved from a three-ton block of Indiana Limestone, it was designed to coordinate with the existing main columns in the Basilica. Designed in three separate pieces so it could be transported, the font holds 20 gallons of water. It was installed in April of 2000, and blessed by Francis Cardinal Arinze.

An alcove near the Chapel of the Immaculate Conception contains a respository for Holy Oils, which are blessed by the Bishop on Holy Thursday. The repository is called the Ambry. It was designed by Father Vincent Crosby, O.S.B.

To the south of main entrance is an icon of Saint Joseph, designed by Father Vincent Crosby, O.S.B., and executed by Kevin Coffey, formerly a resident of Greensburg and now a monk of Saint Procopius Abbey in Lisle, Illinois. This alcove, and the corresponding one containing the Holy Oils, were part of the 1990s renovations. Previously these areas had been storage closets.

The Paschal Candle bears a place of prominence in the rites of Easter, baptism, and Christian burial. It signifies Christ, who brought the light of resurrection to all, dispelling the darkness of sin and death. Blessed at the beginning of the Easter Vigil, the candle is also lit during baptisms, when we die to sin that we might rise to eternal life with Christ; and, at funerals, as a reminder of the promise of eternal life for all who believe. The candle is engraved with a cross. Above the cross appears the Greek letter, *Alpha*, and below it, the Greek letter, *Omega*, to show that Christ is the beginning and end of all things. In the four quadrants created by the cross are found the numerals of the current year to show that all of time belongs to and has been sanctified by Christ. A grain of incense is inserted into the center and each of the endpoints of the cross, representing the five wounds inflicted upon Jesus in his crucifixion.

To the right of the main entrance, in the northeast corner of the Basilica, is the Chapel of the Immaculate Conception. The Chapel's centerpiece is a Carrara marble sculpture of Our Lady of the Immaculate Conception, the work of Italian artist Giovanni Sugari. Originally installed in the sanctuary and later flanking the main doors, the statue is now in its own chapel.

The Stoltzenberg Company of Munich, Bavaria, made the large triptych windows on the north and south sides of the monastic choir stalls, as well as the pictorial windows in the transepts and aisles. The stained glass windows were installed in 1900 after the plasterwork and the interior were finished. There are 27 stained glass windows in the Basilica and 22 tinted glass windows in the clerestory — or upper windows near the ceiling.

The Nativity window depicts the Virgin Mary, her face shining in tranquil joy, tenderly cradling the Christ child on her lap in the stable at Bethlehem. As the Evangelist Luke recounts the birth of the Savior, angels, after announcing the Messiah's birth to shepherds abiding in the fields, raised their voices in praise of God. The Nativity window portrays these angels in their continuous act of praise. While three of the angels adore the Christ child in the foreground, the choir of angels accompanies their glorious anthem in the background to the melodious strains of mandolin, violin and flute.

The letter designations for the stained glass windows correspond to the map provided as part of this book.

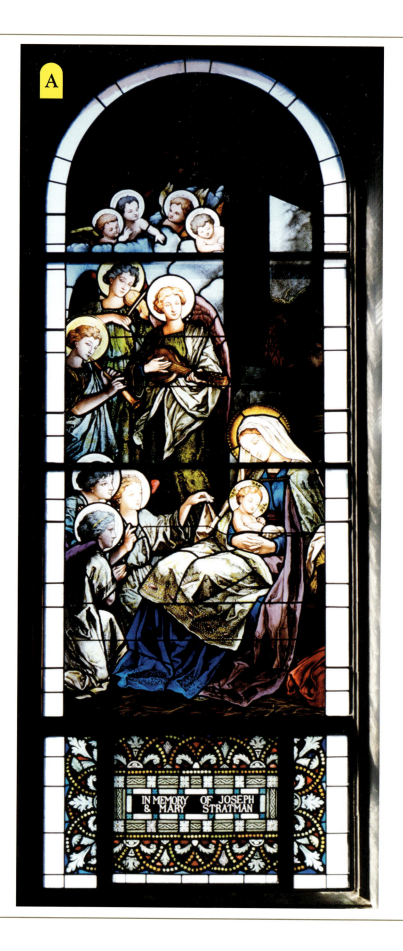

The Epiphany window portrays the visit of the Magi to the Christ child at the stable in Bethlehem. The Gospel of Luke records the visit of wise men from the East, who following a star, traveled to pay homage to the new king whose birth had been prophesied. In the tradition of the Church, this event has been known as the Epiphany, because it marks the manifestation of the Messiah to all nations, of whom the three wise men are emissaries. The Epiphany window portrays the star shining on the infant Jesus, the Light of the World, in the arms of his mother Mary. While Joseph stands vigilant in the background, the three Magi adore the Christ child, having laid their gifts at the Virgin's feet.

This window depicts the Gospel story of the Child Jesus Teaching in the Temple. The Gospel of Luke tells that each year Mary and Joseph made a pilgrimage to Jerusalem for the Feast of Passover. According to the gospel, when he was twelve years old, Jesus remained in Jerusalem after the feast, unbeknownst to his parents. When they returned to the city searching for Jesus, Mary and Joseph found him in the temple among the teachers of the Law. In this window, the child Jesus, dressed in a white tunic, is pictured in the foreground with three teachers, who listen to him attentively as he reaches toward the book of the Law held by one of the men. In the background, Joseph can be seen pointing out Jesus as Mary descends a stairway to find her Son.

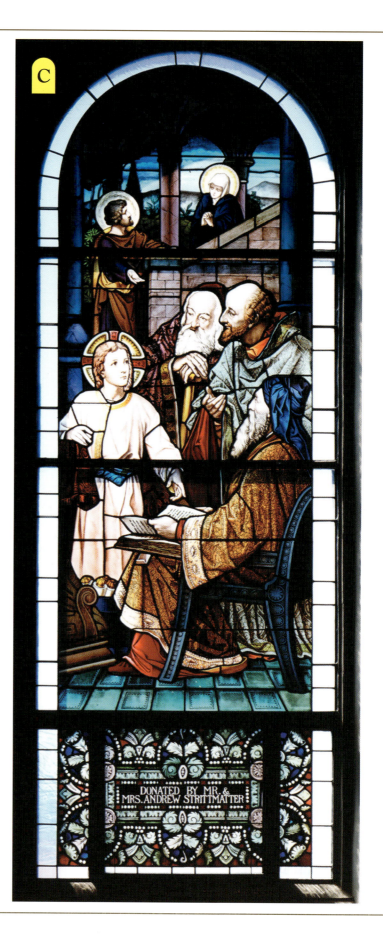

This window portrays the Holy Family: Mary, Joseph and the child Jesus at home in Nazareth. While Mary is shown seated at her handwork, Joseph pauses from his carpentry to point out the child Jesus, who approaches Joseph carrying a pair of crosses he has made from scraps of wood.

This window portrays the Baptism of Jesus in the Jordan by John the Baptist. In the foreground Jesus stands in the Jordan River, with his head bowed and hands folded in a stance of prayer. He wears a red loincloth reminding the viewer of his Passion which is yet to come. John the Baptist, wearing a garment of camel hair (Mk 1:6) holds a staff in his left hand from which a banner hangs bearing the Latin words, *"Ecce Agnus Dei,"* which mean "Behold the Lamb of God," a title by which the Baptist describes Jesus in John's Gospel (1:29). The top of the window shows the Holy Spirit, in the form of a dove, descending upon Jesus through an opening in the clouds, while the golden rays represent a voice from the heavens, which was heard to say, "This is my beloved Son, with whom I am well pleased" (Mt 3:17). In the background, an angel hovers nearby, holding Christ's tunic.

The Transfiguration window depicts an event described in the three synoptic gospels, Matthew, Mark and Luke. These gospels relate that Jesus took three of his disciples, Peter, James and his brother, John, up on a mountain, where they witnessed him transfigured. "His face shone like the sun and his clothes became white as light" (Mt 17:2). On Jesus' left, Moses, holding a tablet of the commandments, represents the Law. On his right, Elijah, with a book in his hand, represents the Prophets. The transfigured Christ stands prominently in the center of the window as the fulfillment of both the Law and the Prophets, while the disciples cower in fear in the foreground.

This window depicts Jesus blessing the children. The gospels of Matthew, Mark and Luke record that people began to bring their children to Jesus so that he might touch them. The disciples did not approve, but Jesus rebuked them, saying "Let the children come to me; do not prevent them, for the kingdom of God belongs to such as these" (Mk 10:14). The window portrays Jesus sitting, holding a toddler on his right knee while his left hand rests in blessing on the head of a second child, whose mother presents her to Jesus. An older woman in the garb of a widow looks on approvingly. A boy stands on Jesus' left, while two disciples are shown standing behind Jesus. In the foreground, a young girl kneels to Jesus' right. In the background, other women with children in arms can be seen approaching.

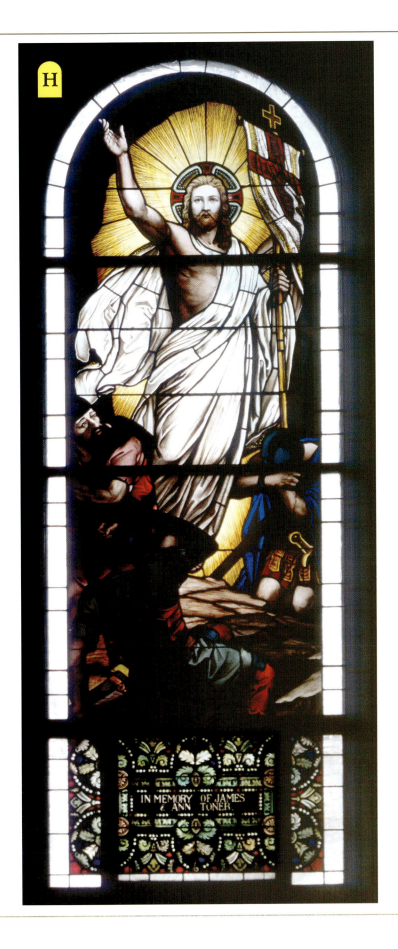

The Resurrection window portrays Jesus victoriously emerging from the tomb dressed in dazzling white. Golden rays of glory emanate from the risen Christ. His right hand is raised in triumph over the grave. Jesus holds a cross in his left hand from which hangs a banner of white with a red cross emblazoned upon it, symbolic of the resurrection. In the left foreground, two of the temple guards look on in astonishment, while a third guard, wearing the uniform of a Roman Centurion, hides his face in fear on the right.

This window illustrates the scene from the Acts of the Apostles, in which Jesus ascended to heaven. The Acts of the Apostles records that after appearing to the disciples and teaching them for forty days after the Resurrection, Jesus called the apostles to Mount Olivet where he admonished them to wait for the Spirit to come to them. In the window, Jesus, dressed in a dazzling garment of white and gold, stands prominently in the center rising on the clouds toward heaven. Two angels, kneeling in prayer and adoration, accompany the ascending Lord. In the foreground, the apostles, looking upward, witness the Ascension.

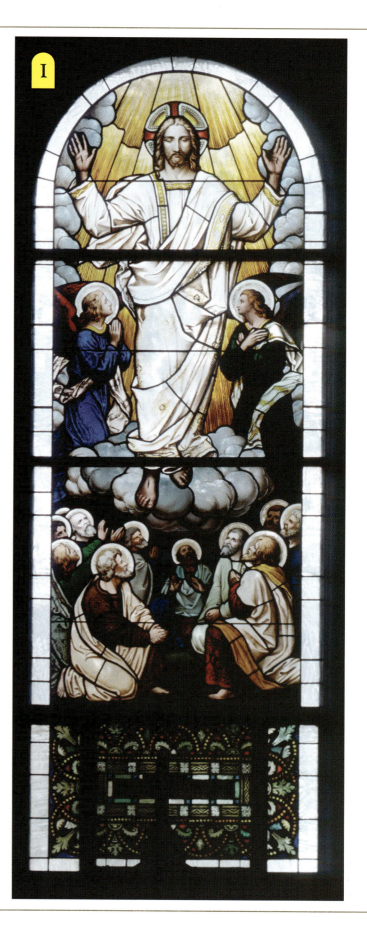

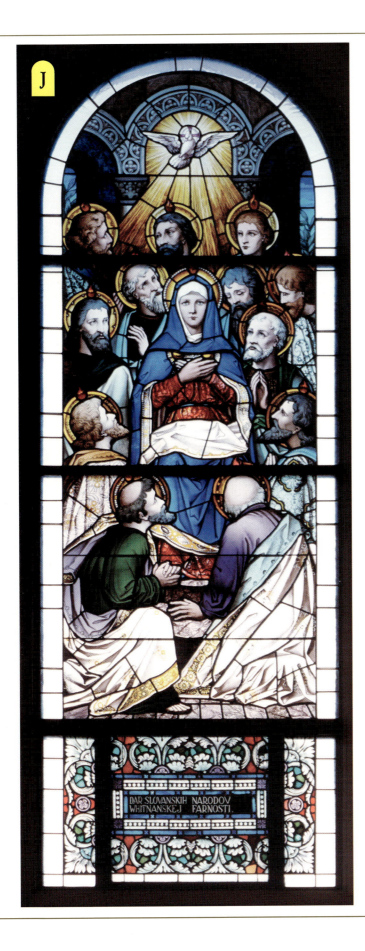

Fifty days after the Resurrection, the Acts of the Apostles tells us, the Holy Spirit descended upon the disciples gathered in the upper room. This window portrays this event, known as Pentecost. The Holy Spirit is shown descending in rays of gold from heaven. The twelve apostles are gathered around the Virgin Mary, who is seated in the center in a posture of serenity and prayer. Tongues of flame are seen resting on each of their heads. The Acts of the Apostles attests that the disciples were filled with the Holy Spirit and began to speak in different languages as they fearlessly began to proclaim the gospel.

The Good Samaritan window portrays a scene from a famous parable found in Luke's Gospel. Jesus uses the story to illustrate the concept of who is our neighbor. According to the parable, when a man is attacked along the road to Jericho, a Samaritan, a traditional enemy of the Jewish people, shows him compassion when two members of the man's own religious leadership pass by without providing assistance. The window shows the Samaritan lifting the wounded man onto his own animal, preparing to take him to Jericho, where the parable tells us, he provided for the man's care. A flask of wine, which, according to the parable, was used by the Samaritan to cleanse the injured man's wounds, sits in the foreground. In the background another traveler can be seen approaching Jericho after having passed the victim without offering assistance.

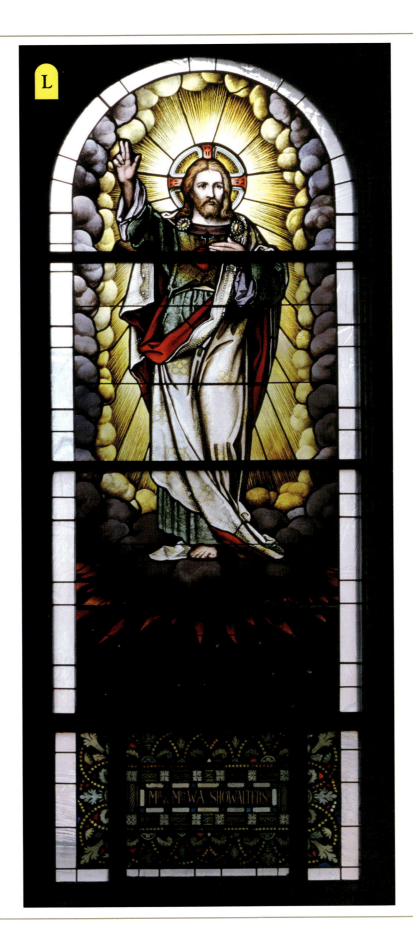

This window presents Jesus returning in glory as foretold in the Acts of the Apostles. The risen Lord is shown standing on clouds resting on a starry nighttime sky. Golden rays of glory shine in the background. Dressed in rich robes, Jesus is shown with his right hand raised in a posture of teaching while his left hand points to his sacred heart, seat of his tender love for humanity whom he redeemed through his incarnation, passion, death and resurrection.

This window illustrates the parable of the Pharisee and the Publican, or tax collector, found in Luke's Gospel. According to the parable, both men came to the temple to pray. The Pharisee was ostentatious, proclaiming his own righteousness. The tax collector was humble, not even daring to look up to heaven as he prayed for mercy. The window shows the Pharisee in the foreground, dressed richly. He points with his left hand to draw attention to the coins he is dropping into the basket of offerings with his right hand. In the background, the Publican can be seen dressed somberly. His head is bowed as he makes his quiet prayer for forgiveness.

Saint Boniface was a Benedictine monk of the eighth century in England. Born of a noble family, he chose religious life over secular pursuits. He is noted for his missionary work to Germany, where he preached the gospel and brought about the conversion of many. Tradition holds that Boniface cut down an oak tree sacred to the god Thor in order to show the powerlessness of the Norse gods. He was ordained a bishop by Pope Gregory II and was elevated to the dignity of archbishop by Pope Gregory III. The window shows Saint Boniface in a church dressed in the vestments of a bishop. He wears the miter of the episcopacy and the pallium of the archbishop. He holds a crosier in his right hand and clutches a book of the Gospels to his heart. The book is pierced by a dagger, symbolizing Boniface's martyrdom for the faith. Saint Boniface converted many souls to Christ and bears the title, Apostle of Germany.

The Good Shepherd window portrays Jesus under one of his many titles from John's Gospel. Dressed in the triumphant colors white and gold, Christ stands holding a shepherd's crook in his left hand, surrounded by a flock of sheep, reminding the viewer of Jesus' words, "I am the good shepherd" (John 10:14). Jesus holds a lamb on his right shoulder, reminiscent of the parable of the lost sheep found in Matthew's Gospel, which illustrates God's love for us using the image of a shepherd, who having a hundred sheep, would willingly leave the other ninety-nine to go in search of the one who has wandered off. In the background, an apple tree stands as a reminder of Adam and Eve, the first to go astray.

This window depicts John the Baptist, whom Matthew's Gospel describes as "clothed in a garment of camel's hair" (Mt 3:4), reminiscent of the prophet Elijah. His right hand is raised as he calls the people of Israel to repentance. In his left arm rests a cross-shaped staff from which hangs a banner bearing the words, *"Ecce Agnus Dei,"* or "Behold the Lamb of God," a title by which the Baptist describes Jesus in John's Gospel (1:29). In his left hand, John the Baptist holds a book, upon which is enthroned a lamb symbolic of Jesus. The lamb holds a white banner emblazoned with a cross in red, a symbol of the resurrection. The book represents the scroll with seven seals described in the Book of Revelation (5: 1-10), which only the triumphant Lamb of God is found worthy to open.

This window portrays the closing scene of the parable of the Prodigal Son recorded in the Gospel of Luke. The parable relates how a man had two sons. The younger son returns to his father's house asking forgiveness after having squandered his inheritance in a foreign land. Illustrating the mercy of God, the man welcomes his son back into his household. The window shows the prodigal son, kneeling in the garb of a beggar in the foreground, while his father stretches his hands in a posture of benediction. A servant can be seen in the background approaching with a robe that matches the father's own garment, a sign of the son's full reinstatement as a member of the household. To the left, the older son is shown returning from the fields where he was working.

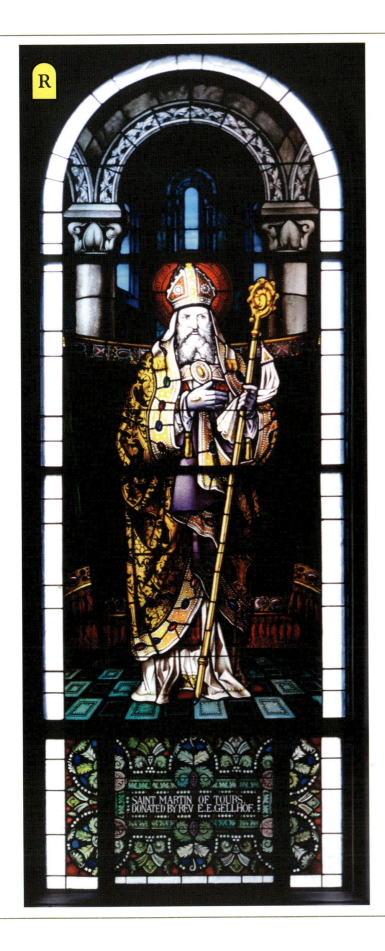

This window is dedicated to Saint Martin of Tours, a bishop of the fourth century. Saint Martin was born to a military family and as a young man was enlisted in the Roman army. According to legend, he split his cloak to share it with a poor beggar. A disciple of Saint Hilary, Saint Martin chose a life of solitude when his military duty was completed, but was made bishop of Tours by popular acclaim. His ministry, marked by zeal and simplicity, is noted for his staunch opposition to heresies that gained popularity during his lifetime. The first chapel at Montecassino was dedicated to him by Saint Benedict.

Saint Benedict and Saint Scholastica were twins. They met once per year at a small house between their two monasteries. On this occasion, the two have spent the entire day praying, studying Sacred Scripture and sharing a meal together. Benedict stands and is preparing to leave. Scholastica asks him to stay a little longer. Benedict refuses, citing that it is not good for monks and nuns to be outside of their monasteries at night. Scholastica pleads for him to stay. He adamantly refuses. Scholastica begins to pray. Suddenly, the winds pick up. The curtain is blowing in the background. Heavy rains begin to fall. The rain comes in the window in the center. The weather has turned foul and unwelcoming. Benedict exclaims, "Woman! What have you done?" Scholastica states that since her brother would not listen, she asked someone who would listen to her — namely, God. The weather was so inclement that Benedict had to stay the night. He and his sister prayed, studied more Scripture and had a meal in the morning. Benedict left later that morning. As he was nearly back to his monastery, he received news that his sister had died. She knew her time on earth was coming to a close and she wanted to spend it with her brother. This window teaches that we must never discount the power of prayer and the virtue of charity.

In August of 1855, Pope Pius IX—now Blessed Pope Pius IX—elevated Saint Vincent to the status of an autonomous Abbey and created the American Cassinese Congregations of Benedictine monks. He declared the Holy Guardian Angels to be the patrons of the American-Cassinese Congregation of Benedictine abbeys. The center panel of this triptych window portrays a Guardian Angel with his arms about a young girl, dressed in blue, and a young boy, who wears a brown tunic, as they make their way along a path. The boy clings to the angel for protection from a red snake, coiled as if about to strike in the lower right foreground of the window, while the girl's upturned face and folded hands suggest a stance of prayer. The scene recalls Psalm 91, verses 11-13:

> *For God commands the angels*
> > *to guard you in all your ways.*
> *With their hands they shall support you*
> > *lest you strike your foot against a stone.*
> *You shall tread upon the asp and the viper,*
> *trample the lion and the dragon.*

The side panels of the window depict scenes from the Book of Tobit. The left panel portrays the Archangel Raphael accompanying young Tobiah on his journey from Ninevah to Rages in Media. The Archangel carries a traveler's staff in his right hand, while his left hand is outstretched in a posture of teaching. Tobiah looks at the Archangel Raphael attentively as he carries his staff in his left hand. His dog, which Scripture records accompanied the pair, frolics in the foreground. In the right panel, Tobiah greets his father Tobit upon his safe return to his parents' home as his mother Anna and the Archangel Raphael look on.

Pope Saint Gregory the Great records in his Dialogues that, when the time came for Saint Benedict to pass from this world, he beseeched his brothers to bring him into the Oratory, or chapel, that he might pray. This triptych window presents that scene. Benedict can be seen in the center panel with his arms outstretched toward the altar in a posture of praise. He is supported by his monks, one of whom holds Benedict's crosier. Other monks kneel or stand about the abbot with expressions of concern as they join Benedict in his final prayer. Saint Benedict died on March 21, 547. His *Transitus*, or passing into heaven, is still celebrated on this date over fifteen centuries later.

This triptych window portrays Saint Vincent de Paul, a priest of seventeenth century Paris. Vincent de Paul was noted for his work among the poor. He is shown in the center panel of the window, dressed in the clerical garb of his day. Standing in a Paris street, Vincent de Paul holds an infant in his left arm while he comforts an urchin with his right hand. The side panels of the window depict the ministries of the Daughters of Charity, a religious order of women founded by Saint Vincent de Paul. The saint is also noted for the founding of several seminaries for the training of clergy. Saint Vincent Parish was already under the patronage of Saint Vincent de Paul when Boniface Wimmer arrived in 1846. Perceiving his own mission to be similar to that of Saint Vincent de Paul, Wimmer never sought to have the patronage changed. Though Vincent de Paul was not himself a Benedictine monk, Saint Vincent Archabbey remains the only Benedictine foundation under his patronage.

The windows in the apse, depicting five founders of religious orders, are the work of the Mayer Co. of Munich.

Saint Romuald was the founder of the Order of Camaldolese Hermits. He lived during the tenth century at a place called *Campus Madoli*. Noted for his strict observance, Saint Romuald is shown in the Benedictine habit, holding a crosier, a symbol of leadership, and a whip, symbol of discipline. The Camaldolese are recognized for their ascetic lifestyle, living in separate cells as hermits, but gathering together for prayer and Mass daily.

Saint Bernard of Clairvaux was a Benedictine monk, abbot and teacher. He helped to found the Cistercian reform in the twelfth century in order to promote a strict observance of Benedictine monasticism. A prolific writer, Saint Bernard is honored as a doctor of the Church. The window portrays Saint Bernard dressed in the white habit of Cistercian monks and wearing the pectoral cross denoting his status as an abbot. He holds a crosier in his left hand. In his right hand, he carries a book and quill symbolic of the rich heritage of writings he composed. At his feet rests a beehive, a symbol of monasticism.

Saint Benedict, Patriarch of Western Monasticism, enjoys a prominent place in the center window of the apse. Saint Benedict founded the monastery at Montecassino about the year 529. He composed a *Rule* for monks that continues to guide monastic life to this day. Saint Benedict is portrayed in this window in the monastic habit, holding a crosier in his right hand, symbolizing his role as abbot, or leader. In his left hand, the saint carries the *Rule* and a broom, symbolic of monastic discipline. At his feet stands a raven holding a piece of bread in its beak. Tradition holds that when some wicked men attempted to poison Benedict, a raven came and took the tainted bread. Saint Benedict is the patron saint of western monasticism, and co-patron of Europe. In 1964, Pope Paul VI proclaimed Saint Benedict the patron of western civilization. His followers have been credited for the preservation of western culture.

Saint Dominic was born Dominic Guzman in Moorish Spain in the thirteenth century. He founded an order of traveling preachers who helped to reconvert Europe to the faith when heresy threatened to overtake the Church. The Order of Preachers is more commonly known as the Dominican Order. This window shows Saint Dominic dressed in the Dominican habit and cloak. His right hand is raised in a posture of teaching. In his left hand, Dominic holds a book of the Gospels and a lily denoting the purity of his preaching. At his feet a small dog sits holding a torch in its mouth. According to tradition, when Dominic's mother was pregnant with him, she had a dream of a dog with a torch in its mouth. The dog was running all over, setting the earth on fire. Saint Dominic's preaching was to set Europe on fire for the faith.

Saint Francis of Assisi was born to a wealthy family and enjoyed a life of ease and excess. As a young man, he experienced a dramatic conversion, which led him to found a group dedicated to preaching and living a life of humility and poverty in imitation of Christ. This initial group grew into the Order of Friars Minor, more commonly known as the Franciscan Order. Saint Francis is depicted in this window in a stance of prayer, dressed in the simple brown habit he chose for his friars in imitation of the clothing worn by poor peasants of his day.

The original rose windows (one in each transept and one over the front doors) are of decorative glass, executed by the Kinsella Company of Chicago. The Basilica is made in a cross or Cruciform shape. The rose windows in the organ gallery and the side galleries highlight this.

The fourteen Stations of the Cross are of an ivory-tint composition with exquisitely modeled figures in half relief, and they come from the Bavarian Art Company in Munich. Each station is surmounted by a wooden cross.

The Stations signify certain scenes in the Passion of Christ, and represent a tradition that reaches back to pilgrimages to the Holy Land in the fourth century. The history of this spiritual exercise can be traced to Saint Francis of Assisi, who wished for people who could not afford to go to the Holy Land to spiritually unite themselves with the earthly places associated with Christ's passion.

Placed at intervals around the walls of the Basilica, the Stations of the Cross start on the north side of the nave near the transept which contains the Reposed Body of Christ. Stations one through seven are on the north side, proceeding to the narthex of the Basilica near the Chapel of the Immaculate Conception. They continue on the south side of the Basilica near the entrance to the Parish Center and end at the transept on the south side of the church in the nave.

4

5

6

Earlier in church history there were more than fourteen Stations of the Cross; however, since the seventeenth century the Church recognizes fourteen Stations of the Cross.

1) Jesus is Condemned to Death
2) Jesus Carries the Cross
3) Jesus Falls the First Time
4) Jesus Meets His Afflicted Mother
5) Simon of Cyrene Helps Jesus to Carry the Cross
6) Veronica Wipes the Face of Jesus

7) Jesus Falls the Second Time

8) The Women of Jerusalem Weep over Jesus

9) Jesus Falls the Third Time

10) Jesus is Stripped of His Garments

11) Jesus is Nailed to the Cross

12) Jesus is Raised on the Cross and Dies

13) Jesus is Taken Down from the Cross and Placed in the Arms of His Mother

14) Jesus is Laid in the Sepulchre

The corpus above the altar was carved at Saint Vincent in the 1860s by an unknown, nineteenth century monk of Saint Vincent Archabbey. It was used as the students' crucifix in the College cafeteria until it was refurbished and placed in the Basilica in August of 1997. It is a Lucan Corpus. This means that there is no crown of thorns on Jesus as He is portrayed in the Gospel of Luke. The concept for the new cross was created by Father Vincent Crosby, O.S.B. Design and execution were by Norbert and Victoria Koehn of Cleveland. The vaulting above the main altar rises to 68 feet.

The altar is under the crossing, supported by four piers. The columns and arches forming the parameter of the crossing are all carved stone. In the vaults of the crossing, which can be seen as representing the heavens, are the four evangelists, painted by Joseph Reiter. The current Sanctuary, which means holy place, is demarcated by four tent poles (large, gray columns, and a canopy (ceiling). Columns symbolize the earth and the canopy symbolizes heaven. There are angels present on the columns, to guide and protect the holy place. The altar platform may be considered to represent the holy Mount Sion or Jerusalem, site of both the cenacle (or upper room) and Mount Calvary. The top step of the high altar is known as the Predella.

Sunlight shines through a rose window, creating a miniature rose window on one of the crosses inscribed on top of the Basilica altar. There are five consecration crosses carved in the altar, representing the five wounds of Jesus, one at each of the four corners and one in the center of the altar.

    This altar is the second main altar that has been in use in the Basilica. The first altar was made of white Carrara marble. It stood as high as the top of the present-day crucifix. It was removed in 1954 — eight years before Vatican II began. The new altar is constructed of two types of marble. The pedestals or feet are two slabs of white Carrara marble. They each weigh two tons. The table top, or *Mensa* in Latin, is a dark green variegated marble. It weighs ten tons. The main altar was designed by Father Rene Gracida, later a bishop, and blessed on February 12, 1956.

Dr. Leo Ravazzi of the Pietrosanto Marble Studio in Italy executed the four sculptured panels on the base blocks. The bottom pedestals are decorated with reliefs of the Four Great Sacrifices of the Old Testament. The top of the Altar represents the Sacrifice of Jesus on the Cross. Thus, the Old and New Testaments are joined. The words *Altare Privilegiatum* appear on the sides. This translates as privileged altar — a special designation previously connecting the granting of indulgences to Masses celebrated at the principal altar of certain prominent churches. The designation was suppressed in 1967, with the clarification that the church offers its suffrages for the dead at every Mass without distinction.

The numbers and symbols on the photos correspond to the Basilica Map:

• Viewed from the nave side, left, The Akedah — The Sacrifice of Abraham and Isaac (Genesis 22).

• Viewed from the choir side, left, The Sacrifices of Cain and Abel (Genesis 4).

• Viewed from the Nave side, right, The Passover Sacrifice of Moses (Exodus 12).

• Viewed from the choir side, right, The bread and wine sacrificed by Melchizedech, the Priest (Genesis 14).

The elevated platform on the south side of the altar is for the chair of the Archabbot. It is the symbolic seat of his jurisdiction as shepherd of the Saint Vincent family. The Archabbot is the Ordinary Major Superior of the Monastery, the Chancellor of the College and Seminary, and the canonical Pastor of the Basilica Parish.

Hanging from the column is the personal coat of arms of Archabbot Douglas R. Nowicki, O.S.B., the eleventh Archabbot of Saint Vincent. The left side of the shield portrays the Saint Vincent coat of arms, while the right side with the hearts represents his personal coat of arms: three gold hearts on a red field; and his motto, *"Cor ad Cor Loquitur,"* or "Heart Speaks to Heart." It refers to the Archabbot's prayer that giving and receiving authentic love may always be the chief characteristic of the Saint Vincent monastic community. This was also the motto of Cardinal John Newman.

The Blessed Sacrament Chapel is a place for silent prayer and meditation before our Eucharistic Lord. The tower, pedestal and tabernacle were created by Norbert and Victoria Koehn of Cleveland, based on a concept by Father Vincent Crosby, O.S.B. The tower is modeled after the Basilica's back spires.

The Sacrament Tower is hand-carved oak and is based on a Medieval concept that was employed in the great cathedrals of Europe. The idea of a Sacrament Tower was utilized to draw attention to the place of reservation of the Blessed Sacrament in these vast ancient churches.

The Tabernacle (Latin for tent) is also composed of hand-carved wood. It has been gilded and inlaid with semi-precious stones. The sides of the Tabernacle depict four Eucharistic scenes from Holy Scripture. The frontispiece of the Tabernacle (top, left) depicts the Emmaus Account in the Gospel of Luke (24: 13-25), *We recognized him in the breaking of bread.* The other scenes, proceeding from the frontispiece are from Chapter 6 of the Gospel of John, "I am the bread of Life," (top, right); the "Manna from Heaven" scene from Exodus (bottom, left); and the *Agnus Dei* or Lamb of God (bottom, right).

The sculpture in the chapel in the north transept is an image of the reposed Christ in death, part of the original side altar in that space. It was retained and placed in a new tomb-like setting designed and executed by Norbert and Victoria Koehn. It is in this transept that monks are waked during their funerals, and lie in repose the night before their Mass of Christian Burial.

As is traditional in all churches in Romanesque style, above the altar in the crossing vaults are the four Evangelists (Gospel writers), by Joseph Reiter. They are depicted with their traditional symbols and painted directly on the plaster of the ceiling:
- Matthew, with an angel.
- Mark, with a lion.

- Luke, with an ox.
- John, with an eagle.

The symbols come from the Book of Revelation (4:1-11).

The Lily is the symbol for both purity and resurrection: purity due to its clean white flowers and resurrection because of its shape in the form of a trumpet that majestically announces Christ's triumph over death.

The rose symbolizes the unending beauty of God. As each petal unfolds, more beauty is revealed to the beholder.

These images are rondels decorating the vaults throughout the Basilica. Marian and Christological emblems are also included.

There are 76 choir stalls in the choir, 38 on each side. This is where the monks of Saint Vincent gather to pray the Liturgy of the Hours and to celebrate Mass. The Liturgy of the Hours is principally composed of the *Book of Psalms*. The monks pray in choral fashion, meaning they face one another, and recite or chant the psalms antiphonally, which means that one side recites or chants a stanza while the other side listens. The monks pray morning prayer and evening prayer in the Basilica and have their daily Mass in the choir area. Midday prayer has been celebrated in the Saint Gregory the Great chapel since 1999.

The mural paintings that flank the sidewalls at the entrance to the apse depict the Four Latin Doctors of the Church. Doctor in Latin means "teacher." The art is the work of Joseph Reiter.

They are:

Saint Augustine of Hippo (north side, top) from Northern Africa. Saint Augustine is the most notable theologian of the early church.

Saint Gregory the Great (north side, bottom). Saint Gregory was a monk who became the first of 50 Benedictines to be elected Pope. He was Pope around the year 600. He wrote the biography of Saint Benedict and is credited with writing down the musical notations which bear his name: Gregorian chant.

Saint Augustine of Hippo

Saint Gregory the Great

Saint Ambrose of Milan (south side, top). Saint Ambrose was only a catechumen when he was elected Bishop of Milan by popular acclaim. Ambrose is responsible for the conversion and baptism of Saint Augustine, and for composing many hymns for the Liturgy.

Saint Jerome (south side, bottom). Saint Jerome was an early theologian and Scripture scholar. He is credited with translating the Bible from Hebrew and Greek into Latin. Latin was the "Vulgar" or ordinary language of the people at the time. Thus the translation has become known as the Vulgate Bible.

Saint Ambrose of Milan

Saint Jerome

In the Dome of the Apse is a starburst depiction of a mystical scene from the Book of Revelation 5: 1-14. There is a Lamb, which represents Jesus Christ, holding the Banner of the Resurrection. A Chalice is at the Lamb's feet, representing Christ's sacrifice on the cross. The Lamb stands upon a Book with seven seals. This represents the revelation of Christ's dominion over all things. The vision takes place within a trefoil, symbolic of the Blessed Trinity. The artist, Joseph Reiter, painted it in a way that suggests that the vision has 'burst' through the church roof.

The Apse Arch contains paintings depicting — in ascending order — the Nine Choirs of Angels. These are the work of Joseph Reiter. The Nine Choirs are as follows:

Beginning with the top center, working down, alternating from left to right. The numbers on the photos correspond to the Basilica map.

1) Seraphim: These are the highest order or Choir of Angels. They are the Angels who are attendants or guardians before God's throne. They praise God, calling, 'Holy Holy Holy is the Lord of Hosts.' The only Biblical reference to the Seraphim is Isaiah 6:1-7. Note the Angel in the top center holding the 'Sanctus Banner.' One of them touched Isaiah's lips with a live coal from the altar, cleansing him from sin. Seraphim have six wings: two cover their faces, two cover their feet and two are for flying.

2) Cherubim: Cherubim rank after the Seraphim and are the second highest in the nine hierarchies. The Old Testament does not reveal any evidence that the Jews considered them as intercessors or helpers of God. They were closely linked to God's glory. They are manlike in appearance and double-winged and were guardians of God's glory. They symbolized God's power and mobility. In the New Testament, they are alluded to as celestial attendants in the Apocalypse (Rv. 4-6). Catholic tradition describes them as Angels who have an intimate knowledge of God and continually praise Him.

3) Thrones: Thrones are the Angels of pure humility, peace and submission. They reside in the area of the cosmos where material form begins to take shape. The lower Choirs of Angels need the Thrones to access God.

4) **Dominions:** Dominions are the Angels of leadership. They regulate the duties of the Angels, making known the commands of God.

5) **Virtues:** Virtues are known as the Spirits of Motion and control the elements. They are sometimes referred to as 'the shining ones.' They govern all nature. They have control over the seasons, stars, moon; even the sun is subject to their command. They are also in charge of miracles and provide courage, grace, and valor.

6) **Powers:** Powers are warrior Angels who defend the cosmos and humans against evil. They are known as potentates. They fight against evil spirits who attempt to wreak chaos through human beings.

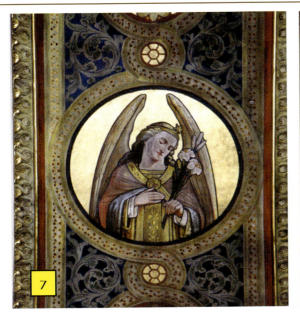
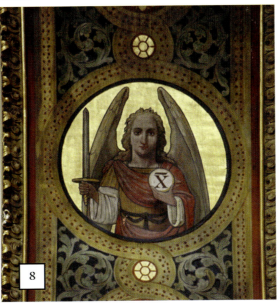

7) Archangels: Archangels are generally taken to mean 'chief or leading angel' (Jude 9; 1 Thes 4:16). They are the most frequently mentioned throughout the Bible. They may be of this or other hierarchies as Saint Michael the Archangel, who is a princely Seraph. The Archangels have a unique role as God's messenger to the people at critical times in history and salvation (Th 12:6, 15; Jn 5:4; Rv 12:7-9) such as the Annunciation and Apocalypse. A feast day celebrating the Archangels Michael, Gabriel and Raphael is celebrated throughout the Church on September 29. A special part of the Byzantine Liturgy invokes the 'Cherubic Hymn' which celebrates these Archangels and the Guardian Angels particularly. Of special significance is Saint Michael as he has been invoked as patron and protector by the Church from the time of the Apostles. The Eastern Rite and many others place him over all the Angels, as Prince of the Seraphim. He is described as the 'chief of princes' and as the leader of the forces of heaven in their triumph over Satan and his followers. The angel Gabriel first appeared in the Old Testament in the prophesies of Daniel. He announced the prophecy of 70 weeks (Dn 9:21-27). He appeared to Zechariah to announce the birth of Saint John the Baptist (Lk 1:11). It was also Gabriel who proclaimed the Annunciation of Mary to be the mother of our Lord and Saviour (Lk 1:26). The Angel Raphael first appeared in the book of Tobit (Tb 3:25, 5:5-28, 6-12). He announces 'I am the Angel Raphael, one of the seven who stand before the throne of God' (Tb 12:15).

8) Principalities: In the New Testament Principalities refers to one type of spiritual (metaphysical) being who are now quite hostile to God and human beings (Rom 8:38; 1 Cor 15:24; Eph 1:21; 3:10; 6:12; Col 1:16; 2:10, 15). Along with the principalities are the powers (Rom 8:38; 1 Cor 15:24; Eph 1:21; 1 Pt 3:22; 2 Thes 1:7); and cosmological powers (1 Cor 15:24; Eph 1:21; 3:10; Col 2:15); Dominions (Eph 1:21; Col 1:16) and Thrones (Col 1:16). The clarity of the New Testament witness helps us see that these beings were created through Christ and for Him (Col 1:16). Given their hostility to God and humans due to sin, Christ's ultimate rule over them expresses the reign of the Lord over all in the cosmos. This is the Lordship of Christ, which reveals God's tremendous salvation in conquering sin and death at the cross, and now takes place in the Church (Eph 3:10).

9) Angels: These Angels are closest to the material world and human beings. They deliver prayers to God and God's answers and other messages to humans. Angels have the capacity to access any and all other Angels at any time. They are the most caring and solicitous in assisting those who ask for help.

The four statues behind the choir represent four important figures in the history of monasticism. These statues were carved by Ferdinand Seeboeck in 1930 (see page 55). The statues depict:

Saint Benedict, left, is the Father of Western Monasticism and Patron of Western Civilization. He is holding a crozier which symbolizes his role as Abbot (shepherd) of a monastery. His statue is on the north side of the choir.

Saint Placid, right, was an early disciple of Saint Benedict. He entered the monastery at the age of eight and died as a martyr. He is holding a palm branch, which is the symbol of martyrs. His statue is also on the north side of the choir.

Saint Maurus, left, was an early disciple of Saint Benedict. He was known to have the gift of healing. Saint Maurus had a great devotion to the Holy Cross of Christ and holds a cross with a relic of the True Cross inside. His statue is on the south side of the choir.

Saint Scholastica, right, is the twin sister of Saint Benedict. She is known as the Mother of women monastics (nuns). She holds a crozier as a symbol of her authority as Abbess (shepherd) of a convent. Her statue is on the south side of the choir.

SAINT VINCENT ARCHABBEY AND COLLEGE, BEATTY, PENNSYLVANIA, SOUTH VIEW.

Saint Vincent College. Beatty, Pennsylvania, Archabbey Church.

ST. VINCENT ARCHABBEY AND COLLEGE, BEATTY, PA.

ARCHABBEY CHURCH, ST. VINCENT COLLEGE, LATROBE, PA.

THE ARCHABBEY CHURCH, LATROBE, PA.

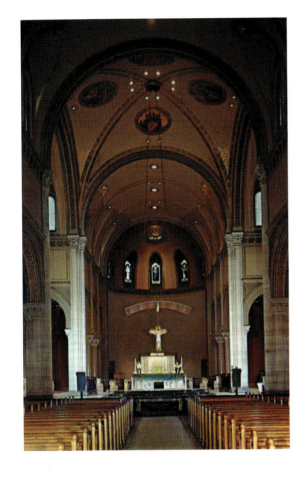

THE ARCHABBEY CHURCH, ST. VINCENT COLLEGE, LATROBE, PENNSYLVANIA

Since its dedication, hundreds of postcards have been produced depicting the Archabbey Basilica. Whether black and white, tinted or full color, these images suggest that the Basilica has been the visible centerpiece of campus since its construction, and a landmark of western Pennsylvania.

The Sportsman's Hall Parish Later Named Saint Vincent
1790-1846

By Omer U. Kline, O.S.B.

Originally published by Saint Vincent Archabbey Press
Latrobe, Pennsylvania
©1990, 2005

Original indenture indicating the sale of Sportsman's Hall and property to Father Theodore Brouwers from Joseph Hunter on April 16, 1790. Note the pink silk ribbon under the diamond-shaped paper bearing the seal of Westmoreland County, Pennsylvania.

1
Father Theodore Brouwers, O.F.M., 1790, To Father Peter Helbron, O.F.M. Cap., 1799

The year 1990 marked the bicentennial of Saint Vincent Parish, Latrobe, Pennsylvania, which was founded in 1790. As one might suppose, its beginnings were modest, especially in comparison with the magnificent Saint Vincent Basilica that serves as a place of worship at the heart of a campus that includes a parish, a Benedictine archabbey, a seminary and a college sponsored by the Benedictines.

The most logical date for the humble beginning of what was to be the great enterprise of Saint Vincent is April 16, 1790. On this date Father Theodore Brouwers, O.F.M., purchased the 300 acres of land called "Sportsman's Hall Tract" and thus founded Sportsman's Hall Parish. The parish was later placed under the patronage of Saint Vincent de Paul and so was called Saint Vincent Parish. To add to the significance of this event, Saint Vincent is the first Catholic parish in Pennsylvania west of the Allegheny Mountains; and, as Father Andrew Arnold Lambing, foremost historian on things Catholic in the Pittsburgh area of that day, said: "It is the cradle of Catholicity in Western Pennsylvania." Father Brouwers was, therefore, not only the first resident pastor of the Sportsman's Hall Parish, but also the first Catholic priest to establish a permanent residence in western Pennsylvania.

Father Brouwers' life story is a very intriguing one, packed into fifty-two years of life. He was born in Rotterdam, Holland, in 1738, and pronounced vows as a Franciscan Friar at twenty years of age. He was ordained a priest on June 5, 1762, and taught at Franciscan seminaries in Holland and Belgium until 1776. It was in this epochal year of American independence that Father Brouwers was appointed superior of a missionary band that was sent to Curaçao, a Dutch island-colony in the West Indies off the coast of Venezuela. In Curaçao Father Brouwers had the authority and title of Prefect Apostolic. On this "hot and soggy island" he labored and ministered for eleven years amid the most trying conditions. His departure from Curaçao is shrouded in mystery; we know only that he left in 1787, and was next heard from in January 1789 in Philadelphia. Here he stayed for a few months, and became aware that the Catholic settlers of western Pennsylvania—in particular, those who had located in the area of the Newton (incorporated as the Borough of Greensburg in 1799) in Westmoreland County—strongly desired the ministry of a priest. It was in the autumn of 1789 that Father Brouwers was commissioned by Bishop John Carroll to care for the spiritual needs of these neglected Catholic settlers. The latter had been selected by Pope Pius VI in 1784 to be "Superior of the Mission" of the newly independent United States of America; and, in this year 1789, he was named first Catholic bishop of the newly-established Diocese of Baltimore, which comprised the thirteen original states of the Union. As such, Bishop Carroll was empowered to appoint Father Brouwers the first resident pastor of the Catholic faithful in western Pennsylvania. This year had already been made most memorable in American history by the inauguration, on

Drawing of the Sportsman's Hall Parish plant as it appeared in 1831, the year after the arrival of Father James Stillinger. On the hillside above the large tree was the grave of Father Theodore Brouwers, O.F.M. (now in the Saint Vincent Cemetery). The church was the one built by Father Peter Helbron, O.F.M. Cap., in 1810. To the right is the parochial residence—consisting of Sportsman's Hall with an addition.

Original indenture indicating the sale of Sportsman's Hall and property to Father Theodore Brouwers from Joseph Hunter in April of 1790.

April 30, 1789, of General George Washington as the first president of the United States.

Father Brouwers wasted little time in the autumn of 1789 in making preparations to set out for his new parish; but, before leaving Philadelphia on August 7, 1789, he purchased a tract of land in western Pennsylvania consisting of approximately 170 acres, from Arthur O'Neill of Chester, Pennsylvania—the tract was thus called "O'Neill's Victory." This land is located along the eastern bank of the Loyalhanna Creek near the present town of New Alexandria in Derry Township. Through the years it became known at Saint Vincent as the "Seven Mile Farm," and in 1970 it was purchased by the Commonwealth of Pennsylvania under the right of eminent domain for projected use in the expansion of Keystone State Park.

Father Brouwers arrived at "O'Neill's Victory" during the middle of the month of November 1789, and became disenchanted with that property as a place for his headquarters. He found that the land was not as fertile as he had expected and that the location was almost twelve miles from the greater number of his scattered flock. In fact, during the winter of 1789-1790, Father Brouwers became convinced that "O'Neill's Victory" was not a good place to build a church and a priest's house. Since he found there no suitable place for divine services, he took up living quarters with the Christian Ruffner family, in whose house he said Mass and performed other pastoral services for the Catholics of the area. The Ruffner house was located about three miles from Newtown (present-day Greensburg), near the present town of Crabtree (close to historic Hannastown).

This reliance on Christian Ruffner was not accidental. The three brothers, Christian, Simon and George Ruffner, along with John Probst, John Young and Patrick Archibald, on March 10, 1789, had purchased an acre and a half of land in Newtown, where they began to build a small log church that was destined never to be completed. But this purchase was significant since this plot was the first property in Pennsylvania west of the Allegheny Mountains to be owned by the Catholic Church, one on which the Blessed Sacrament Cathedral parish plant is now located. This event is significant in the history of the Sportsman's Hall Parish. During the years following the Revolutionary War, a group of Catholic pioneers—including those named above—had come from the eastern Pennsylvania Catholic settlement of Goshenhoppen near Philadelphia and located along the "Great Road to Ft. Pitt" (i.e., the Forbes Road), with a concentration in the present-day Greensburg area. These hearty settlers were overwhelmingly of German Catholic ancestry and had been promised that a Catholic priest would visit them occasionally and that eventually a resident pastor would be sent. In fact this colony was visited, in June 1789, for the first time by a Catholic priest in the person of Father John Baptist Cause, an Alsatian Franciscan, who had his headquarters in Conewago in Adams County near Gettysburg—called the "Gateway of the Faith." Father Cause, in the absence of any church building, said Mass in the house of John Probst, a few miles northwest of Newtown (later known as Greensburg) near present-day Harrison City. This Mass was the first said in a permanent Catholic settlement in western Pennsylvania. But Father Cause remained only a few days, so that the little colony had assembled only once for divine services before he returned to the east; he would, however, return to the Sportsman's Hall Parish, in the autumn of 1790, under very different circumstances as will be related later.

One of the Catholic pioneers who settled in the

The Fraser Purchase to John Fraser of Bedford reads: "Whereas it appears that the commanding officer of Fort Pitt has been authorized to give permission to sundry persons to settle on different stages on the Roads leading to Fort Pitt, for the better accommodating and Supplying of His Majesty's troops, employed in this communication, I do therefore permit you to settle and improve on a certain place above Ligonier known by the name of the Fourteen Mile Run ... in Consideration of that grant from the Crown you are to pay as an acknowledgement Twenty Shillings Sterling per annum ground rent, if demanded. ..."

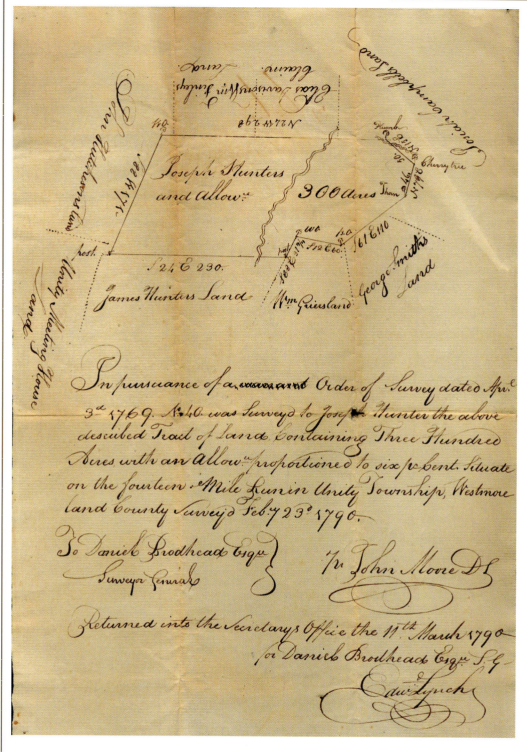

"The Survey of February 23, 1790," used in drawing up the "Patent" of March 12, 1790 in which the "Sportsman's Hall Tract" was sold to Joseph Hunter who, in turn, would sell it to Father Theodore Brouwers, O.F.M., on April 16, 1790. This "Tract" contains approximately 300 acres, intersected by Fourteen Mile Run, and composes the core of the present Saint Vincent campus.

area in 1788 was Henry Kuhn, the brother of Christian Ruffner's wife, Ottilia. It was these two parishioners, Christian Ruffner and Henry Kuhn, who played such a prominent role in the brief pastorate of Father Brouwers. While living at the Christian Ruffner house during the winter of 1789-1790, Father Brouwers made himself thoroughly acquainted with his Catholic flock and with his surroundings in general. During this same time, Father Brouwers found in Henry Kuhn a friend and confidant who gave him good advice during this time of adversity. It was Henry Kuhn who was influential in getting Father Brouwers, in the spring of 1790, to abandon his original intention of building a house and a chapel—and so locating the parish center—at "O'Neill's Victory." And it was this same Henry Kuhn who at this time acquainted Father Brouwers with a more desirable tract of land that was for sale, and urged him to buy it. This tract of approximately 300 acres in Unity Township, about seven miles east of Newtown (present-day Greensburg), had been patented on March 12, 1790, by a certain Joseph Hunter; it had been called Sportsman's Hall early on, a name given it originally by a Harrisburg gentleman, who had used it as a hunting ground. This tract of land along Forbes Road "above Ligonier known by the name of the Fourteen Mile Run" had originally been purchased in 1766, by John Fraser, an Indian trader, who received it in the name of King George III of Great Britain. Father Brouwers visited the Sportsman's Hall property and found it very much to his liking. Thus it was, on April 16, 1790, that a deed was drawn up and signed at the county seat, whereby the "tract of land called 'Sportsman's Hall'" was transferred from Joseph Hunter to "Theodorus Browers" for the sum of about £475 (about $2,000) in Pennsylvania money, a large sum for those days but a bargain at something less than $6.00 an acre.

Father Brouwers soon moved to the newly-purchased property. He at once engaged a carpenter to build a house of hewn logs, one and one-half stories high and seventeen feet square, which was known as "Sportsman's Hall," called after the name of the tract itself. This building was to serve as a home for the pastor of the parish for nearly forty years, and additions to the building would increase its length to approximately twenty-four feet. Thus this house became the first residence of a Catholic pastor in western Pennsylvania, and one of the rooms served as the first church. There were several other structures built on the property: a house for Christian Andrews, who together with his wife Maria, attended to the farm; there were also some barns and stables. But Father Brouwers continued to say Mass each Sunday at Christian Ruffner's house; he traveled the five miles on horseback.

It was, however, not long until the rigors of this life on the frontier began to take its toll on Father Brouwers' delicate constitution. Although he was only fifty-two years of age, his health began to fail and he suffered periodic attacks of fainting. In fact, on a Sunday in June 1790, Father Brouwers became so ill while offering Mass that he was able to conclude the service only with great difficulty. He became so alarmed that he sent to Newtown (present-day Greensburg), which had become the seat of Westmoreland County in 1785, for a capable officer to assist him in drafting his Last Will and Testament. William Maghee, the County Registrar, answered the call, but the contents of this first Will and Testament will never be known since Father Brouwers recovered and the document was not preserved. Although he was able to resume some of his duties, during early autumn he had a serious relapse and so wrote to Father James Pellentz of Conewago, one of the Vicars General of the Diocese of Baltimore, with the request that a priest be sent to take care of the Sportsman's Hall Parish during the time of his incapacitation. Arriving in the latter part of September 1790, Father John Baptist Cause—the same priest who had visited Newtown (present-day Greensburg) in June, 1789—was sent. Father Cause read Father Brouwer's Will and was not satisfied with some if its provisions. In an incredible action, Father Cause threatened to deny the dying Father Brouwers the last rites of the Church unless he would, among other demands, bequeath all his movable property to the Catholic parish at Conewago. And so the services of William Maghee were called for once more, and several revised wills were drawn up, in which concessions were made at the insistence of Father Cause. In the meantime Father Brouwers' condition was daily becoming more grave, so much so that Mr. Maghee intervened and put an end to further concessions being made. On account of these delays, the Last Will and Testament of Father Theodore Brouwers was written and executed on October 24, 1790, only five days before his death. On October 29, 1790, Father Brouwers died; and, according to a provision in this Will, his body was laid to rest in a plot overlooking Sportsman's Hall—since 1869, his remains have lain at rest under the massive stone cross in Saint Vincent Cemetery.

The Last Will and Testament of Father Brouwers named Christian Ruffner and "Henry Coons" [Kuhn] as Executors, and they attempted to carry out their duties by following the instructions concerning the burial of Father Brouwers, Masses to be said for his intention, and the disposal of his property. In doing so they were guided by the provision that bequeathed all of his real estate "to a Roman Catholic priest that shall succeed me in this said place, to be entailed to him and to his successors in trust and so left by him who shall succeed me to his successors and so in trust and for the use herein mentioned in succession for ever." There was little doubt in the mind of Father Cause that he was that successor; and immediately after the death of Father Brouwers, he took possession of the latter's real estate and personal property. Father Cause occupied the Sportsman's Hall log house and held divine services there for the parish congregation. In the meantime he sent to Conewago for a wagon and a team of four horses; and, when they arrived, he packed up the personal effects—i.e., books, clothing and furniture—of Father Brouwers and sent them on their way to Conewago—in accordance with a provision of the Last Will and Testament. At this time Father Cause stayed on at Sportsman's Hall Parish, and it soon became apparent that what he wanted was authorization to draw out of the

Present-day monument "in memory of the Ruffner brothers, Simon, Christian, and George, pioneer Catholics, who, with their families, were a vital part in the founding and fostering on this site of the first Catholic parish church in Western Pennsylvania."

The Last Will and Testament of Father Theodore Brouwers, O.F.M., as drawn up and executed on October 24, 1790 by William Maghee, the Registrar of Westmoreland County.

Philadelphia bank the money that Father Brouwers had deposited there. This sum of money was considerable, a deposit of $1,146.00 at the time of Father Brouwers' death—a small fortune in those days when a man's yearly salary might be $100.00. The Will had not authorized Father Cause to withdraw this money, and so he asked the Executors for the Power of Attorney to do so. At first Christian Ruffner and Henry Kuhn, the Executors, were reluctant to do so; but the deceptive Father Cause finally persuaded them by stating that he was doing them a favor and would bring the money with him upon his return to Sportsman's Hall Parish from a trip that he had to make to Conewago and Philadelphia. Furthermore, he told them that, if they would not grant his request, he would never return. And, once armed with the Power of Attorney in writing, Father Cause set out posthaste for Conewago, where he spent the winter of 1790-1791. He took with him the remaining personal belongings of Father Brouwers, and left the congregation of Sportsman's Hall Parish without the services of a priest in the interim.

Father Cause did go to Philadelphia in the spring of 1791 and presented the bank with the draft of $1,146.00, which was honored for the full amount. Not only did Father Cause not return to Sportsman's Hall Parish, but he at once appropriated the money for his own use, spending it wildly. The celebrated example was his purchase of a theatrical show, entitled "Panorama of Jerusalem," with which he traveled about from town to town, leading a life quite unworthy of his priestly vocation. It was then that Father James Pellentz of Conewago, in his role as a Vicar General, dispatched a message to Father Brouwers' Executors at Sportsman's Hall Parish to inform them of Father Cause's actions. Father Pellentz advised them to have Father Cause arrested and lodged in jail at York, Pennsylvania. The Executors, nevertheless, had to make the arduous trip to York where a peaceable settlement was reached. Father Cause found bail, gave a bond of £261 payable to Father Pellentz; and, in the same bond, he relinquished all claims against the Executors.

Father Cause would no longer be heard from at the Sportsman's Hall Parish, but not so in the vast Diocese of Baltimore. In a celebrated sermon by Bishop John Carroll on Sunday, February 19, 1792, Father Cause was suspended and excommunicated, the immediate cause for which was his pastoral service to a group of German nationals in Baltimore, after he had been forbidden by the bishop to minister to them. Bishop Carroll was patient with Father Cause until the end, and Father Cause, on May 2, 1793, wrote to the bishop asking for absolution and volunteering to go as a missionary to a remote part of the diocese. Bishop Carroll, on June 4, 1793, gave a favorable reply, but there is no information available on whether Father Cause responded and was reconciled to the Church. Consequently this mysterious figure fades from the annals of history without a clue as to when or where he died.

In the meantime the Executors of the Last Will and Testament of Father Brouwers, Christian Ruffner and Henry Kuhn, in accordance with a proviso in the Will, held, on July 18, 1791, a public sale of Brouwers' livestock and farm implements, with the proceeds going to Christian Andrews and his wife in payment for their work on the Sportsman's Hall farm. But there was not to be peace at the Sportsman's Hall Parish while the difficulties occasioned by Father Cause were being resolved in the east. The saga began with the arrival, on May 2, 1791, of Father Francis Rogatus Fromm, O.F.M., who at once took possession of the Sportsman's Hall property and began to exercise his ministry.

Father Fromm had been born in Germany in the late 1740s, had been professed as a Franciscan in Würzburg and was later ordained, circa 1773. He worked in the Archdiocese of Mainz for sixteen years, and then abruptly came to the United States in 1789 "unsolicited, unexpected and unknown"—as Bishop Carroll was later to write. But in 1789 Father Fromm carried with him a letter of recommendation from the Vicar General of the Archdiocese of Mainz, and so Bishop Carroll accepted him for assistance in the growing German settlements of Conewago and Lancaster, Pennsylvania. It was in Lancaster that Father Fromm met Father Cause in 1790, and so he became aware of the opportunity for position and property at the Sportsman's Hall Parish that awaited Brouwers' successor. In the meantime, Bishop Carroll, upon his return from England and his August 15, 1790, episcopal consecration, acceded to the request of the parishioners that he remove Father Fromm from his Lancaster pastorate, largely because of his brusque manner. Bishop Carroll then advised him to return to his German homeland. But the cunning Father Fromm was now determined to become Father Brouwers' successor.

And so, against the explicit orders of Bishop Carroll, Father Fromm, in April 1791, headed for Westmoreland

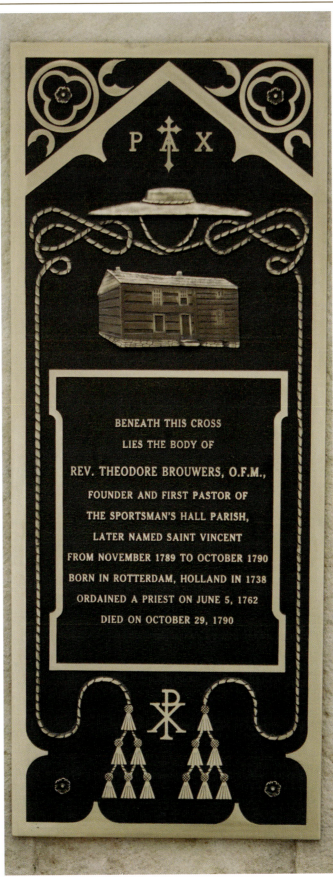

Unity Township Road 898, which leads to Saint Vincent Cemetery, honors Father Theodore Brouwers, O.F.M., founder and first pastor of the Sportsman's Hall Parish, later named Saint Vincent. The cemetery itself has a plaque in honor of Father Brouwers on the stone cross underneath which he is now buried.

"Sportsman's Hall," a hewn log structure, built under the pastorate of Father Theodore Brouwers, O.F.M., in 1789. It served as the first parochial residence and church for the Sportsman's Hall Parish. Additions were constructed to the building from time to time.

County. Father Fromm presented himself to the Sportsman's Hall Parish congregation, and gave them every indication that he had been designated as the successor of Father Brouwers. The parishioners, in turn, welcomed Father Fromm's pastoral ministry, as they had been without the services of a priest for seven or eight months. Father Fromm took advantage of this good will, and soon after his arrival had the members of the congregation accept a document that acknowledged him as the successor to Father Brouwers and as their elected pastor "for the time of his life." Also, Father Fromm was intent on drawing up a written agreement, to be dated July 2, 1791, explaining the manner in which he had taken possession of Sportsman's Hall. Part of Father Fromm's intent was to have the Executors of Father Brouwer's Last Will and Testament sign this document, which they did without qualms, as he had made such a good impression on them and as they thought that he had come to the parish with the good grace of Bishop Carroll.

The next event in this story was Father Fromm's return to eastern Pennsylvania, in that same month of July 1791, in order to procure articles needed for his parish. While in the east he wrote to Bishop Carroll telling him that he had taken possession of the Sportsman's Hall property and that he had been chosen pastor by the parish congregation. Father Fromm now boldly requested Bishop Carroll to sanction all of these proceedings so that he might consider himself the lawfully constituted successor to Father Brouwers. But Bishop Carroll would not hear of it, and evidently called upon Father Pellentz, his Vicar General at Conewago, to send another priest to minister to the Sportsman's Hall Parish. This conjecture is based on the fact that, on August 11, 1791, in a long letter written in Philadelphia, Father Fromm, who evidently was beginning to feel uneasy about his position, said to the Brouwers' Executors, Christian Ruffner and Henry Kuhn: "Do not allow any priest, whom Father Pellentz may send, to take possession of Father Brouwers' house, otherwise we may lose everything."

By the time Father Fromm returned to the Sportsman's Hall Parish in September 1791, the congregation had begun to suspect that things were not as they should be with this priest. They tried to get rid of him, but he tenaciously held on to the Brouwers' property. In 1794 matters came to a crisis with the parishioners insisting that Father Fromm should become reconciled to the bishop or vacate the position of pastor. But he then entered into a written agreement with the congregation, stipulating that he continue as pastor for certain sums of money which they agreed to pay; and, that he give up the parish after one year, if in the meantime he should fail to obtain Bishop Carroll's sanction.

What Father Fromm had not told the people of Sportsman's Hall Parish was that Bishop Carroll had already notified him on May 13, 1793, that all powers of church ministry that the bishop had formerly granted to him were now revoked. Nearly a year passed before Father Fromm acknowledged his bishop's letter. And, in the meantime, Father Fromm, fearing that his written agreement of 1794 with the Sportsman's Hall parishioners would militate against his holding on to the Brouwers' property, managed to get his hands on the document, tore off his signature and announced: "I am not your priest, and you are not my congregation." The executors of Brouwers' will then entered into a law suit in order to have Father Fromm ejected from the property. But there would be a long delay before this case would be tried in the Court of Common Pleas of the Fifth Circuit of the State of Pennsylvania in Westmoreland County. Bishop Carroll, learning of these happenings, wrote from Conewago on August 5, 1795, to both the Sportsman's Hall Parish congregation and to Father Fromm. The bishop officially informed the parishioners that Father Fromm had "never been commissioned to exercise pastoral functions" for them, and so was "suspended from celebrating Holy Mass." Bishop Carroll also promised to secure a pastor for them as soon as possible. In his August 5, 1795, letter to Father Fromm, Bishop Carroll affirmed the suspension until the charges were answered. The bishop's August letter brought an immediate response from Father Fromm, who promised to mend his ways. In fact Bishop Carroll, in an October 18, 1795, letter to Father Fromm, promised to reinstate him as a pastor of another congregation, if he would freely relinquish Brouwers' property. But, alas, before the week was out, Father Fromm himself informed Bishop Carroll that he was continuing to administer the Sacraments and had secured a lawyer to defend his occupancy of the Brouwers property.

Bishop Carroll's response to this situation was to fulfill his promise to the Sportsman's Hall parishioners to send them a lawful pastor. He sent Father Lawrence Sylvester Phelan, O.F.M. Cap.—sometimes called Whalen or Whelen—described as "a mild-mannered and wonderfully patient Capuchin," to attend to the Sportsman's Hall Parish. Upon Father Phelan's arrival, he energetically began ministry to the parish and the delicate task of dealing with Father Fromm during the law suit. As Father Fromm still retained possession of the Brouwers' property, Father Phelan was obliged to reside in the home of Simon Ruffner. That Father Phelan "did not find Westmoreland a land flowing with milk and honey," is evident from the following excerpt of a letter that he wrote, on October 17, 1795, to Bishop Carroll:

"Your reverence can have no conception of my distress here, even for the necessaries of life, for really I have not anything like a sufficiency of food, and such as I get is poor and filthy. Most of the Irish, who, though poor, were by far the most generous, have now quit this settlement; five or six German families remain, whose chaplain I may call myself, since I cannot pretend to travel for want of a horse. These people, indeed—abstraction made of religion—are the last of all mankind for sentiments of humanity. The poor man I live with has not been paid what was promised for my board, and whether he intends it or not, he treats me accordingly. Perhaps he can't help it. Bread is the sole support of his family. Morning, noon, and night, flour and water, or bread and water, with a little burnt grease thrown over it is the support of his starved and almost naked large family. Since my arrival, the only meat they had was a little pig about twenty or thirty pounds, and a calf ten days old, of which we have eaten this whole week till

Transcription of a portion of the letter appointing Father Fromm pastor of the Sportsman's Hall Congregation.

> # Sportsman's Hall
> ### and
> ## St. Vincent Abbey.
>
> ### III.
> ### Trial of Father Fromm.
>
> The records of the trial of Father Fromm are of unusual interest and importance. They give a legal standing to the principle that a member of a religious organization must abide by the regulations of that organization. The rights of Bishop Carroll, which Father Fromm had denied and defied, were recognized and upheld by judge and jury and thus a precedent was established, which gave great promise of good to ecclesiastical discipline.
>
> Westmoreland County. December Term 1798.
>
> **Lesse of the Executors of Theodoras Browers**
> **v Franciscus Fromm.**
>
> Browers was a German Catholick Priest, who after a Residence in a Danish Westindia Island, had a few years before his Death Removed into Pennsylvania and superintended a Catholick Congregation near Greensburg in Westmoreland County, and Owned Two Plantations there, which by his Will Dated 24. of October 1790, he Divised as follows — to a Roman Catholick priest that shall Succeed me in this said place, to be Entailed to him and his Successors in trust and so left by him Who shall succeed me to his successors and so in trust and for the use herein Mentioned in succession forever, and that the said priest for the time being shall strictly and faithfully say four Masses, Each and Every year forever. (Viz) One for the soul of the Reverend Theadoras Browers on the Day of his Death in Each and Every Year forever, and three Others, the following Days in Each Year as aforesaid at the Request of the Reverend Theodorus Browers, and further it is my will that the priest for the time being shall Transmit, the land so left him in trust as Afforsaid to his successor Clear of all incumbrances as Afforsaid.
>
> The will Directed the Payment of Debts and funeral Expences, and the Erection of a Tombstone on the Grave of the Testator on the premises. the Ejectment was brought for the land thus Devised

Page from the Saint Vincent Journal recounting the trial of Father Fromm.

it became green and musty from want of salt. When I arrived first, they had about a dozen hens, of which I must have eaten eight, as they still have four. Thus have I spent five months of a most rigorous Lent, that threw me into diarrhea, that, in such wretchedness and cold, made a most penitential winter."

But the greater Lenten penance for Father Phelan was attempting to bring a solution to a situation that found two factions in the parish pitted against each other to the extent that both were taking recourse to the civil courts. When, on October 11, 1795, someone shot through the window of Father Fromm's bedroom in what was probably a desperate attempt to convince him to leave Sportsman's Hall, he promptly brought suit against several members of the congregation and against Father Phelan himself, charging them with attempting to take his life. The court ignored the case, but Father Fromm was sufficiently frightened so that on December 16, 1795, he drew up his Last Will and Testament—later proven invalid because of his claim to be the legitimate successor of Father Browers. But there was still a strong contingent, including Henry Kuhn, who even at this stage agreed to retaining Father Fromm as their priest. It was this group, together with Father Fromm himself, who signed a letter that was sent to Bishop Carroll on January 23, 1796. This letter was conciliatory in tone and promised to abide by the bishop's decision either to retain Father Fromm or to send him elsewhere. But during all of this time the civil suit brought by Father Fromm continued, and Father Phelan, in total discouragement, "kindly but forcibly" informed the parishioners that, with the consent of Bishop Carroll, he was leaving them for another mission. And so, in mid-1796, Father Phelan withdrew from the Sportsman's Hall Parish. It is known that in 1805 he was the resident priest at the "Buffalo Creek Mission" in Armstrong County (now known as Sugar Creek), and that he remained there for several years. There is but a sketchy account of Father Phelan's later years. It was evident in a letter from him to Bishop Carroll on May 7, 1807, that he was "laboring zealously" at Chambersburg in south-central Pennsylvania. Also, it is known that Father Phelan returned to Ireland in 1811, and died in 1824 at Saint James Chapel House, Dublin, when he was seventy-two years of age.

After the departure of Father Phelan from the Sportsman's Hall Parish, Bishop Carroll sent Father Patrick

Lonergan, O.S.F., to the Westmoreland County Catholic settlement, and requested that he remain there during the trial of Father Fromm. The year was 1796 and Father Fromm was still in possession of the Brouwers holdings. Father Lonergan found it virtually impossible to accomplish anything under the circumstances and so turned his attention to establishing a Catholic colony elsewhere. He, therefore, purchased large tracts of land at West Alexander in Washington County. But he did not succeed in attracting Catholic settlers and sold these lands only to purchase other tracts in and about Waynesburg in Greene County. Father Lonergan did get a number of Catholic families from Sportsman's Hall to settle at this Greene County colony. It can be established by a letter dated November 1, 1805, from Father Lonergan to Bishop Carroll, that the former was still in Waynesburg on that date. But this colony was also a failure; Father Lonergan sold all of the land except that on which Saint Ann's Church still stands, and traveled down the Mississippi River to New Orleans, where he died—"at what time and at what age had not been ascertained."

While Father Lonergan was engaged in these activities, the suit that the Brouwers Executors, in concert with the Sportsman's Hall congregation, had initiated to eject Father Fromm from the property and to recover it for the legitimate authority of the Catholic Church, continued. Father Fromm had the advice and support of a number of the prominent citizens of the locality; but, as the court case proceeded, Father Fromm began to sense the weakness of his position. Furthermore, he became more and more deeply in debt; and, in mid-1797, was forced by his creditors to vacate the Brouwers property that he had usurped. And at long last the case came before Judge Alexander Addison, president of the Courts of Common Pleas of the Fifth Circuit, at the Westmoreland County December Term, 1798. The jury, under the direction of Judge Addison, gave a verdict against Father Fromm, which was a vindication of the contention that the congregation of the Sportsman's Hall Parish was fully under the supervision—both temporal and spiritual—of the Catholic Bishop of Baltimore. Thus the rights of Bishop Carroll, which Father Fromm had denied and defied, were recognized and upheld. In the verdict Judge Addison decreed that the Bishop of Baltimore "had the sole episcopal authority over the Catholic Church of the United States." And he continued by stating that, without authority from Bishop Carroll, "no Catholic priest can exercise any pastoral functions over any congregation within the United States." This court trial and verdict, the records of which are preserved at the Westmoreland County Courthouse, became notable, since they established in the civil courts the authority of a Roman Catholic bishop.

Father Fromm next appealed the ruling to the Superior Court, then holding sessions in Philadelphia. He was required to appear there in person, and so made the long journey over the mountains in the spring of 1799. During the hot summer in Philadelphia and before his case had reached the court calendar, Father Fromm fell victim of the dread disease of yellow fever, then raging in Philadelphia. He was taken to the hospital but soon died. There is no evidence whether he was reconciled to the Church before his death, but Father Alexander Wyse, O.F.M., writing in 1983, observed that Father Fromm's papers are preserved in the Baltimore Cathedral Archives, "as would hardly be the case had he not handed them over as a sign of his submission to the Church which, in headier days, he had served with such gross self-seeking and so little credit." And so in a Philadelphia hospital in 1799 the first phase of the history of the Sportsman's Hall Parish came to a close.

2. Father Peter Helbron, O.F.M. Cap., 1799, To Father James A. Stillinger, 1830

The second phase of the Sportsman's Hall Parish began on November 17, 1799, with the arrival of Father Peter Helbron, O.F.M. Cap., who had been appointed by Bishop John Carroll of the Diocese of Baltimore as pastor of the Westmoreland County congregation. Father Helbron thus became the second resident pastor—Father Fromm had not been a lawfully appointed pastor—of the Sportsman's Hall Parish.

Father Helbron was a native of Germany (born circa 1750)—from the neighborhood of Trier—and was a member of the Capuchin Order. Little else is known of his early life, except the fact that he had seen service in the Prussian army and had become an expert horseman. His ability to ride would be put to a genuine test during his extensive missionary travels throughout western Pennsylvania. The qualities that characterized this priest-friar have been captured by a contemporary who spoke of Father Helbron as "a man of culture and refinement, punctili-

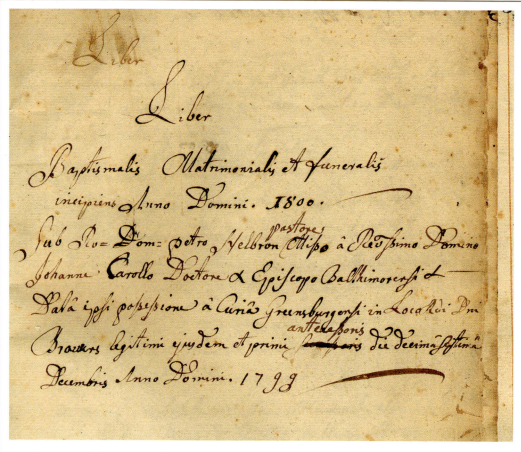

Portion of first page of Father Peter Helbron's Register.

ously neat and precise in his priestly attire and duties, with a dignity and commanding presence."

It was this Father Peter Helbron who came to Philadelphia, along with his priest-brother, Father John Baptist (Charles) Helbron, O.F.M. Cap., landing on October 14, 1787, after a transatlantic voyage. The two had come to America to work among the German immigrants in the missions of Pennsylvania, in response to a letter in a German newspaper.

Father John Carroll, who was then "Superior of the Mission" in the United States, welcomed the two German Capuchins and appointed them to the congregation in Goshenhoppen, Berks County, where they were welcomed by the many German Catholic settlers. Indeed Father Peter Helbron was appointed pastor at Goshenhoppen on November 12, 1787, and remained there until he became pastor of Holy Trinity Parish, Philadelphia, after his brother, Father John Baptist Helbron, left for Europe in the autumn of 1791. The latter had been pastor of Holy Trinity Parish from 1789 until he embarked for Europe to raise money in an attempt to defray the enormous debt on the parish. But Father John Baptist Helbron was destined never to return to America, since he was guillotined in Bayonne, France, on November 25, 1793, at the age of forty-seven, a victim of the French Revolution.

Father Peter Helbron's five-year pastorate of Holy Trinity Parish was a stormy one. His courage would be tested by financial worries, by the dreadful yellow fever plague of the 1790s—which would claim Father Fromm as one of its victims in 1799—and by the turmoil in the American Catholic Church of that day which was known as trusteeism.

The trustee system had been and would continue to be a phenomenon in the Catholic Church of the United States. Through this system church property was held and administered by an elected group of predominantly lay trustees. The trouble with trusteeism usually began when these trustees assumed the right of appointment and dismissal of parish priests, often under the threat of withholding financial assistance. Before Father Peter Helbron took over the pastorate of Holy Trinity Parish from his priest brother, the latter had had much difficulty with the trustees. But in 1791 Father Peter Helbron was elected by the parish trustees to succeed his brother. Surprisingly, Bishop John Carroll—who had experienced a lifetime of clashes with the trustee system in order to gain ownership of Church property and control of pastoral appointments—readily gave his assent to the election of Father Helbron, as he approved of the choice and did not want to challenge the trustees at this time. There was no clash at Holy Trinity Parish with the trustees until 1796, when they defied Bishop Carroll and elected the Rev. John Nepomucene Goetz, an Austrian immigrant, as their pastor. Father Helbron took issue with the trustees, but was "dismissed and discharged" by them. It was then that Father Helbron took up residence at Saint Joseph Parish, where he provided priestly ministry to this little parish and also to those members of the Holy Trinity congregation who had remained loyal to him. In the meantime the Parish of Holy Trinity was in schism until 1802. And so it was that, after three years at Saint Joseph, in 1799 Father Helbron gave up hope of being restored to his rightful position as pastor of Holy Trinity Parish and accepted Bishop Carroll's appointment to the Sportsman's Hall Parish.

With the arrival of Father Helbron to his new mission on November 17, 1799, there opened a new chapter in the history of the Church in western Pennsylvania.

Indeed Father Helbron began the real organization of a permanent parish at Sportsman's Hall, since he was able to bring order out of chaos. But the beginnings were not easy as Father Helbron exchanged a Philadelphia parish riddled by trusteeism for a wilderness tract of land that had on it one leaky building seventeen feet square, called "Sportsman's Hall," inherited from Father Brouwers. In this structure he was expected to live and also to conduct religious services. In fact Father Helbron had immediate difficulty even in obtaining possession of the Brouwers estate. Mr. Topper, Father Fromm's agent, refused to hand over the property to Father Helbron. But recourse was taken via legal proceedings and Mr. Topper was ousted by due process of law. Father Helbron thus was able to take peaceful possession of the properties.

He wasted little time in beginning his priestly ministry among the parishioners of Sportsman's Hall Parish. The estimate in 1799 was that there were seventy-five communicants for the congregation. It was soon made clear to him that the scandalous conduct of Father Fromm, his predecessor, had played havoc with the faith of the people. But Father Helbron was undaunted; he at once began to familiarize himself with the conditions of the place, to study the people and to learn their needs. His gentle kindness and his firmness easily won a way into the hearts of his people, commanding their respect and gaining their support and cooperation with his plans and endeavors.

Father Helbron, with his characteristic energy, soon began to improve the Sportsman's Hall Parish plant. This was evident when the congregation built for him, in 1800, a house, 26 by 28 feet, which offered better accommodations for both the priest and people. After a short time an addition was built to the house to serve as a chapel—thus it became the first church of the settlement. Father Helbron "blessed it in the name of Jesus, and entitled it the Chapel of the Holy Cross." But this space, although it served as a place of worship for ten years, soon proved to be too small. Father Helbron offered his unfinished house as a chapel, but the parishioners were determined to build a new church on the spot which Father Brouwers had selected for that purpose. And, in order to raise the necessary funds, the parishioners were called upon to voluntarily pledge contributions—73 persons offered to contribute $206.50, according to a list preserved in the Saint Vincent Archives. Lumber was plentiful and there was a lot of voluntary labor and so the work on the 26 by

Baptisms recorded in Father Peter Helbron's <u>Register.</u>

Marriages recorded in Father Peter Helbron's Register. *The records are complete except for one entry, which was physically cut out of the register book.*

40 foot structure made steady progress. Henry Kuhn, the ever-active parishioner, did, however, have to journey across the Alleghenies on horseback to Carlisle to buy the nails needed. And so it was, that, in 1810 the people of the Sportsman's Hall Parish had a church of their own—rough hewn as it was—in which to worship.

One of the remarkable facts about Father Helbron's pastorate is that he received no salary from his congregation—he asked none and expected none. What was presumed was that the farm would yield for him a comfortable living, but Father Helbron exercised poor judgment as a farmer. He kept too much livestock on the parish lands, and would not sell when prices were fair, and was not punctual in paying those workmen who did the farming. As he grew older and more feeble, his lack of finances became more acute. In fact he was ultimately compelled to appeal to his congregation for assistance. Father Vincent Huber tells us: "A subscription was taken up for him and a handsome sum realized."

While Father Helbron was caring for the spiritual and temporal needs of the parishioners, he did not neglect those Catholics who lived in other parts of Pennsylvania west of the Allegheny Mountains. He visited the Catholics of at least seven counties before he received any assistance in the form of a fellow missionary priest. These seven counties formed a semicircle with the western slope of the Allegheny Mountains, namely: Westmoreland, Fayette, Washington, Greene, Allegheny, Butler and Armstrong Counties. How much further north Father Helbron traveled in his missionary journeys can only be surmised from the following expression in one of his letters to Bishop Carroll: "As far as the lake," which speculation would tell us was Lake Erie. Within the seven-county area Father Helbron founded mission stations or erected mission churches. These missions, which he established or assisted in establishing, were at Pittsburgh, Brownsville, Slippery Rock and Buffalo Creek (later called Sugar Creek). It should be especially noted that credit for having paved the way for the first Catholic Church in Pittsburgh should be given to Father Helbron. A Colonel O'Hara had presented him with "a fine lot" on which to build a church, and $1,000.00 had been collected for that purpose. The church here spoken of was Old Saint Patrick's in which Father S. Badin of Kentucky celebrated Mass on December 10, 1807, and reported that he had "found thirty Catholic families in the town." This church stood just in front of what was later the Union Station of the Pennsylvania Railroad.

One of the things that Father Helbron did from the time of his arrival at the Sportsman's Hall Parish in the autumn of 1799 was to keep a record of baptisms, marriages and funerals—something that had not been done previously. These records, reputed to be "the oldest in this part of the United States," are preserved in the Saint Vincent Archives and have been a valuable source of information not only concerning the parishioners, but also concerning all of the missionary ministrations of Father Helbron in western Pennsylvania. Because of the value of this source, it was originally published between 1915 and 1917 and then reprinted in 1985 under the title, *Catholic Baptisms in Western Pennsylvania, 1799-1828: Father Peter Helbron's Greensburg Register*. The work of copying from the original book was done by Father John Miller, O.S.B.—no small feat because of the German and Latin script and because of the often poor handwriting. The English translation was made by Dr. Lawrence F. Flick, M.D. From these records we learn that, during Father Helbron's pastorate at Sportsman's Hall Parish, from 1799 to 1815, there were 825 baptisms, 47 marriages and 9 funerals.

The year 1799 was an important one for Catholicism in Pennsylvania west of the Allegheny Mountains, not only because of the beginning of the over sixteen years of missionary ministry of Father Peter Helbron, but also because of the arrival at McGuire's settlement (now Loretto) in Cambria County of the celebrated prince-priest, Father Demetrius Gallitzin. Father Gallitzin was a prince from Russian nobility who had converted to Roman Catholicism in his youth. He found his way to America and was ordained a priest in 1795, the first priest to receive all sacred orders in this country. And so it was that in 1799, at the age of thirty, Father Gallitzin began a missionary apostolate that would witness the growth of Catholic communities in the Allegheny Mountains, an apostolate that would continue until his death forty-one years later in 1840.

From 1799 until Father Helbron's death in 1816, he and Father Gallitzin remained friends and gave assistance to each other despite distance and difficulties. They would exchange visits, prolonging them to days and even weeks. How fortunate it was that Father Gallitzin and Father Helbron had such a good relationship, since these two pioneer pastors were the only priests laboring in Pennsylvania west of the Alleghenies until 1807. And so we have the picture of the young Russian prince-priest and the elderly German Capuchin helping each other. A good illustration can be found in the letter which Father Helbron wrote to Bishop Carroll on November 22, 1806, concerning the laying of the cornerstone for Old Saint Patrick's Church in Pittsburgh; he noted that Father Gallitzin would assist him in the ceremony. And then Father Helbron wrote in his labored English syntax that Father Gallitzin was "the only help to me...and I to him." And during the next year (1807) Father Gallitzin wrote to Bishop Carroll that Father Helbron was to visit him at Loretto during his severe illness and "stay with me till I gain sufficient strength to discharge my duty." The story of "Prince Gallitzin" has often been told and he well deserves the honored title of "The Apostle of the Alleghenies." Father Helbron has not been so celebrated, but in the contention of Father Felix Fellner, O.S.B., the

The year 1799 marked the arrival of Father Demetrius Gallitzin, a prince of Russian nobility, and the first priest to receive all sacred orders in the United States. Prince Gallitzin was a friend of Father Peter Helbron. Each man gave assistance to the other in their pastoral work, between 1799 and 1816, in spite of the distance and difficulties.

The number of parishioners who had made their "Easter duty," i.e., gone to confession and communion during the Eastertide, as recorded in Father Peter Helbron's Register.

preeminent historian of Saint Vincent, Father Helbron also "deserves justly the name of 'The Apostle of Western Pennsylvania.'"

But Father Helbron's years as a missionary priest at Sportsman's Hall Parish were drawing to a close. He was already over sixty years of age upon his arrival in 1799. The years and the long and difficult missionary journeys had taken their toll on his once-robust body. Bishop Michael Egan, O.F.M., of Philadelphia, which had become a separate diocese in 1808, noted Father Helbron's advanced age during an 1811 visitation to the western part of the Diocese of Philadelphia. But Father Helbron preferred his work in the comparative peace of western Pennsylvania to the trustee troubles of Philadelphia. During his sixteen years at Sportsman's Hall, he frequently journeyed to Philadelphia to pick up supplies and to attend to business affairs, but he refused offers to have him return to his former pastorate at Holy Trinity Parish, where he had experienced so much turmoil with trusteeism.

In these latter years—1811 to 1816—Father Helbron must have felt that his days were drawing to a close and he preferred to die in his beloved Sportsman's Hall Parish. But it was not to be. Around 1811 a tumor developed in Father Helbron's neck which baffled the local medical doctors. Such was the concern of the congregation, fearing the imminent loss of their pastor, that they raised money to defray the cost of a trip by Father Helbron to Philadelphia to seek more advanced medical and surgical treatment. In 1816, he traveled to Philadelphia, had the tumor removed, but the operation did not have the hoped-for results. Father Helbron realized that his strength and life were ebbing away so he set out for his beloved home at Sportsman's Hall, three hundred miles away. When he arrived in Carlisle, he was too ill to journey further. He went to the home of Thomas Hagan, a Catholic, and spent his final days there, where Thomas' wife, Mary, provided him with nursing care. He died on April 24, 1816, and was buried in a little plot of ground that adjoined the Saint Patrick's Church in Carlisle.

Father Helbron had time during his final illness to draw up his Last Will and Testament. In it he bequeathed all his real and personal property "unto Mary Hagan wife of Thomas Hagan to hold to their heirs and assigns [in trust] for the use of the Catholic Church in the borough [of Carlisle] for ever. . . ." Since Thomas Hagan had been named Executor, he came to Sportsman's Hall and sold all of the personal effects of Father Helbron. After all debts had been paid, there was a balance of $325.58, which Mr. Hagan used a year later to purchase a lot and a stone house next to Saint Patrick's Church in Carlisle.

With the death of Father Helbron, the parish of Sportsman's Hall and the missions in western Pennsylvania suffered a severe loss. What he had meant to these Catholic pioneers was put into words by one of his biographers, Father Gerard Bridge, O.S.B., who wrote of Father Helbron in 1916:

"The works that he left behind during the sixteen years of his ministry; his zeal in the care of souls; his arduous labors for the spread of God's Kingdom; the fidelity with which he served the people, and the love which he constantly manifested towards the lowest of his flock; these are the stones in the monument which he erected with his own hands and by which a grateful people hold his memory in loving remembrance and lasting benediction."

And so it was that the fruitful ministry of Father Helbron came to an end in the spring of 1816, and once more the congregation found itself without a resident pastor.

For a year and a half after the death of Father Helbron, the Sportsman's Hall Parish was visited by at least two priests. The first, the celebrated Father Gallitzin, came at least once, since he recorded a baptism on October 14, 1817, in the parish register. A more consistent priest-visitor, who ministered to the spiritual needs of the people of the parish, was Father William Francis Xavier O'Brien, the first resident pastor of Old Saint Patrick's Parish in Pittsburgh. He made pastoral visits in May, July and November of 1816; and, in February, April and August of 1817. Father O'Brien had forty-nine baptisms at the parish during these six visits. He was no stranger to the parish for he had visited Father Helbron there in 1808, 1809 and 1815. During his 1816-1817 visits Father O'Brien urged the parishioners to finish the interior of the house that had been built for Father Helbron in 1800; the congregation not only completed the work on the house; they also added a room to it. In addition, it was during this period of time that the parishioners took up a subscription for the purpose of providing a more permanent altar in the church that had been built in 1810. This subscription list, dated May 15, 1816, and still preserved in the Saint Vincent Archives, contains seventy-three names of parishioners who collectively promised to pay $310.00—thus proving the campaign was a success. It is worthy to note that many Irish names appear on the list. A number of these Irishmen were employed as laborers in building the many turnpikes in western Pennsylvania.

This nineteen-month period at the Sportsman's Hall Parish without a resident pastor came to an end on November 27, 1817, when Father Charles Bonaventure Maguire, O.S.F., in his own words, "obtained possession of the benefice." He had been appointed pastor of the Sportsman's Hall Parish by Father Louis de Barth, Administrator of the Diocese of Philadelphia. There was an Administrator of the Diocese because Bishop Egan had died on July 22, 1814, and it would be six years until his successor, Bishop Henry Conwell, was appointed, consecrated a bishop, and took possession of the diocese.

Father Maguire had had a remarkable life in the almost fifty years before his arrival at Sportsman's Hall. Although born and raised in Ireland, he went to the University of Louvain in Belgium for higher studies, which culminated in ordination to the priesthood. He also joined

Saint Patrick's Church in Carlisle, where Father Peter Helbron is buried.

the Order of Saint Francis of the Strict Observance. His early priesthood was spent in pastoral ministry in various parts of the Netherlands and Germany; and he became a linguist of considerable ability, acquiring especially a remarkable knowledge of the German language. He next found himself in France during the frenzy of the French Revolution. Father Maquire was one of those clergymen who sided with the French government against the revolutionists during the latter part of the Reign of Terror. On one occasion he was seized and was being dragged to the guillotine when he was rescued and managed to escape. Next, Father Maguire emerged in Rome where he taught Theology at the College of Saint Isidore for six years. But in the year 1815 he was again in Belgium and this time he ministered to the wounded and dying after the Battle of Waterloo. It was shortly thereafter that Father Maguire, distressed with the disturbed condition of affairs in the Old World, decided to enter the missionary field on this

Monument to Father Peter Helbron at Saint Patrick's Church, Carlisle, Pennsylvania:

"In memory of Rev. Peter Helbron born 1756 died in Carlisle 1816 a pioneer priest of Pennsylvania his remains repose under the church."

side of the Atlantic Ocean. He arrived in Philadelphia early in the year 1817; and, after his appointment as pastor of the Sportsman's Hall Parish, he set out for western Pennsylvania.

When Father Maguire arrived at Sportsman's Hall on November 27, 1817, as the third resident pastor, he found little to commend it. All of Father Helbron's personal goods, furniture, provisions, livestock and farming implements had been sold and the proceeds had been given to Mary Hagan in trust for the Church at Carlisle—in accord with the provisions of Father Helbron's Will. And so Father Maguire was obliged to make a considerable outlay of money to buy livestock for the farm and the necessary implements to till the land. Also, a circular barn, that had been built in Father Fromm's time, was in a dilapidated condition. Father Maguire requested the congregation to build a new barn; they hired a carpenter and the new barn was soon completed. To manage the farm, Father Maguire engaged his own brother and had his sister keep house for him. Also, he leased the best parts of the farm to David Mulholland for a term of seven years. But in general the farm proved to be unprofitable for Father Maguire, due largely to a sudden depreciation in farm products. And so he was soon faced with personal debts, despite the salary that he received from the congregation.

Father Maguire's pastoral ministry, on the other hand, was well received and offered much promise. During the more than two years of his pastorate there was general satisfaction with his spiritual service. This favorable ministry and the growth in population of the area caused the congregation to increase rapidly. Father Maguire kept an accurate record of baptisms, marriages and funerals at Sportsman's Hall Parish, just as Father Helbron had done.

Father Maguire's handwriting was always legible and his knowledge of languages prevented him from mangling proper names as his predecessor had done. These records have been preserved in *Father Peter Helbron's Greensburg Register*. There was indeed much enthusiasm for Father Maguire's pastorate, especially when he told the parishioners that he would remain as their pastor as long as he lived. It was during this burst of enthusiasm that he announced that he would go to Europe to collect money so that a new brick church could be built near the cemetery further up on the hill. But, in a turn of events, he never did make the European trip.

Indeed this bubble of euphoria soon burst, when, in the spring of 1820, Father Maguire moved to Pittsburgh to become pastor of Old Saint Patrick's Parish to replace the same Father William F.X. O'Brien, who had ministered intermittently at Sportsman's Hall Parish since 1808. Father O'Brien had a delicate physical constitution and the duties at the Pittsburgh parish were so demanding that "his strength became so exhausted that he was no longer able to continue his labors." So, in the spring of 1820, Father O'Brien, at only thirty-eight years of age, retired and went to live at Mount Saint Mary's College in Emmitsburg, Maryland. Father Maguire, during his tenure at Sportsman's Hall Parish, had visited Father O'Brien at Saint Patrick's Parish on more than one occasion; and, familiar with the parish and convinced of its promising future, he seized the opportunity to be the pastor. Father Thomas Heyden, writing at Bedford, Pennsylvania, on a later date, related this part of the story: "Moved by the wants of the Catholics of Pittsburgh, he [Father Maguire] was transferred, or transferred himself thither, for there was no great order in those days—he made the church at Pittsburgh what it is." He did have an illustrious career as pastor of Saint Patrick's, and died there, on July 17, 1833, of cholera during the epidemic that gripped the people of Pittsburgh.

Although Father Maguire lived in Pittsburgh from the spring of 1820, he made occasional visits to the Sportsman's Hall Parish, and provided the people with the opportunity to receive the Sacraments. Also, Father Maguire's brother and Mr. Mulholland retained possession of the farm at Sportsman's Hall until after the appointment of Father Maguire's successor as pastor in 1821.

The resignation of Father Maguire as pastor was a great disappointment to the congregation, and the fact that he left behind a debt of $242.83 added bitterness to disappointment. The reaction of the congregation was to take the administration of the properties of "Sportsman's Hall" and "O'Neill's Victory" into their own hands. They were convinced that the various pastors had bungled the farming operation. And so it was that a petition to the Pennsylvania State Legislature was drawn up and signed by nearly all of the members of the congregation requesting it to vest the management of the two tracts of land in a board of trustees. Father Maguire was able to get a counter-petition drawn up and had this protest sent to the Legislature but it was to no avail. The petition from the congregation was granted in an Act of Assembly, dated March 7, 1821. The actual text stated that the pastors had abused the trust placed in them by the last Will and Testament of Father Brouwers, and so the two tracts of land were put into the hands of a board of trustees—five were named.

The great significance of this Act of Assembly was that the trustee system that had wreaked so much havoc on the Catholic Church in eastern Pennsylvania and elsewhere was now introduced into western Pennsylvania. It was probably the first and only instance in which the Pennsylvania State Legislature directly appointed a board of trustees to manage church affairs. And, as such, this action on the part of the Legislature was puzzling, and was not consistent with the American principle of the separation of church and state. Some excuse for the Act of Assembly may be found in the unfortunate condition of the "Sportsman's Hall" and "O'Neill's Victory" tracts of land at the time when the petition was made and granted. It would not be until eleven years later (1832) that this Act of Assembly would be reversed by the Supreme Court of Pennsylvania. It was then that the Last Will and Testament of Father Brouwers was interpreted to mean that these lands were the private property of the pastor, held by him in trust not for the congregation, but for his successor in the pastoral charge to whom he was required to "transmit the land so left to him in trust as aforesaid to his successor clear of all incumbrance." But this decision was made in 1832; and in the meantime Father Maguire's successor as pastor of the Sportsman's Hall Parish would be called upon in 1821 to face the challenges of the trustees appointed by the State Legislature.

The fourth resident pastor of the Sportsman's Hall Parish was Father Terrence McGirr, D.D. Little is said

Father Charles B. Maguire, O.S.F., third resident pastor of Sportsman's Hall Parish, 1817-1821.

about his actual appointment to the pastorate, most probably because Bishop Henry Conwell was only in the process of taking over the Diocese of Philadelphia after it had been without a bishop for over six years. In any event Father McGirr arrived on the scene and took charge of the congregation in the beginning of March 1821, when he was thirty-nine years of age. Father McGirr was a native of Ireland who had been educated for the priesthood at Saint Patrick's College, Maynooth, where he received the degree of Doctor of Divinity. It is not certain when he arrived in America, but we do know from church registers in Philadelphia that he ministered in that city off and on from 1813 until 1820. It is also known that Father McGirr was in Pittsburgh in 1814, where he bought a lot adjoining Old Saint Patrick's Church and built a house. Father Vincent Huber, O.S.B., writing in 1892, described the new pastor of the Sportsman's Hall Parish as follows:

"Father McGirr was a singular character; he was good at heart, faithful to his duties, ready for every hardship, humble, obliging and kind to the poor; but his outer deportment was not in keeping with the dignity of his priestly character. In conversation he was rough, uncivil, unreserved, harsh and often

This version of the Sportsman's Hall postcard was partially colorized.

extremely overbearing and imperious."

When Father McGirr arrived in March 1821, Father Maguire's brother still occupied the parish house and retained possession of the tracts of land—in the name of Father Maguire. For this reason Father McGirr lived for several months in Youngstown, a hamlet two miles away along the "Pennsylvania Turnpike" which followed the Forbes Road. And, when Mr. Maguire vacated the parish house, Father McGirr moved in and assumed management of the tracts of land, without paying much attention to the board of trustees. He also engaged his brother, Bernard McGirr, as farmer. The trustees, at first, showed surprise at their pastor's independent actions but did not protest because of the favorable first impression that he had made on them. The trustees, however, gradually began to insist on their supposed rights and made it very unpleasant for Father McGirr, whose impetuous nature was beginning to manifest itself. Father McGirr's irritable and resentful temper asserted itself particularly in his Sunday sermons. He also antagonized the parishioners by saying Mass at a very early hour without consulting them about a time convenient for them. All of these happenings did not bode well for Father McGirr, whose nine years at Sportsman's Hall Parish were "marked by almost continual strife and dissension."

The major difficulties that Father McGirr had as pastor of Sportsman's Hall Parish centered around the board of trustees, who called themselves "the trustees and wardens or vestrymen of the Roman Catholic Congregation in Unity Township." These self-styled church trustees at their first formal meeting, which took place on May 1, 1822, established rules and regulations "for the good and uniform conduct and management of said congregation." They soon took action in the form of resolutions declaring that it would be "illegal, for the clergyman or present incumbant [sic], for the time being, to superintend at any Election for Trustees." Moreover, "no Relatives of the present Clergyman by marriage or otherwise or of any other known person or persons living on the plantations belonging to the said Congregation, shall be considered Eligible [sic] to serve or to be Elected a Trustee for the said Congregation." This board of trustees even went so far as to appoint a committee of three, whom they authorized to demand from Rev. Terrence McGirr all the personal property he has received from the Catholick [sic] Congregation." And further, the trustees appointed a treasurer who was empowered to receive the entire income from the two tracts of land—i.e., "Sportsman's Hall" and "O'Neill's Victory"—and was not allowed to disburse any of the income without the written consent of the majority of the trustees.

And so the stage was set for the inevitable clash between Father McGirr and the trustees. The occasion was when Father McGirr rented the lands at "O'Neill's Victory" to a person who was not looked upon with favor by the trustees. The trustees, in turn, leased the farm to a man named George Aaron and gave him first possession. Next, Father McGirr, in the autumn of 1826, brought suit of ejectment against George Aaron. The case was tried in the Westmoreland County Court of Common Pleas, and then removed to the Circuit Court in the same county. After a delay of three years the case was decided against Father McGirr, who appealed to the Pennsylvania Supreme Court. In an 1830 decision Judge C.J. Gibson sustained the judgment of the lower court by holding "that the devise was for the maintenance of a priest, in ease of the congregation." This long drawn-out series of adverse court decisions, occupying almost the entire tenure of Father McGirr's pastorate placed him at the mercy of the trustees upon whom he was dependent for his very livelihood.

Matters for Father McGirr went from bad to worse. Already in the early 1820s the parish congregation, through the trustees, had petitioned Bishop Henry Conwell of Philadelphia to remove Father McGirr from the pastorate and to send them another priest. But Bishop Conwell did not even answer this request; the presumption is that the aged prelate had troubles enough in the city of Philadelphia to occupy all of his attention. In fact Bishop Conwell was summoned to Rome in 1828; and, during his long absence, Father William Matthews was Administrator of the Diocese of Philadelphia. It was during this time that Father Matthews was presented with a petition, drawn up and signed by a number of the parishioners of Sportsman's Hall Parish, asking for the removal of Father McGirr. This petition embodied a number of scandalous accusations against Father McGirr that were never substantiated. And, in an incredible bit of irony, the previous pastor, Father Charles Maguire, signed the petition. And this petition was sufficiently convincing to Father Matthews to have him pen a letter to Father Maguire with directions to investigate the charges and another letter to Father McGirr, directing him to abide by the decision of Father Maguire. Thus, in his 1892 account of these proceedings, Father Vincent Huber observed: "In this way one of the accusers was appointed to act as judge and it was therefore not difficult to foresee the outcome of the trial."

Father Demetrius Gallitzin, who from his Allegheny Mountain parish in Loretto served as Vicar General of the western part of the Diocese of Philadelphia from 1821 to 1830, now came to the rescue of the beleaguered Father McGirr. Father Gallitzin was a friend and confidant of Father McGirr; he recognized under the rough and rugged exterior a priest of real worth whose friendship was worth seeking. In fact Father Gallitzin had repeatedly visited the Sportsman's Hall Parish during Father McGirr's troubled pastorate in the interests of peace, but without avail. But this so-called "trial" of Father McGirr filled Father Gallitzin with indignation. He thus considered it his duty to intervene and to obtain justice for an innocent, though possibly imprudent, friend. And so in November and December of 1828, Father Gallitzin wrote long letters to both Father Maguire and Father Matthews in protest. In both letters Father Gallitzin acted in his capacity as Vicar General; he was particularly insulted that Father Matthews had taken action in a matter in the western part of the Diocese of Philadelphia without even consulting the Vicar General. These protests on the part of Father Gallitzin evidently had the effect of prolonging the stay of Father McGirr at Sportsman's Hall Parish, but the adverse conditions remained and the ultimate removal of Father McGirr was inevitable.

A word seems to be in order about the ministry of Father McGirr as a missionary priest for over nine years during all this turmoil. Throughout his tenure, Father McGirr was faithful to the performance of his pastoral duties at the Sportsman's Hall Parish, and he continued the practices of Father Helbron and Father Maguire in making missionary visits to other parts of Westmoreland County, and to Armstrong and Butler Counties as well. In 1822, Father McGirr decided to erect a small church, 26 by 44 feet, under the title of Our Lady of Mount Carmel, on a plot of land near the settlement known as New Derry, which was about six miles north of Sportsman's Hall. Father McGirr's intent was to serve the Irish Catholic farmers and coal miners who had settled in this area. And, although Father McGirr held services occasionally in this rough hewn church, it never developed as a separate parish, but became part of Saint Martin Parish, which was founded in 1856. Another place visited by Father McGirr was Saint Patrick Church in Cameron's Bottom, Indiana County. This Church had been founded from Loretto by Father Gallitzin in 1820. There was something predictive in Father McGirr's visiting Cameron's Bottom, since he would minister to these people in his later years, from 1834 until 1842.

Father McGirr, during his nine-year pastorate, continued the practice of recording baptisms and marriages in the book that had been initiated by Father Helbron and continued by Father Maguire—later printed as *Father Peter Helbron's Greensburg Register*. But it is regrettable that Father McGirr's recordings were defective and difficult to read. What had been said by Father Thomas Middleton, O.S.A., of Father McGirr's writing in the register of Saint Augustine Church in Philadelphia might also be said in this instance: "It is a very noticeable hand; the worst almost I have ever been perplexed to decipher, and one you could apparently read as easily upside down as any other way." And what records that Father McGirr did leave behind were evidently incomplete, since entire pages were left blank. He wrote no records of deaths or burials, none of mixed marriages and none of the baptisms of adults. The first entry in this historic record book was made on March 8, 1821; and the last was made on May 10, 1830. Father McGirr had recorded ninety-eight infant baptisms and forty marriages.

By the time of Father McGirr's last entry in the record book on May 10, 1830, his days as pastor of Sportsman's Hall Parish were numbered. The board of trustees, on November 9, 1829, had taken recourse to the civil court in an attempt to get rid of their pastor, but the situation was resolved before the court case had been pursued. The key to this part of the story was the designation, on February 25, 1830, of Father Francis P. Kenrick to be Coadjutor Bishop to Bishop Henry Conwell in the Diocese of Philadelphia, with jurisdiction over the government of the diocese. This appointment prompted the board of trustees at Sportsman's Hall, on September 4, 1830, to petition Bishop Kenrick to remove Father McGirr and to "supply our congregation in Westmoreland County with another clergyman in his place." The trustees were aware of the impending visitation of Bishop Kenrick to western Pennsylvania. In fact Bishop Kenrick arrived in Youngstown at 4:00 a.m. on October 19, 1830, after an overnight stage coach ride from Bedford. Fortunately the *Diary and Visitation Record* of Bishop Kenrick has been preserved and so the following are the actual words of the decision made concerning the pastorate of Father McGirr:

"There has been much trouble between the Rev. Terrence McGirr and the faithful under his charge, so that he can no longer exercise the pastoral office among them without evident peril to souls. I counseled him, therefore, to resign the charge within one month from the nineteenth day of October; otherwise I would be forced to remove him."

And thus the pastorate of Father McGirr at Sportsman's Hall Parish came to its agonizing end. He left in the late autumn of 1830 and journeyed to Loretto to be with the only confidant he appeared to have, Father Gallitzin. It was in these Allegheny Mountains that Father McGirr was to spend the last twenty-one years of his life. Father Gallitzin made sundry attempts to get Father McGirr back into active ministry. In fact there is mention in Bishop Kenrick's *Diary and Visitation Record* that he had given Father McGirr, on May 23, 1834, "charge of the congregation of St. Joseph in the place known as 'Hart's Sleeping Place,' also St. Patrick's in the place called 'Cameron's Bottom.'" It is also known from the Diary that the old clashes between Father McGirr and the people arose again at Cameron's Bottom, and that Bishop Kenrick got him to agree to give up this charge in September 1842.

It appears that Father McGirr spent the remainder of his life on a farm along the Ebensburg-Wilmore road. He lived there with his brother, who managed the farm under his direction. This closing decade of Father McGirr's life was evidently quiet and undisturbed, and he died peacefully on August 11, 1851—over eleven years after the death of Father Gallitzin. Father McGirr, at the time of his death, was sixty-nine years of age. He was buried in the little cemetery in Ebensburg next to the Catholic Church—then called Saint Patrick's; now under the patronage of the Holy Name of Jesus. Even to this day, his grave is easily identifiable in the cemetery, since there is a prominent tombstone fittingly inscribed:

Repose to the soul of a priest of God
REV. TERRENCE McGIRR
born A.D. 1782
In the parish of Clogher, Co. Tyrone, Ireland
ordained a priest A.D. 1806
At the College of Maynooth, Ireland
died
on the 11th day of August, A.D. 1851
<u>*Requiescat in pace.*</u>

But during all of these years from 1830, the congregation of the Sportsman's Hall Parish was being well shepherded. It was in November of 1830, that Bishop Kenrick had appointed, as pastor, Father James A. Stillinger.

3. Father James A. Stillinger, 1830, To Father Boniface S. Wimmer, O.S.B., 1846

With the appointment of Father James Ambrose Stillinger by Bishop Francis Patrick Kenrick in November 1830, to succeed Father Terrence McGirr as pastor, a new and renowned era of the parish began. Father Stillinger arrived at his new assignment on November 18, 1830, and noted in his own handwriting that he began "the discharge of the duties of holy ministry" on the First Sunday in Advent, November 28, 1830. In the era of missionary labor Father Stillinger's field of pastoral ministry was more broad than the Sportsman's Hall Parish. In fact Bishop Kenrick had appointed him, at the same time, to be the first pastor of the recently organized Saints Simon and Jude Parish in Blairsville, a borough that had been incorporated in 1825 and that was approximately fifteen miles to the northeast of the Sportsman's Hall Parish.

There was also an understanding with Bishop Kenrick that the Catholics residing in all of Westmoreland County were in Father Stillinger's care. And, in 1832, he was directed by Bishop Kenrick to visit, when possible, the few Catholics residing east of the Allegheny River as far north as the New York State line, a distance of 110 miles. In August of 1833, Father Stillinger accompanied Bishop Kenrick on visitation in western Pennsylvania; it was during this trip that they conducted religious services at the recently organized Saint Peter's Parish in the thriving borough of Brownsville. On August 4, 1833, Bishop Kenrick wrote in his *Diary and Visitation Record*: "In order to meet the needs of the faithful, the Rev. J.A. Stillinger promises that he will visit this congregation four times a year." And, in 1834, Father Stillinger further promised Bishop Kenrick to attend to the spiritual needs of the Catholics residing in all of Fayette County, and of Greene and Washington counties as well.

One of the reasons that such a great and expansive pastoral burden had been placed on the shoulders of Father Stillinger was the small number of priests that were officiating in Pennsylvania west of the Allegheny Mountains at that time—Father Stillinger said that there were only three plus himself. Another reason why this large burden was given to Father Stillinger was the fact that he was twenty-nine years of age and had been a priest for only nine months at the time of this 1830 assignment, and thus was filled with youthful vigor.

But, if the story of Father Stillinger in western Pennsylvania is to be understood, the early happenings which prepared him for this role should be traced. To do so there is an invaluable source, the autobiographical letter that Father Stillinger wrote, around the year 1870, to Father John A. Watterson, then President of Mount Saint Mary's College in Emmitsburg, Maryland. (A first draft of this letter is on file in the Saint Vincent Archives.) Father Watterson—later Bishop of the Diocese of Columbus, Ohio, from 1880 until 1899—had been a member of the Blairsville congregation and so a good friend of Father Stillinger, who had urged him to write "a sketch of his life." In this autobiographical account—which he interestingly wrote in the third person—Father Stillinger stated that he had been born in Baltimore, Maryland, on April 19, 1801, a son of parents who had been born in America from German and French lineage. For some reason that he did

Father James Ambrose Stillinger, fifth resident pastor of Saint Vincent Parish, 1830-1844. Photograph from a portrait of Father Stillinger on display at Saints Simon and Jude Parish, Blairsville.

not give, James Stillinger, from the age of eleven, lived in the Philadelphia area with his paternal grandparents, who had taken "him to themselves." When his grandfather died in 1812, "he was variously employed in several respectable families" while he was growing up—from the age of eleven to the age of fifteen—and attempting to go to school when he had a chance. In 1816 James Stillinger "was employed for a short time in a German printing office where he learned to read German by setting type." It was this knowledge of German that would serve him so well during his many years of pastoral endeavor. In 1817 he began an apprenticeship of nearly four years—from the age of sixteen to the age of nineteen—in the printing office of Robert G. Harper in Gettysburg, Adams County, Pennsylvania. And it was while working in Gettysburg that the personal narrative of the priestly vocation of James Stillinger began to unfold.

In his autobiographical account, Father Stillinger traced the origins of his vocation to the priesthood. He noted that early in life it had been suggested that he study for the priesthood, but his response was that, "if he had the desire he had not the means," and "that it would be more satisfactory to him to learn a trade and by honest industry earn the means to pay his way, if he wanted to take such a step." What follows in the autobiographical letter of Father Stillinger is a long account of the steps that led him to Mount Saint Mary's College and Seminary, Emmitsburg, Maryland, in November 1820. It all began when he visited Mount Saint Mary's on Sunday, July 19, 1818—prophetically the feast of Saint Vincent de Paul—to attend Mass. There he met Father John Dubois, S.S., a Sulpician priest who was to become in 1826, Bishop of the New York Diocese. Thus began the relationship that, for over the next two years, would foster his priestly vocation. And, in the spring of 1820, James Stillinger asked Mr. Harper to relieve him of his apprenticeship in the Gettysburg printing office; it took six months for Mr. Harper to release him of his indenture after having found other apprentices to take his place.

So it was that James Stillinger, in November of 1820, arrived at Mount Saint Mary's, where he was to remain for ten years. Father Stillinger, in his autobiographical account, tells of these formative years in the following modest and brief passage: "How he conducted himself is for others to say. It is sufficient to say he had the good will of his superior and not an enemy that he knew of." This firsthand account continued by giving the following succinct rendition of the events that brought Father Stillinger to western Pennsylvania in November 1830:

"He was ordained on the 28th day of February 1830 by Archbishop Whitfield (of the Archdiocese of Baltimore), and the 72nd priest ordained in Baltimore. He returned to Mt. St. Mary's a few days after his ordination and attended to the mountain congregation and Liberty until November following, when he was appointed by Bishop Kenrick Pastor of SS. Simon's and Jude's Church, Blairsville, Indiana County, Pennsylvania. St. Vincent's then called "Sportsman's Hall," near Youngstown, and all Westmoreland County was added to his charge."

Father Stillinger did not display reluctance at being assigned to the missions in the western part of the Diocese of Philadelphia during the first year of his priesthood, but there must have been concern in having him leave Mount Saint Mary's, as indicated by the letter of November 8, 1830, from Bishop Francis P. Kenrick to Father John B. Purcell, then President of Mount Saint Mary's College, who, in 1833, was to become Bishop of the Diocese of Cincinnati. This letter reads:

"Notwithstanding my most sincere intentions to meet your wishes, expressed in Conewago, concerning Rev. Mr. Stillinger, I am forced to take him from you. The congregation of Westmoreland seems absolutely to require him, whose piety, and knowledge of the German tongue render him peculiarly adapted to fill the vacancy which has occurred. Had you witnessed the tears of the good people, you would scarcely hesitate to give them this good Pastor, who may console them for years of spiritual desolation. I, who am charged with their salvation, could not but feel the most anxious solicitude to give them one whom I deem the most proper to heal their wounds. Do not, I pray you, put an obstacle in the way of so much good. If you have any claims, are you not rewarded for your sacrifice by the consideration that you have formed a worthy priest, whose prayers will draw down benedictions on his benefactors."

This letter of Father Stillinger's bishop is not only a reasoned account of why this young priest should be assigned to the missions of western Pennsylvania, but it is also a commendation of his priestly character. The young Father Stillinger must have been an impressive person. He has been described as "tall in stature, dignified in bearing, kind in manner, and firm in determination." He was, in carrying out his duties as a priest, "zealous, pious, punctual, and practical." And a further insight tells us that Father Stillinger's "condescending manner easily won the hearts of his people, while his firm and resolute will gained their confidence and guarded the rights of the pastor." He was always preparing to undergo any hardship for the good of his people.

An even fuller description of Father Stillinger was given in 1914 by Father Andrew Arnold Lambing, the historian from Pittsburgh who had known him personally. He spoke of Father Stillinger's powerful frame that carried "at his heaviest nearly 300 pounds." His physical strength was demonstrated by the strength of his grip, so that "in shaking hands he could almost crush the hand of a strong man." Father Lambing continued his description of Father Stillinger by saying: "His countenance was of the German cast, though his accent betrayed little of his Teutonic extraction." Father Stillinger's voice was distinctive; Father Lambing describes it as "soft and gentle and devoid of the metallic ring and fullness that distinguish the orator, yet he possessed a fervor that few could find it in their hears to resist." The account also speaks of Father Stillinger's sparkling and playful eyes, which attracted the young and filled them "with confidence, while inspiring them with respect." This, then, was the young priest who appeared on the scene in Westmoreland and Indiana Counties in November 1830, to begin what was to be a forty-three year missionary apostolate.

When Father Stillinger took charge of the Sportsman's Hall Parish on November 25, 1830, he found that the parish buildings and lands—in fact both tracts, "Sportsman's Hall" and "O'Neill's Victory"—were in the hands of the board of trustees that had been entrusted with management by the Pennsylvania State Legislature in an Act of Assembly on August 7, 1821. These trustees "evinced a disposition not only to manage the temporalities with an independence too often characteristic of such persons, but also to control the pastor to an extent that would deprive him of the freedom necessary for one in his position." The best demonstration of this dominance by the trustees was the fact that the house at Sportsman's Hall Parish where Father Stillinger expected to reside was occupied by the person in charge of the farm, and so the pastor decided under the circumstances to live in Blairsville. He resided in Blairsville until 1835 when the new parochial residence at Sportsman's Hall was ready for occupancy.

But from the onset Father Stillinger took a firm stand with the trustees at the parish and gave them "to understand that he considered himself capable of managing his own affairs." He accomplished by his firmness and prudence what Father McGirr had not been able to do with his gruffness and obstinacy. What Father Stillinger did was to insist that all interference in the management of the estate of Father Brouwers should cease. In this position Father Stillinger was earnestly supported by Bishop Kenrick. When the latter paid his first visit to Sportsman's Hall Parish in August of 1831, he drew up a comprehensive document in which he corrected the false impressions about the estate and the Last Will and Testament of Father Brouwers, and instructed the congregation on their duties toward their pastor. This instruction is of so much importance in this issue that it is here quoted in its entirety:

"*Bishop Kenrick, having gratified the Congregation of Sportsman's Hall, in providing them with an excellent Pastor, expects that the Congregation will on their part respect the Pastor's rights and leave the property entirely under his management.*

"*It was originally purchased, not by the Congregation with their money, but with the money of the Revd. Mr. Brouwers,*

who bequeathed it to the Catholic Pastor for support. The Will of the dying Man should be sacredly guarded. In extraordinary circumstances the Legislature created a corporate Body to protect the Pastor's rights, by preserving the Farm from devastation during the Vacancy of the Pastorship; but these circumstances being changed, it does not appear Just or conscientious to use a Charter obtained in that emergency, particularly as its use would defeat the disposition of the Will. The dying Man meant to leave his successors in the Pastorship an honorable and independent Maintenance, subject to no control. The Congregation has therefore no right to interfere, under any pretext, since the property is not theirs. As several Congregations are now destitute of a Pastor who, if sent to them, would be left free of all Lay interference, the bishop cannot consent to oblige the Rev. Mr. Stillinger to remain in the Sportsman's Hall Congregation should the Management of his property be denied him. Rev. Mr. Stillinger will consent to suffer the present Occupants to remain during the Term for which they rent the Farms, provided the Trustees forthwith cease from all interference, and leave him to manage his affairs by himself or by such persons as he may appoint. August 24, 1831."

These instructions were received by the board of

Rev. Norbert A. Gerstl, O.S.B. (1859-1939), also painted a version of the Sportsman's Hall campus.

Monument to Father James Stillinger in the Roman Catholic cemetery in Blairsville.

trustees, and by the Sportsman's Hall Parish congregation generally, with respectful submission. In fact shortly thereafter the trustees posted a notice that, at the next meeting at which trustees were elected, a vote of the congregation would be taken regarding whether future trustees would be appointed by Bishop Kenrick and Father Stillinger or whether to discontinue the elections. This meeting of active members of the parish was held on May 28, 1832, and it was unanimously decided that no more elections for trustees should be held, but that "it should go by appointment, and that it should rest with the Right Rev. Bishop and the Pastor to make the appointments." The records of this May 28 meeting that proclaimed the above-mentioned decision were signed by the four trustees, namely: Jacob Coon, George Miller, Conrad Henry and John Rogers. Thus, this vexatious question was settled to the great satisfaction of all. And Father Stillinger, having secured for himself such "liberty of action," soon gained the confidence and good will of his parishioners. Nor do we have any evidence to show that any further friction over this matter ever developed again between Father Stillinger and the congregation. As a postscript it should be noted that, also in 1832, the Supreme Court of Pennsylvania reversed the 1821 Act of Assembly that had granted to the board of trustees such extraordinary powers.

With the matter of the trustees settled, peace and harmony were restored to the Sportsman's Hall Parish, and the congregation began to increase rapidly. Thus it was that the little rough hewn Church of the Holy Cross, built in 1810 during the pastorate of Father Helbron, proved to be too small. In addition—as Father Stillinger reminisced in his 1870 autobiographical letter—this church was "in a decayed state, and rudely built." Father Stillinger also saw the need for a residence in which the pastor could live; the only present accommodation for the priest was a "rickety log shanty"—thus giving an added reason why Father Stillinger lived in Blairsville during these years. Thus Father Stillinger, in the summer of 1833, proposed to the congregation the erection of a more substantial church and a parochial residence. To this proposition the people gave their ready assent. Also Bishop Kenrick was very supportive of these plans; he wrote in his *Diary*, after he had visited and administered confirmation at the Sportsman's Hall Parish on August 25, 1831, that the congregation was looking forward to the building of a new church and priest house—the latter because, in Bishop Kenrick's words, the pastor "should reside there." Bishop Kenrick freely granted permission for the construction; in a letter, under the date of July 4, 1833, he wrote to Father Stillinger: "As to the erection of a new church at Sportsman's Hall, you have my free permission to undertake it, as I rely on your judgment as to its practicability." And then Bishop Kenrick added the following encouraging statement: "The docility of these good people deserves to be rewarded by exertions on our part to console them and give them the benefits of Religion."

Little time was wasted; at a parish meeting on July 24, 1833, it was unanimously decided to erect a substantial brick church and a parochial residence. At this same meeting a subscription list was compiled, with one hundred and three persons subscribing a total of $4,162.00. This published list of subscribers offers a cross-section of the membership at the Sportsman's Hall Parish in 1833—characteristically the list is headed by Rev. J.A. Stillinger with a donation of $500.00.

Father Stillinger wasted no time in having the plans prepared; he then called for bids on the proposed construction. Several bids were received and the Pittsburgh firm of Anthony Kerrins and Jonathan Wilson, Master Builders, secured the contract. The articles of agreement were drawn up and signed by the builders and Father Stillinger on October 4, 1833. By this contract Kerrins and Wilson pledged themselves to build a brick church, gothic in design, approximately 50 by 85 feet, for the sum of $5,850.00. It was soon ascertained that this contract had not been sufficiently specific as to details, and that the builders, in whom Father Stillinger had full confidence, had not done their work well. Already at the time of construction the foundation walls began to give way and many other serious defects were noticeable. The builders made some repairs but the work remained unsatisfactory. Thus the balance of approximately $1,400.00 that was due to the builders was withheld for damages. The builders brought suit to force payment; but, dragging out as such lawsuits do, it was only in August 1843, that a jury reached a verdict in favor of the congregation. And, although the 1833 contract had set the cost of the church at $5,850.00, it had actually cost more than $9,000. This dramatic increase in cost was due largely to the installation of altars, pews, bells and other furnishings in order to ready the church for divine services. An organ was purchased and installed in the new church at a cost of approximately $700.00, of which $619.25 had been raised by a separate subscription. In the summary, at the time of the dedication of the church, the congregation found itself burdened with a debt to the amount of $5,928.27.

But this debt did not dampen the joy of the solemn dedication of the completed church on July 19, 1835, by Bishop Kenrick. In his *Diary and Visitation Record* he describes the church as spacious and beautiful (*"ampla et pulchra"*). He further noted that "a very great multitude of people" had gathered for the occasion. Father Stillinger celebrated the Mass of dedication and Bishop Kenrick preached. As it was the custom of Bishop Kenrick to name churches after the saint whose feast occurred on the day of the dedication, and as this church was dedicated on the feast of Saint Vincent de Paul, he named it Saint Vincent Church—the name that has endured for over one hundred and fifty years. The day's celebration continued on into the afternoon when the Office of Vespers was chanted. At this afternoon service there was a sermon preached in German by Father Peter Lemke to accommodate the large crowd of German immigrants and their families. Father Lemke was at that time an assistant to the aging Father Gallitzin in his vast Allegheny Mountain missionary territory; he would later play a prominent role at Saint Vincent under the Benedictines. Bishop Kenrick stayed overnight and, on July 20, 1835, confirmed fifty-five persons in the newly dedicated Saint Vincent Church. In his *Diary* on this date Bishop Kenrick, after noting that "nearly one hundred" had "received Holy Communion on this same day," paid the following tribute to Father Stillinger and the parishioners of Saint Vincent Parish: "God grant that the consolation which I experienced here by reason of the piety of the priest in charge and the good will of the people under his care may long endure."

This Saint Vincent Church was to have a glorious existence of one hundred and twenty-eight years. From 1835 until the consecration of the Saint Vincent Archabbey Church on August 24, 1905, the venerable Saint Vincent Church would serve as the place of worship for the parish. It was also the monastery church for the Benedictines from 1846 until 1905. From 1905 until early in the 1960s the Saint Vincent Church was used principally by the students of the seminary, college and preparatory school and so was popularly called the "Students Chapel." But the life of this venerable structure came to a violent end when it was destroyed in the great fire of January 28, 1963.

At the same time in the early 1830s when the Saint Vincent Church was being constructed, Father Stillinger turned his attention to the erection of a parochial residence. The same construction firm, Kerrins and Wilson, that was building the church, erected this house. It was a two-story brick structure 40 by 40 feet, that was located approximately one hundred and fifty feet north of the church. It was erected at a cost of $2,600.00. Father Stillinger was able to move into this parochial residence in the summer of 1835, and so he transferred his living quarters from Blairsville. For the next nine years he would continue to live at Saint Vincent Parish, while also attending to the congregation at Saints Simon and Jude Parish in Blairsville.

Father Stillinger's vast mission to the Catholics of such a large area of western Pennsylvania must have been most taxing. In his autobiographical letter of 1870, he stated: "The labors and privations and sufferings of these missions were surely sufficient for anyone's zeal if he were blessed with the physical strength to endure them." But in the same letter Father Stillinger reminisced—writing in the third person—that "after a few years he was relieved from visiting these distant places by others being appointed to attend to them, as he had quite sufficient to occupy his time in serving the Catholics in the two large counties

Yet another version of Sportsman's Hall was reproduced in a painting by Rev. Norbert A. Gerstl, O.S.B. (1859-1939).

of Indiana and Westmoreland." In fact we know from a letter, dated July 31, 1835, that Bishop Kenrick wrote from Pittsburgh to Father Stillinger in Blairsville that Father John O'Reilly would visit Saint Peter's Church in Brownsville once a month; and so, that Father Stillinger would henceforth be "free from the troublesome ride" to Brownsville.

This concentration of Father Stillinger on the two parishes of Saints Simon and Jude and of Saint Vincent was evident during Bishop Kenrick's visitation in 1838. On July 28, 1838, Bishop Kenrick recorded in his *Diary and Visitation Record* that he had confirmed forty-two persons in the Church of Saints Simon and Jude, to which he added the following tribute: "The congregation enjoys peace in the exercise of piety, under the pastoral care of Rev. James Ambrose Stillinger, who has charge here now for nine years past, and has won the loyal affections of the people." Bishop Kenrick then noted that there were approximately one hundred families in the Blairsville parish, where during the year there had been thirty births, six marriages and four deaths.

Bishop Kenrick then went on to give similar information concerning the congregation at Saint Vincent; he noted that there were approximately one hundred and fifty families, and during the year there had been thirty-five births, seven marriages and five deaths. Bishop Kenrick was to return to Saint Vincent Parish during his 1839 visitation, when he confirmed ninety-four persons on Sunday, June 24, 1839. On that occasion Bishop Kenrick wrote in his *Diary* of Father Stillinger that he was "strong in the affections of the people by reason of his good life" and that he was "held in high esteem also by those who are outside the fold." Three years later, on July 14, 1842, Bishop Kenrick returned once more to Saint Vincent Church and confirmed ninety-five people. And, as part of the same visitation, Bishop Kenrick was in Blairsville at Saints Simon and Jude Parish on Sunday, July 17, 1842, to confirm sixty-five people. Of particular interest is the fact that the sermon at both Confirmations was preached by the Very Rev. Michael J. O'Connor, pastor of Saint Paul's Church in Pittsburgh and Vicar General to Bishop Kenrick for western Pennsylvania.

The significance of Father O'Connor's presence is that Bishop Kenrick had been urging, since 1835, that the Diocese of Philadelphia be divided and that the Diocese of Pittsburgh be erected to serve the western part of Pennsylvania. It became evident that, when Bishop Kenrick sent Father O'Connor to Pittsburgh in July 1841, he was grooming him to be the first Bishop of Pittsburgh. The eight-year wait was over on August 11, 1843, when the Diocese of Pittsburgh was established and Father O'Connor was named the first bishop. He was consecrated in Rome on August 15, 1843, but would arrive in his newly established diocese only on December 20, 1843. Father Stillinger must have been pleased with these developments, because, when he first heard the news in a letter from Father Thomas Heyden of Saint Thomas Parish in Bedford, who had received the report directly from Bishop-elect O'Connor, Father Stillinger, in his September 25, 1843, reply to Father Heyden, said that "we have one with whom we can act.... I feel confident he will spare no pains to make our diocese one of the foremost in the union, and I think it can be done." What makes this exchange of correspondence interesting is the fact that Bishop Kenrick had noted in his *Diary* on June 26, 1837, that he had included the names of Father Heyden and Father Stillinger in the recommendations for future Bishop of Pittsburgh—in fact he had already suggested Father Stillinger's name on July 25, 1835. But six years had elapsed and Bishop O'Connor was now the ecclesiastical superior of both the above-named pastors. Their eyes would now turn west rather than east.

While all of these events were occurring, Father Stillinger was continuing his faithful ministry in his dual pastorate. Although he had taken up residence in the new brick house at Saint Vincent Parish in the summer of 1835, he did not neglect the congregation at Saints Simon and Jude Parish. He had lived there from the time of his appointment in 1830 until 1835. In his autobiographical account of 1870, Father Stillinger tells us that there was a church being built in Blairsville when he arrived in late 1830. The church was the work of a small but enthusiastic group of Catholics who, in fact, had sent in June 1830 a delegation to Pittsburgh to meet the newly consecrated Bishop Kenrick and to petition him to send them a priest. Bishop Kenrick not only agreed to send them a pastor as soon as it would be in his power to do so, but he stopped in Blairsville on his way to Philadelphia on July 1, 1830, and administered the Sacrament of Confirmation for the first time in the town. Father Stillinger's arrival, then, was the fulfillment of Bishop Kenrick's promise to send a priest to the Catholics in Blairsville. Father Stillinger not only took up residence in Blairsville on November 28, 1830, but he saw completion of the building of the little church. Bishop Kenrick tells us in his *Diary and Visitation Record* that he had blessed this church on October 28, 1830, the feast of Saints Simon and Jude—under whose patronage he placed it. But it was only approximately 30 by 40 feet, and soon became too small for the growing congregation.

And so, in 1841 and under the direction of Father Stillinger, work was begun on a new church, 50 by 115 feet, with a tower and spire 120 feet high. This new church was made of brick and was modeled after the Gothic style of architecture. After eighteen months of construction it was completed. On October 2, 1842, the new Saints Simon and Jude Church was solemnly dedicated by Father Michael O'Connor, pastor of Saint Paul Parish, Pittsburgh and Vicar General for the western part of the Diocese of Philadelphia, having been delegated by Bishop Kenrick. At the conclusion of the dedication ceremony, Father Stillinger celebrated a High Mass at which Father Thomas Heyden of Bedford preached an eloquent sermon. To enhance Saints Simon and Jude Church, Father Stillinger, in 1859, installed nine large and beautiful oil paintings that he had obtained from Germany. The church was destined to serve for almost one hundred and thirty years, until it was razed in the early 1970s to make room for a new church that was dedicated on May 28, 1973.

There was a close bond between Bishop O'Connor and Father Stillinger which was revealed in many ways. When the pastorate of Saint Michael Parish in Loretto was made vacant by the resignation of Father Peter Lemke in 1844, Bishop O'Connor asked Father Stillinger to take charge of Saint Michael's which was the domain of the legendary Father Demetrius Gallitzin until Father Gallitzin's death on May 6, 1840. Bishop O'Connor, in his letter to Father Stillinger in which he asked him "to accept Loretto," demonstrated his great confidence in Father Stillinger by stating that he was "most anxious to place a person there on whose judgment and good conduct I could place the fullest reliance." But Bishop O'Connor left the decision in the hands of Father Stillinger, who respectfully declined the offer.

Yet another evidence of the esteem and confidence of his bishop was accorded to Father Stillinger, when, by letter dated July 10, 1845, Bishop O'Connor called upon him to serve as the first Vicar General of the Diocese of Pittsburgh. This appointment Father Stillinger accepted although he declined Bishop O'Connor's offer to have him reside in Pittsburgh. He preferred to remain in his beloved Blairsville—to which he had moved, in 1844, from Saint Vincent Parish—even though he was called upon to serve as Administrator of the Diocese during Bishop O'Connor's trip to Rome and other parts of Europe from July 23, 1845 until December 13, 1845. We have every reason to believe that Father Stillinger served actively in his capacity as Vicar General and that Bishop O'Connor showed much confidence in him. But a difference of opinion arose between the two over an issue involving money that the brother of Father Stillinger had loaned to Saint Vincent Parish, and had not been repaid after Father Stillinger moved to Blairsville. This situation—blown out of proportion—precipitated Father Stillinger's resignation as Vicar General, which Bishop O'Connor reluctantly accepted on November 30, 1848. Father Andrew Arnold Lambing wrote the following observation about this incident: "But both had too much piety and good sense to permit this to be more than a passing ruffle of their sincere regard for each other." There is every reason to believe that the remaining twelve years, during which they labored together in the Diocese of Pittsburgh,

Bibliography

Bridge, O.S.B., Gerard. *An Illustrated History of St. Vincent Archabbey.* Beatty, Pennsylvania, 1922.

Bridge, O.S.B., Gerard. "The Rev. Peter Helbron, O.F.M. Cap., Pioneer Missionary of Western Pennsylvania," *Saint Vincent College Journal,* XXV (May 1916), 591-603.

Catholic Baptisms in Western Pennsylvania, 1799-1828, Father Helbron's Greensburg Register. Baltimore, 1985 (Reprinted from *Records of the American Catholic Historical Society of Philadelphia* in installments between September 1915 and December 1917).

Fellner, O.S.B., Felix. *Abbot Boniface and His Monks.* (Privately published at Saint Vincent Archabbey, Latrobe, Pennsylvania, 1956), 5 volumes.

Fellner, O.S.B., Felix. "Chapter I: Early Catholicity in Western Pennsylvania," *Catholic Pittsburgh's One Hundred Years,* ed. William Pur-

were amiable.

One other matter concerning Father Stillinger and the Saint Vincent Parish that should be mentioned, was his concern for education. The prime example was his dream of opening a college and seminary on the Sportsman's Hall tract of land. Indication of this dream can be found in the July 6, 1831, letter of Father Simon Gabriel Brute, S.S., from Mount Saint Mary's College, to Father Stillinger. Father Brute—who was to become Bishop of the Diocese of Vincennes, Indiana—told him: "As for that good idea of a little college and seminary at Sportsman's Hall... you do well to submit it to your bishop." Father Brute had advised early communication with Bishop Kenrick, since this type of idea would require much thought and preparation in the hope that its time would come. That time was eleven years later, when, while on visitation at Saint Vincent Parish, Bishop Kenrick noted on July 14, 1842, in his *Diary and Visitation Record,* that the plan to use the Sportsman's Hall property and the buildings thereon for a college and seminary was acceptable to both Father Stillinger and to Father Michael O'Connor, the Vicar General. In fact both Bishop Kenrick and Father O'Connor had entered into communication with Father John Timon, C.M., superior to the Vincentians in the United States and later the first Bishop of Buffalo, concerning the staffing of this proposed educational institution. But Father Timon eventually responded that he did not have, at the time, the manpower to staff such a college and seminary. The main drawback to this plan, however, appeared to have been the forecast that, in the impending division of the Diocese of Philadelphia, such a Sportsman's Hall college and seminary would most probably be in the territory of the new Diocese of Pittsburgh. But, with Father O'Connor, who would become the first Bishop of Pittsburgh one year later, the idea was germinal and would reach fruition with the coming of the Benedictines to Saint Vincent Parish in 1846.

Father Stillinger had also shown other interests in education. When, in 1835, the Saint Vincent Church and parochial residence were built, he had also directed the construction of a small one-story brick structure, located approximately 250 feet to the southeast of the church. Father Stillinger had hoped to use this building for school purposes, but such was not the case, at least in those early years. This little building would figure prominently in the next decades of the annals of Saint Vincent. Father Stillinger, further, in his 1870 autobiographical letter, demonstrated his interest in education by laying claim to having "purchased by his own funds" the farm two miles from Saint Vincent on which Saint Xavier Academy was to be built. But, major credit for the impetus of founding this institution of secondary education really belongs to others.

We know that, in November 1844, Father Stillinger transferred his place of residence from Saint Vincent Parish to Saints Simon and Jude Parish. But, just as he had done while living in Blairsville from 1830 to 1835, he continued to minister to the congregation at Saint Vincent Parish from November 1844 until the appointment of a pastor to succeed him. An indication of this contemplated move was given by Bishop Kenrick in his March 23, 1843, letter to Father Stillinger in which he spoke of the latter's "desire to be relieved from the charge of St. Vincent's congregation," but it would take several years and a change in diocese and bishop to effect this transfer. Bishop O'Connor, not long after his installation as Bishop of Pittsburgh, appointed Father Michael Gallagher as the sixth resident pastor of Saint Vincent Parish.

Thus came to an end the fourteen-year pastorate of Father Stillinger at Saint Vincent Parish. He kept faithful records of baptisms, marriages and funerals in the parish, and these records are preserved in the Saint Vincent Archives. Between the years 1830 and 1844 there were 597 baptisms recorded over Father Stillinger's signature, 124 marriages and approximately 140 deaths of adults and children. What a record of pastoral service was thus made by Father Stillinger to the Saint Vincent Parish while he was also pastor in Blairsville and ministering to diverse missionary stations. Also to the credit of Father Stillinger was the harmonious adjustment to the difficulties with the trustees at Sportsman's Hall. But it is with surprise that one learns from Father Lambing, writing in 1914, that Father Stillinger's agreement with the Saint Vincent Parish congregation, that he "should receive $200.00 a year with a certain part of the produce of the farm," was not fully honored. In a letter which Father Stillinger wrote to Bishop O'Connor after leaving Saint Vincent, he stated that, after laboring there for fourteen years, instead of getting $2,800.00 he had received only $700.00.

But Father Stillinger continued his friendly relationship with the congregation at Saint Vincent Parish, and also with the Benedictine community that arrived in

1846, during the twenty-nine years that he remained in his pastorate at Blairsville. It was at Father Stillinger's parish house in Blairsville that Father Boniface Wimmer, O.S.B., and his group of Benedictine aspirants stayed overnight in the journey on foot from Carrolltown, Pennsylvania, that brought them to Saint Vincent to found a monastery on October 18, 1846. And it was this same Father Stillinger who, on October 24, 1871, was able to be present at Saint Vincent Abbey for the festivities which marked the twenty-fifth anniversary of the coming of the Benedictines to America.

It seems incredible that Father Stillinger was pastor of Saints Simon and Jude Parish for forty-three years. When he moved to Blairsville in 1844, he had the commodious church that had been dedicated in 1842. But, again, with his interest in education, he kept working on the project of building a parish school in Blairsville until, in 1855, he was instrumental in the construction of a one-room school, over which he placed a lay teacher in charge. Father Stillinger later replaced this school with a two-story brick building that served until 1949. He was not able to secure a religious community to serve the parish school until shortly before his death in 1873. He built a large brick convent near the church in the summer of 1872, and then secured a number of Sisters of Charity from Altoona, Pennsylvania, to occupy this convent in January 1873 and to take charge of the parish school.

Once Father Stillinger had returned to live in Blairsville in 1844 and had given up the pastorate of Saint Vincent Parish, his field of labor gradually diminished. He did, however, continue to care for the Catholics in the town of Indiana, where he supervised the building of a church, which in 1847 was dedicated by Bishop O'Connor and placed under the patronage of Saint Bernard. In 1852, the Benedictines from Saint Vincent began to care for Saint Bernard Parish and so the pastoral labors of Father Stillinger were henceforth confined exclusively to Blairsville.

So it was that Father Stillinger lived the final twenty-one years of his life—from age fifty-one to age seventy-two—in comparative peace and quiet with the good people of his congregation in Blairsville. He feared that he might become so feeble in his declining years that he would have to resign the pastorate, but he was spared that distress. Although, in the summer months of 1873, there had been a more rapid decline in health "than should have proceeded from old age," Father Stillinger died suddenly on the morning of September 19, 1873, at the age of seventy-two. He had died of heart failure in the sacristy of the church after having said Mass. His congregation and the entire Blairsville community were shocked by his sudden death, as he had administered the affairs of the parish up until the end and, in fact, had made his customary visit to the parish school the afternoon before. After the Funeral Mass, the late Father James Ambrose Stillinger was laid to rest in a place he had chosen behind the church. His remains have since been moved to the Saints Simon and Jude Cemetery on the outskirts of Blairsville. Father Andrew Arnold Lambing, the Pittsburgh church historian who knew Father Stillinger personally, has given us an appropriate encomium for this great priest, when, in 1880, he called him: "A man who figured more conspicuously than any other in the history of the Church in Westmoreland and Indiana Counties."

Father Michael Gallagher, who succeeded Father Stillinger as pastor of Saint Vincent Parish, had been a missionary priest in western Pennsylvania since his ordination in 1837. He was an immigrant who had been born in Drommore, Ireland, in 1806. He came to the United States when he was fifteen years old, and was employed at Keating's Mills in Manayunk, a suburb of Philadelphia. Later on Bishop Kenrick received him into the old Fourth Street Seminary in Philadelphia to study for the priesthood. And immediately after his 1837 ordination, Bishop Kenrick sent Father Gallagher to Brownsville, the center of a missionary field that included Greene, Washington and Fayette counties and a part of Somerset County, with an occasional visit into Virginia. During the years that he labored in this vast area, Father Gallagher resided in Brownsville, since Saint Peter's Church was the only one in that district. In April 1839 this church burned down, and Father Gallagher, undaunted, commenced the building of the stately stone edifice that still stands today.

It was shortly after the building of the new Saint Peter's Church had been completed and it had been consecrated that Father Gallagher was transferred to Saint Vincent. We know from Bishop Kenrick's *Diary and Visitation Record* that Father Gallagher accompanied the bishop on his eighth visitation in 1837, on the latter's way to the Brownsville assignment. During Bishop Kenrick's ninth visitation in 1838, he "confirmed about thirty persons in the Church of St. Peter, Brownsville." The bishop at that time noted that Father Gallagher was the pastor in resi-

---

cell. Pittsburgh: Catholic Historical Society of Western Pennsylvania (1943), 3-24.

Fellner, O.S.B., Felix. *Phases of Catholicity in Western Pennsylvania During the Eighteenth Century.* Latrobe, Pennsylvania, 1942.

Fellner, O.S.B., Felix. *The Loyalhanna Valley in History.* Latrobe, Pennsylvania, 1954 (originally published in *The Latrobe Bulletin* during the city's 1954 centennial year).

Fellner, O.S.B., Felix. "The Rev. Theodore Brouwers, O.F.M., Missionary in the West Indies and the Pioneer Priest in Western Pennsylvania," *Records of the American Catholic Historical Society of Philadelphia*, XXIV (December 1914), 356-363.

Fellner, O.S.B., Felix. "Trials and Triumphs of Catholic Pioneers in Western Pennsylvania as Revealed by Their Correspondence," *Records of the American Catholic Historical Society of Philadelphia*, XXXIV (September 1923), 195-261 and XXXIV (December 1923), 287-343.

Guilday, Peter. *The Life and Times of John Carroll, Archbishop of Baltimore (1735-1815)*. New York, 1922.

Haas, O.S.B., Louis. *St. Vincent's*. St. Vincent's Print, Latrobe, 1905.

Healy, R.S.M., Kathleen. "The Early History of the Sisters of Mercy in Western Pennsylvania," *The Western Pennsylvania Historical Magazine*, LV (April 1972), 159-170.

Huber, O.S.B., Vincent. "Sportsman's Hall," *Records of the American Catholic Historical Society of Philadelphia*, III (1888), 142-173.

Huber, O.S.B., Vincent. "Sportsman Hall and St. Vincent Abbey," *St. Vincent's Journal*, I-III (1892-1894), passim.

Lambing, Andrew A. *A History of the Catholic Church in the Dioceses of Pittsburgh and Allegheny*. New York, 1880.

Lambing, Andrew A. Vol. I, *Brief Biographical Sketches of the Deceased Bishops and Priests Who Labored in the Diocese of Pittsburgh from the Earliest Times to the Present With*

Drawing of the Saint Vincent Parish plant as it appeared in 1846, upon the arrival of Father Boniface Wimmer. In the top center is the Saint Vincent Church, built in 1835 by Father James Stillinger. To the right is the parochial residence, also built in 1835. In the center is the historic Sportsman's Hall. To the extreme left is the school house which had also been built in 1835, and which served as the first monastery for Father Wimmer and his followers.

dence and that "he works with great zeal, and gratifying results." And, in 1839, when Bishop Kenrick was on his tenth visitation during which he dedicated Saint Ann's Church in Waynesburg, he noted in his *Diary* that Father Gallagher was also in charge of that church but not able to be present for the ceremony "because he had broken his leg by a fall from a horse." This part of Bishop Kenrick's Diocese of Philadelphia became, in August 1843, the Diocese of Pittsburgh under Bishop O'Connor.

Father Lambing states that Father Gallagher arrived at Saint Vincent Parish to take up his new duties in the latter part of 1845. That may well be so, but we do know that there are entries in the records of baptisms, marriages and funerals over the signature of Father Michael Gallagher as early as December 1844 and January 1845. And, knowing that Father Stillinger gave up the pastorate of Saint Vincent Parish in November 1844, we can conjecture that Father Gallagher came to the parish prior to being installed as the new pastor. In addition there is preserved in the Saint Vincent Archives, in Father Gallagher's own handwriting, his financial record, entitled "Account with St. Vincent's Church from Nov. 1844 to Nov. 1846," further evidence of his 1844 arrival. There was also an occurrence in the spring of 1845 that leads one to believe that Father Gallagher had already taken possession of the parochial residence that had been vacated by Father Stillinger. This happening involved the Sisters of Mercy who had come to Pittsburgh from Ireland in 1843.

Early in 1844 Henry M. Kuhn, the son of the Henry S. Kuhn who had played such a prominent role in the early history of Saint Vincent Parish, offered to convey for the consideration of one dollar the title of his 108 acre tract of land to Bishop O'Connor, provided a school for girls would be established there. Bishop O'Connor then entered into an agreement with the Sisters of Mercy whereby the property was transferred to them in exchange for their promise to found such a school. The problem at this time, however, was that there was no building on Mr. Kuhn's farm suitable for use as a convent and school. It was then that Father Gallagher, as pastor of Saint Vincent Parish, which was one and one-half miles northeast of this farm, offered his pastoral residence to the Sisters to be used as a convent and academy until a new building on their own farm would be erected. Father Gallagher, in turn, moved into the small one-story house that Father Stillinger had built for school purposes. The Sisters accepted this offer of the pastoral residence and, on April 28, 1845, opened Mount Saint Vincent Academy for Young Ladies in this two-story brick building containing twelve rooms, to which Father Gallagher added—for benefit of the Sisters and their students—a kitchen, dining room and two classrooms. And so in these quarters the Sisters of Mercy operated Mount Saint Vincent Academy for two years until, on May 14, 1847, they were able to move into a three-story brick building that had just been completed on their own property. At this time the name of the academy was changed to Saint Xavier's. Father Gallagher is remembered during the years from 1845 to 1847 not only as the first chaplain of the Academy, but as the spiritual counselor to the Sisters of Mercy and their students. It is also worthy to note that the Sisters taught the children of Saint Vincent Parish in a small day school conducted in the sacristy of Saint Vincent Church.

Shortly after his arrival at Saint Vincent Parish, Father Gallagher became a party to the renewal of a plan that a minor seminary be established at Saint Vincent. He proposed that a community of religious brothers be engaged to work the land, and in this way support not only themselves but also the students who would attend the minor seminary. Nothing came of this proposal but Bishop O'Connor was supportive of Father Gallagher. Bishop O'Connor, however, was convinced that the success of this proposed school would depend not so much on the brothers as upon the priests who would be placed in charge. But Bishop O'Connor also realized that he would need help from outside of the Diocese of Pittsburgh to supply the number of priests that such a venture would require. And so it was that Bishop O'Connor, in April 1845, contacted Bishop John Baptist Purcell of the Diocese of Cincinnati, who had offered, on one or two previous occasions, to join with Bishop O'Connor in the establishment of a minor seminary program. In a letter, dated April 30, 1845, Bishop O'Connor reminded Bishop Purcell of this offer and then extended to him an invitation to join the Saint Vincent venture on a partnership basis. The immediate result was that Bishop Purcell loaned Father Joseph O'Mealy to work with Father Gallagher toward the establishment of this minor seminary. The two pursued the project for more than a year but made little progress. It was at about this time that Bishop O'Connor learned about the impending arrival of Father Boniface Wimmer, O.S.B., and his band of eighteen followers to Pennsylvania, an event that would alter plans for the Sportsman's Hall Parish.

Father Boniface Wimmer had come to the United States from Metten Abbey in Bavaria with the expressed intent of transplanting the Benedictine Order from Europe to North America. He had at first gone to Carrolltown, Pennsylvania, a town that Father Lemke founded in 1840, since Father Lemke had been instrumental in his

Archabbot Boniface Wimmer, O.S.B.

coming to America and had gone to New York to meet him. Near Carrolltown was property on which Father Gallitzin, about the year 1830, had built a church named Saint Joseph's at Hart's Sleeping Place, a church that Father Lemke was in charge of. It was at Saint Joseph's that Father Lemke arranged to have Father Wimmer settle with his followers on September 30, 1846. But Bishop O'Connor contacted Father Wimmer, had him come to Pittsburgh, and, after the two had inspected the holdings, offered him the Father Brouwers properties in Westmoreland County. Furthermore, the parishioners of Saint Vincent Parish, at the suggestion of Bishop O'Connor, had also urged him to come. The decision was then made to move to the new property, and thus it was that Father Wimmer arrived on October 18, 1846.

Father Gallagher had been present that October day in 1846 when Bishop O'Connor and Father

an Historical Introduction. Pittsburgh, 1914.

Lambing, Andrew A. *Historical Researches in Western Pennsylvania, Principally Catholic.* Pittsburgh, 1884.

"Looking Backward: St. Xavier's Farm Before the Sisters Came and After," *St. Xavier's Journal,* XXXVI (April-June 1926), 6-11.

Melville, Annabelle M. *John Carroll of Baltimore, Founder of the American Catholic Hierarchy.* New York, 1955.

Moosmuller, O.S.B., Oswald. *St. Vincenz in Pennsylvanien.* New York, 1873.

Nolan, Hugh J. *The Most Reverend Francis Patrick Kenrick, Third Bishop of Philadelphia, 1830-1851.* Philadelphia, 1948.

Oetgen, Jerome. *An American Abbot, Boniface Wimmer, O.S.B., 1809-1887.* Latrobe, Pennsylvania, 1976.

Schroth, S.J., Raymond A. (ed.). "The Excommunication of Reverend John Baptist Causse: An Unpublished

> Sermon by Bishop John Carroll of Baltimore," *Records of the American Catholic Historical Society of Philadelphia*, LXXXI (March 1970), 42-56.
>
> Selle, O.S.B., Paulinus J. *Building Constructions at St. Vincent, An Historical Treatise* (B.A. Degree Thesis). Latrobe, Pennsylvania, 1936.
>
> Shea, John Gilmary. *Life and Times of the Most Rev. John Carroll, Bishop and First Archbishop of Baltimore.* New York, 1888.
>
> Szarnicki, Henry. *Michael O'Connor: First Catholic Bishop of Pittsburgh, 1843-1860.* Pittsburgh, 1975.
>
> Tourscher, O.S.A., Francis E. (ed.). *Diary and Visitation Record of the Rt. Rev. Francis Patrick Kenrick, Administrator and Bishop of Philadelphia, 1830-1851.* Lancaster, 1916.
>
> Wyse, O.F.M., Alexander. "Brouwers' Bequest: The Friars in Colonial Pennsylvania," *The Provincial Annals (of the Holy Name Province of Franciscans)*, XXXII (1983), 224-231.

Wimmer were on their tour of inspection. And so, on October 18, Father Gallagher, being privy to the transaction, turned Saint Vincent Parish over to Father Wimmer. This change in the pastorate became definite when, on October 21, 1846, Bishop O'Connor wrote the formal document which reads as follows: *"To all whom it may concern. We do hereby appoint the Reverend Boniface Wimmer, O.S.B., pastor of the Roman Catholic Congregation, worshiping at Saint Vincent Church, Unity Township, Westmoreland County, vacant by the resignation of the Rev. M. Gallagher, and we confer upon said Rev. B. Wimmer all rights and privileges appertaining to said office of pastor of said Congregation, this appointment to hold good until revoked by us or our Successor or until a new appointment."* It should be said to the credit of Father Gallagher that he not only accepted the new pastor and his followers but also agreed to stay on at the parish to assist with the English-speaking parishioners, since Father Wimmer and his followers were not yet conversant in the English language.

It had been mentioned earlier that Father Gallagher, in the spring of 1845, had moved to the small schoolhouse so that the Sisters of Mercy could use the Saint Vincent Parish parochial residence for Mount Saint Vincent Academy. When Father Wimmer and his band of eighteen candidates arrived in October 1846, this arrangement was continuing and so they were obliged to take up temporary residence with Father Gallagher in this crude dwelling, which had not yet been plastered and had a leaky roof. In two rooms and a garret twenty people had to live and function until other arrangements could be made. But the story of Boniface Wimmer and the founding of the first Benedictine monastery in the United States belongs to a future installment of the Saint Vincent Story.[1]

Father Gallagher did remain at the Saint Vincent Parish through the winter and spring. In fact he formally entered the novitiate for the Benedictine Order on December 8, 1846. We also know that he assisted Father Wimmer in teaching Theology to the four clerical novices. Father Gallagher must have had a change of heart, since he left Saint Vincent in the autumn of 1847—his last entry in the baptismal register of Saint Vincent Church was on October 3, 1847. Father Wimmer was quick to inform Bishop O'Connor of this departure, stating that Father Gallagher had "left the Order and the house and the Diocese, and departed for Philadelphia, where he intends to remain for the future." And then Father Wimmer added: "We separated in peace and charity."

We owe credit to Father Lambing, writing in 1914, for information about the remainder of Father Gallagher's life. (Father Lambing, in turn, credits Father Thomas A. Middleton, O.S.A., for providing these facts about Father Gallagher's life.) Father Gallagher did go east, where he joined the Augustinians at Villanova, Pennsylvania. He went through the novitiate there and pronounced Solemn Vows on August 16, 1849. He was then engaged in pastoral ministry to Saint Augustine Parish, Philadelphia. In 1861 he was transferred to Saint Mary's Parish in Lawrence, Massachusetts, from which he administered Saint Augustine Church in Andover—four miles away—while establishing other missions. It is also known that he died on August 25, 1869, at the age of sixty-three, and was buried in the priests' plot of Saint Mary's Cemetery in Lawrence, Massachusetts. And so Father Gallagher lived on for twenty-three years after that memorable day in October 1846, when he handed over the pastorate of Saint Vincent Parish to Father Boniface Wimmer and thus set in motion what Father Vincent Huber called "a new epoch" in the history of the Saint Vincent Parish congregation. From now on the parish at Saint Vincent would be inseparably linked with the Benedictine monastery and educational institution that would flourish on this hallowed hill.

---

[1] Oetgen, Jerome, *An American Abbot: Boniface Wimmer, O.S.B., 1809-1887.* First edition, 1976. Second edition, 1997.

Oetgen, Jerome, *Mission to America: A History of Saint Vincent Archabbey, The First Benedictine Monastery in the United States.* First edition, 2000.

Saint Vincent's.
Souvenir of the Consecration of the
New Abbey Church, August 24, 1905,
on the Fiftieth Anniversary of the
Elevation of Saint Vincent's to an Abbey.

By Louis G. Haas, O.S.B.

Originally published by St. Vincent's Print
Latrobe, Pennsylvania
©1905, 2005

Editor's Note: Father Omer U. Kline's history of the Sportsman's Hall Parish expanded upon the work of Father Louis G. Haas' early history of the parish. Thus, this excerpt from Haas' work omits those sections and picks up where Father Omer's history left off: with the arrival of Boniface Wimmer at Saint Vincent, and the work leading up to the construction and dedication of the Basilica.

Introduction

The consecration of the New Abbey Church, on the fiftieth anniversary of the elevation of our monastery to an abbey, forms a signal epoch in the history of St. Vincent's, and furnishes the occasion for this little sketch giving a short account of the first Catholic settlement in Western Pennsylvania, and of the advent, the establishment, and the growth of the Benedictines of the American Cassinese Congregation in the United States.

Saint Vincent's: A Benedictine Monastery

It was on the 18th of October, 1846 that Boniface Wimmer, accompanied by four theological students and fourteen laymen, arrived at St. Vincent's. Father Wimmer was a member of the Benedictine Order and affiliated with the Abbey of Metten, Bavaria. His followers were candidates for the same Order, which he came to establish in the United States.

Boniface Wimmer first saw the light of day on January 14, 1809, in the small village of Thalmassing, near Ratisbon (today's Regensburg), and received in baptism the name of Sebastian. His rudimentary education was acquired in the parish school of his native town, and at the age of eleven he was sent to Ratisbon to study the classics. Testimonials, still extant, show that the conduct of young Sebastian and his progress in the various branches were all that could be desired. At the age of nineteen he entered the University of Munich, then one of the most famous institutions of learning in Europe—having such men of international reputation as Goerres, Doellinger, Allioli, etc., occupying professorial chairs.

While at Munich pursuing the scientific course, the young man exhibited no disposition for the priesthood but, on the contrary, was strongly inclined to enter upon a military career. As a matter of fact, on three different occasions he endeavored to join the Bavarian Volunteer Battalion, which was organized for the purpose of helping Greece in her struggle for independence; but, from some cause or other, each attempt he made to reach the recruiting office, failed—Divine Providence had mapped out a different course for him. In referring to this period of his life, Abbot Wimmer never omitted to mention that he had a good, pious mother, who seemed to have had higher aspirations for her son than a worldly career, and who faithfully prayed for him.

Gradually, Sebastian began to realize it to be God's will that he enter the ecclesiastical state. Accordingly, after passing a satisfactory examination, he entered the "Georgianum" in Munich, where for two years he diligently devoted himself to the study of theology! During this period he became more firmly convinced that his future usefulness in life could be accomplished only in the Holy Priesthood. He therefore applied for admission into the Diocesan Seminary at Ratisbon and there completed his theological course. While at Ratisbon, he was under the spiritual guidance of the saintly Coadjutor-Bishop George M. Wittmann, who directed the young aspirant till the day of his ordination, which took place August 1, 1831.

After his ordination, Father Wimmer spent one year as chaplain at the shrine of the Holy Virgin at Altoetting in the diocese of Passau, and here it was that he conceived the idea of becoming a Benedictine.

Louis I, King of Bavaria, had just then granted permission for the re-opening of the Benedictine monastery at Metten-on-the-Danube, which together with many other monasteries of Bavaria and other German States had been suppressed nearly thirty years before. The monks had been dispersed, their property confiscated and sold, the proceeds flowing into the State coffers, that had been sorely depleted during the wars with Napoleon.

Two monks of the old Abbey of Metten, both saintly men, survived the period of secularization. With joyful hearts they took possession of their beloved cloister, giving expression to but one wish and prayer: that God would deign to send them worthy candidates for the Order. Their prayers were heard. In September, 1832, five priests entered the novitiate at Metten. Among them was Father Wimmer who, when invested with the habit of St. Benedict, received the name of Boniface.

From the time of his solemn profession, on December 29th, 1833, until his departure for America, Father Boniface was variously occupied in the care of souls, and in teaching in the institutions of the Order at Metten, Augsburg, and Munich.

Father Boniface's Project to Become a Missionary

In the early forties of the last century the yoke of bureaucracy had almost crushed out political and religious liberty in Continental Europe. As a result, vast numbers of Europeans emigrated from the Fatherland to America, to seek not only a livelihood but to enjoy the boon of civil and religious freedom which was denied them at home.

These immigrants settled in the country districts, where conditions for future pleasant homes were most favorable. The one great want which they keenly felt was the absence of spiritual guides. In the "Annals of the Faith," in various periodicals and newspapers, articles appeared from time to time, deploring the loss of faith among a large portion of the German immigrants, owing to the want of a German-speaking clergy. Father Boniface realized the necessity of providing for the spiritual welfare of his countrymen in America and with characteristic energy labored to better their condition.

He published an article in one of the leading journals of Bavaria, stating, in language plain but forceful, his views in regard to the American missions and suggesting an effective method of supplying the great want of priests. He advocated the establishment of a Benedictine colony in the United States for the education of young men to the priesthood. He desired an American clergy for the American mission. The effect of this article was that men of the highest rank in State and Church, such as King Louis of Bavaria, Coadjutor-Bishop, afterwards Cardinal, Reisach of Munich and the directors of the Louis Mission Society, became interested in the movement and urged that Father Wimmer should in person put his proposed plans into execution. The abbot and community at Metten, though reluctant to lose so valuable a member, gave their consent to Father Boniface's undertaking, and bade him God speed.

About this time, Father Boniface met Peter Henry Lemke, a German priest, who had since 1834 labored in the American missions as associate of Rev. Demetrius Gallitzin and had come to the Fatherland in quest of priests for his countrymen in Western Pennsylvania. Father Lemke informed Father Boniface of the condition of the German Catholic settlers in the newly-erected diocese of Pittsburgh, and he magnanimously offered him a large tract of land adjacent to the present borough of Carrolltown, in case he should come to America. Father Boniface accepted the generous offer and forthwith wrote to Bishop O'Connor of Pittsburgh for admission into his diocese. The Bishop, in reply, commended his project and most cordially invited him to come, expressing at the same time an earnest desire that a Benedictine monastery be established in the Pittsburgh diocese.

Accordingly, Father Boniface prepared for his departure to America. As before stated, he had eighteen followers, willing to sacrifice home and its endearments in order to labor in God's vineyard in the New World. The little band of missionaries was greatly assisted financially by the Louis Mission Society (Ludwigs Missions-Verein) through its manager, the Court Chaplain Joseph Mueller, who furnished 6000 florins. Bishop Ziegler of Linz gave 500 florins; others contributed lesser sums; while still others donated sacred vestments, altar linen, books, and similar necessary and desirable articles.

After making a spiritual retreat of several days as an immediate preparation for their departure, Father Boniface and his companions left Munich on July 25, 1846. At Rotterdam they embarked on the sailing vessel "Iowa," and, after the voyage, arrived at New York, September 16. During his stay in New York, Father Wimmer met with very little encouragement as to his proposed plans. Many of the most prominent priests of the city expressed the opinion, that his undertaking was nothing more than a wild and venturesome scheme, with no possibility of successful results. They endeavored to dissuade him from making the western journey; but here the resoluteness and determination of will of Father Boniface asserted themselves. "I will make the attempt," he said, "and I trust, God will help." As soon as their baggage, consisting of forty-two boxes, had been taken out of the custom house, he and his followers set out for the West. They traveled by rail from New York to Philadelphia, thence by canal to Hollidaysburg, from where, after having engaged wagons to carry their belongings, they made their way on foot to Carrolltown. The trip from New-York to Carrolltown had taken them eleven days. Little had they imagined that the place, bearing the name of the illustrious archbishop of Baltimore, was nothing more than a wild waste of wilderness studded here and there with a log hut, and a little log chapel three miles away.

Shortly after his arrival at Carrolltown, Father Boniface journeyed to Pittsburgh to present himself to Bishop O'Connor. The Bishop cordially received the new missionary, again warmly commended his undertaking and expressed his appreciation of the plans to found a monastery and seminary in his diocese. He stated, however, that the location at Carrolltown was ill-suited for the project, and offered him the property at St. Vincent's, deeming it more desirable and better adapted for the ultimate success of the enterprise. The Bishop and Father Boniface visited St. Vincent's. Its natural advantages, the fertility of soil, the running brooks and rolling lands were most inviting, and favorably impressed Father Boniface.

When the future superior of St. Vincent's monastery returned to Carrolltown, he observed a spirit of dejection among his followers; they seemed to realize the futility of laboring on the rugged mountain top and the utter impracticability of founding and maintaining a monastery in those barren regions. Hence, when Father Boniface described the place offered by the Bishop, they unanimously asked that the new site be accepted. A petition also reached Carrolltown from St. Vincent's congregation, entreating Father Wimmer to locate in their midst; whereupon it was decided to accept the Bishop's generous offer. Thus it was that on October 16, 1846, the little band was once more in motion, to complete what in God's design was to be the last part of their journey. After traveling afoot for two days they arrived at St. Vincent's, the future field of Father Boniface's and their life's labor.

The only building available for their reception was a one-story brick schoolhouse with roof unfinished and walls unplastered. The two rooms that constituted this building were at once arranged to afford temporary accommodations. The one room served as a combination kitchen, refectory and community-room; the other was divided into two apartments, the first which was a bedroom for Father Boniface and Father Gallagher, and the second a study and recitation room for the four students. The garret served as dormitory. The pastoral residence, erected by Father Stillinger in 1835, was at the time occupied by a small community of Sisters of Mercy, who were to retain possession until their own building, then erecting two miles south of St. Vincent's—the modest beginning of St. Xavier's Academy—should be ready for occupancy.

The Formation of a Benedictine Community

The 24th of October, 1846, stands out as the first milestone in the history of St. Vincent's Monastery. For on that day the four students and fourteen lay brothers were invested with the habit of St. Benedict; the daily chanting of the Divine Office was begun; and the order of the day, continuing practically unchanged to the present, was introduced.

The circumstance that, at the first clothing with the garb of St. Benedict, there were eighteen candidates to be invested, and only six habits at disposal, did not detract from the solemnity and impressiveness of the occasion. After each group of six had been invested, they retired to the sacristy to exchange the habit with their waiting brethren.

The first year of religious life for the young community was naturally a period of trial and suffering. Crowded for room, needing money for clothing and other necessaries of life, having no source of income and no established credit, their treasury depleted; their condition was anything but encouraging.

The next year, however, affairs assumed a different aspect. Charles Geyerstanger, one of the four novices, who had completed his theological studies in Europe, was ordained March 7, 1847. He has the distinction of being the first Benedictine priest ordained in America. In the same year Father Peter Lechner, a Benedictine of Scheyern, Bavaria, came to St. Vincent's with eighteen candidates for the Order. He also brought a substantial purse of 5000 florins as a second donation from the Louis Mission

Society, which greatly relieved the financial condition of Father Boniface and tended to establish his credit with the public. Father Lechner was an ascetical and learned man, eminently fitted for the posts of master of novices and professor of theology to which he was appointed. With such an efficient co-laborer, Father Superior Boniface found time to regularly visit the Catholic settlements at Greensburg, Indiana, and Saltsburg.

The New Buildings

The growing community of St. Vincent's naturally could not be, for any length of time, housed in the cramped quarters that the little schoolhouse and parochial residence offered. The demand for room increased day by day. "But," Father Boniface asked himself, "where shall I build?" This was a very important question, if we consider that, thus far, his appointment as pastor of St. Vincent's was at the pleasure of the Bishop. Neither Father Boniface nor the Order had any permanent claim on the land willed by Father Brouwers for the use and support of the temporary incumbent in the pastorship. Negotiations were therefore opened with Bishop O'Connor towards the adjustment of this matter. The outcome was that Bishop O'Connor, who on February 15th, 1848, issued a document formally authorizing the foundation of a Benedictine monastery at St. Vincent's, vesting the pastorship of the congregation in each succeeding superior of the community forever and conveying the lands at St. Vincent's in perpetuity to the Order of St. Benedict.

The way being now clear, Father Boniface and his monks at once set about making preparations for the erection of their new home. A brickyard and a sawmill were erected and a limestone quarry opened. Finally, on the feast of St. Michael, September 29th, 1848, the cornerstone of the monastery was laid and blessed. This day brought new life into the struggling community and we are not surprised to be told that all, including Father Superior Boniface himself, aided with their hands' work in the erection of the building. Brother Stephen was the master mason and Brother Andrew the head carpenter.

Despite the energy and industry brought to the work, the building was not completed when winter set in. A temporary roof was erected over the walls and the first floor put to use as a refectory. That the good monks were often unpleasantly reminded of the temporary character of their overhead shelter, we may infer from the fact that during the rainy season they were often forced to partake of their frugal fare under the protection of a friendly umbrella.

Though often handicapped in the choice of materials, the early builders wrought well. The original structure is still staunch and doing good service, and, forms part of the northeast front of the present buildings.

Year after year, as circumstances required, buildings were added until the structure assumed the present form. And St. Vincent's is still expanding, as is shown by the wing now erecting east of the gymnasium.

The large brick barn, familiar and dear to the heart of the "old boys" of St.Vincent's, which served the triple purpose of shelter for domestic animals, of storehouse for the products of the farm, and of auditorium for theatrical entertainments and annual commencements, was built in 1849. In 1878, after the completion of the splendid barn at the foot of the hill, the old structure was converted into workshops. It housed the blacksmiths and tinsmiths, the carpenters and cabinetmakers, the printers and bookbinders, until in 1901, owing to its proximity to the new church, the old landmark was razed to the ground.

The steam flour mill came into existence in 1854, and its three burrstones are still grinding away, producing material for the proverbially "good old St. Vincent's bread."

Solemn Profession

When the existence of a monastery at St. Vincent's was fully assured, as far as it could be by episcopal authority, Father Superior Boniface allowed three of the novices to pronounce their solemn vows. The impressive ceremony took place on April 15th, 1849. The three young men were Benedict Haindl, Placidus Doettl and Celestine Englbrecht; all three have completed life's course. Father Celestine lived to celebrate his golden jubilee as priest, and, after a long and edifying career, died at Erie, October 2, 1904.

The papal decree, issued by Pius IX, in July 1848, authorizing the establishment of a Benedictine monastery at St. Vincent's and constituting the superior thereof the pastor in perpetuity of the St. Vincent's parish, did not arrive till the feast of the Guardian Angels, 1850.

The Opening of the College and Seminary

Father Boniface's original design to erect a college and seminary for the education of young men now began to materialize. The opening of the incipient institution was rather disheartening; times were poor, room was scarce and the luxury of good meals an unknown quantity. Father Boniface candidly admits that the beginning of the College was a failure. He says: "At first we had little success with the boys; our diet did not suit them, and most of them left us. Gradually others came; they had more endurance and remained with us."

The formal opening of the College took place in September 1849, with Rev. Thaddeus Brunner as Director and thirteen enrolled students. Within five years the number of students increased to over ninety.

The Scholasticate

Following the example of St. Benedict and the ancient traditions of the Order, Father Boniface opened a separate department, called the Scholasticate, for the education of young men who aspired to enter the Order. On November 13, 1851, the first Scholastics, seven in number, were invested with the Benedictine habit. At this writing, two of these still survive: namely, Right Rev. Boniface Krug, Archabbot of Monte Cassino, Italy; and Right Rev. Leander Schnerr, Archabbot of St. Vincent's.

The Scholasticate still flourishes. At present it numbers sixty-five pupils, and from it the community of St. Vincent's is chiefly recruited.

The Scholastics pursue the classical course in conjunction with the students of the College; otherwise they are separated from them. They are trained in the spirit of their future calling and are therefore to some extent subject to monastic discipline. In the early days and for many years after, manual labor, such as planting and harvesting corn, digging potatoes, and other work of a similar character, largely entered the routine of the Scholastic's career; so that the scriptural injunction, to eat the bread in the sweat of the brow, was often literally fulfilled by the coming Benedictine.

The Ridge

The purchase, in 1850, of an extensive tract of land on the Chestnut Ridge must be chronicled here. This property was desirable not because of the fertility of its soil, but because of its valuable timber. Father Boniface considered that this secluded spot would also afford a place of recreation for professors and students during the vacation months, where they could repair to enjoy the rural charms of nature and inhale the invigorating mountain air.

A substantial stone house was subsequently built and within recent years a very pretty frame chapel erected, making the Ridge a place of beauty and pleasure. What happy reminiscences cling to the lovely mountain retreat. What old student of St. Vincent's has not a story to tell of nights spent in the hayloft, of chestnuts and buttermilk, of copperheads and rattlesnakes, of mirth and merriment in the rustic park, of breakneck excursions along rugged mountain paths to the Bear Rocks and Devil's Bridge!

A Trip to Europe

The community at St. Vincent's being in a fairly settled condition, Father Boniface, in 1850, undertook a trip to Germany, to visit his friends and benefactors, with a view of obtaining new members for his monastery and of securing further financial aid. In both of these objects he was very successful. Considerable sums were contributed by a number of wealthy persons, as also by the directors of the Louis Mission Society. The generosity of King Louis deserves special mention. He had on previous occasions shown his approval of Father Boniface's undertaking by making substantial contributions; and now again the king, though no longer occupying the Bavarian throne, made him a donation of 10,000 florins; he also gave a large collection of books, mostly of an ascetical or devotional character, so that the Brothers at St. Vincent's might be well supplied with suitable reading matter.

Father Boniface returned to America in 1851, accompanied by twenty-one candidates for the Order.

Thus the foundation of Father Boniface began to assume dimensions that astonished all who had witnessed its

humble beginnings. In order to give to his work a proper standing in the face of the law and to enjoy civil protection in the possession of the property, a charter, giving corporate rights to the Benedictine community, was asked for and obtained from the State Legislature, in 1853.

St. Vincent's Abbey

The year 1855 will be forever memorable in the annals of St. Vincent's; for on August 24th of that year, Pius IX raised the monastery to the dignity of an abbey and appointed Father Boniface its first abbot.

The bringing about of this happy event involved a good deal of trouble and anxiety on the part of Father Boniface. It was found necessary that he should go to Rome in person. He did so in February 1855, and submitted a memorial to the Sacred Congregation giving a full account of his work and of the status of his community.

Pleading his case before the Propaganda, Father Boniface set forth that, from the very day he was sent to America, he considered it to be his mission in establishing the Benedictine Order in America, to found not merely one single house, but with God's help other centres of missionary and educational activity, particularly for the training of young men for the holy priesthood. He further declared that, in order to base this great work on a solid foundation, it was in his mind pre-eminently desirable that the mother house should have consistency and durability which the rank and dignity of an abbey alone could give.

Bishop O'Connor, although he ever showed himself the fatherly friend and ready helper of Father Boniface, in this instance made opposition on the ground that, as he thought, the time had not yet come to raise St. Vincent's to the distinction of an abbey.

The Propaganda carefully examined the bishop's objections, which were in part supported by Archbishop Bedini who, in 1853, had visited St. Vincent's when he found the material, and to a certain degree also the spiritual edifice in the formative stage, giving to the whole an appearance of immaturity and instability. On the other hand, King Louis, Archbishop Reisach, and other influential men interposed their good offices in favor of the petition of Father Boniface and his community.

Finally, upon the official recommendation of Abbot Pescetellli, the Procurator-General of the Cassinese Congregation, the Propaganda decided to report the matter favorably to the Pope; whereupon the decree was duly issued by which St. Vincent's was made an abbey and Father Boniface appointed first abbot, his incumbency to last for a term of three years, after which an election by the Chapter should take place according to the provisions of St. Benedict's rule.

The papal decree, erecting St. Vincent's Abbey, also ordained that the houses to be founded from St. Vincent's should coalesce and form one congregation, to be named the American Cassinese Congregation of the Benedictine Order, and observe, in addition to the Holy Rule, the statutes of the Bavarian Benedictine Congregation.

It was a day of rejoicing and thanksgiving for the members of the monastery, when on the 6th of December, 1856, their beloved Superior returned as their abbot.

Here it may be of interest to cast a glance at the statistics of St. Vincent's for the year in which it became an abbey. At that time we find belonging to St. Vincent's, twenty-one priests, fifteen clerics, twenty-two novices and one hundred and twelve lay brothers. The number of students, including seminarians and scholastics, was one hundred and ten; their names are preserved in a written catalogue, dating from the same year.

Of the twenty-one priests, only ten resided at St. Vincent's; the rest were stationed at various places doing missionary work, chiefly among German Catholics. Two resided at Butler, three at St. Mary's, two in Cooper's Settlement, three at Carrolltown, and one at Indiana. These priests have all gone to their reward; of the one hundred and twelve lay brothers, only five still survive.

The ecclesiastical as well as the secular authorities had done all that was necessary to establish Abbot Wimmer's foundation on a firm and solid basis. Hence from this time on we find an increased and well-directed activity among the members of the Order. The Seminary and College received every attention. The professorial staff became more efficient; the number of useful books in the library increased rapidly; the physical laboratory was furnished with a variety of apparatuses. At this time the musical department received a very valuable accession in the person of Joseph Moritz Schwab, a graduate of the Conservatory of Munich.

In 1858 the term for which Abbot Boniface had been appointed expired. Accordingly, after a week's spiritual retreat, conducted by Father F.X. Weninger, S.J., the first election for abbot was held on September 18th of that year. Abbot Boniface was almost unanimously chosen, and the Holy See confirmed him as abbot for three years.

This term having ended, the Chapter for the second time proceeded to elect an abbot, and with the same result as in 1858. The confirmation now given by the Holy Father was for an indefinite time (*ad beneplacitum Apostolici Sedis*).

St. Vincent's During the War

The War of the Rebellion, that brought distress and sorrow to every family in the land, did not fail to disturb the peaceful life of Abbot Boniface and his community.

At the outbreak of the war there were several Fathers stationed in the care of souls in Confederate territory: viz., in Richmond, Va., Nashville, Tenn., and San Jose and surrounding missions in Texas. They were entirely cut off from all communications with their mother house; for, during the greater part of the war, it was well-nigh impossible to get through the lines.

Money was so scarce that in a letter from this period, Abbot Boniface writes, "one scarcely gets to see any money." All necessaries of life soon rose to prohibitive prices, necessitating a reliance for support on the various crops of the farm. Coffee made from roasted acorns and barley, corn bread and mush, were staple articles of table fare in those days.

Besides this, St. Vincent's was called upon to furnish its quota of men for the army. Father Meinrad Jeggle, then at Erie, Father Valentine Lobmayer, at Johnstown, Father Benno Hegele, at Newark, and Brother Martin Beck, Sacristan at Carrolltown, were drafted; however, the parishes which they served raised funds to buy substitutes for them. At St. Vincent's five lay brothers were drafted: viz., Leo Christ, Bonaventure Gaul, Ildephonse Hoffmann, George Held, and Ulrich Barth. Through personal intervention of President Lincoln, these brothers were, soon after being mustered in, detailed to the Hospital Corps. The experience gained by Bro. Bonaventure in this branch of the service, coupled with his great charitableness, fitted him to become, in after years, the trusted and successful healer of cuts and bruises, sprains and fractures. Many of the "boys" between '65 and '96 hold him in grateful remembrance for kindly and efficient aid rendered in cases of hurts and ills liable to overtake the frisky boy on the campus or in the gymnasium.

St. Vincent's was also represented in the Confederate army. Father Emmeran Blueml, who, at the outbreak of hostilities, was pastor of the German parish at Nashville, joined the 10th Regiment of Tennessee as chaplain. He served as such with great courage and devotion until August 31, 1864, when, at the battle of Jonesborough, he was struck and killed by an exploding bomb, whilst in the act of ministering to a dying officer in the rear of the line of battle.

There were stirring times in the College on many a day during the war. In 1861, the register of the College contained the names of twenty-three students whose homes were in the Confederate States and most of whom were, by force of circumstances, compelled to remain at the College until the war was over. That these boys were loyal to the South is attested by the fact that the old College campus—yea, even the study-hall—witnessed many a fierce engagement between the "Yanks" and "Rebs," as they "affectionately" called each other. When news of a decisive action between Union and Confederate forces came in, Union cheers met with Confederate yells and the conflict was on, until the appearance of the prefect forced the belligerents to a temporary truce.

And yet, during all this strenuous period, these same boys worked hard at their books, vied with one another in friendly rivalry for academic honors and distinctions, and most of them have made their mark in life, both North and South.

Abbot Wimmer's Second Trip to Rome

In January, 1865, Abbot Boniface set out on a journey to Rome, which he was compelled to undertake because affairs of the greatest importance connected with his monastery required that he appear personally before the Roman authorities. Not all of Abbot Wimmer's measures and undertakings, however well-meaning and large-hearted their author, had met with unqualified success and applause. On the contrary certain unfavorable reports had reached Rome, and it was to give a full account of his work and administration that he determined to repair to the Eternal City.

The Roman court, with the most rigid minuteness and with traditional slowness, investigated every detail bearing on the spiritual and temporal condition of Abbot Wimmer's foundations. All the points on which accusations against him were based, received most careful attention, which, of course, consumed considerable time, so that Abbot Boniface was detained in Rome over sixteen months; at the end of which time the Sacred Congregation arrived at a decision altogether favorable to the Abbot, and his patience thus sorely tried was rewarded by a happy termination of his case.

Pius IX on this occasion showed marked signs of his personal good will toward Abbot Wimmer, whom he confirmed for life as Abbot of St. Vincent's and President of the American Cassinese Congregation. In addition, a petition asking for the elevation to an abbey of the westernmost Benedictine foundation was granted and thereby the priory, then known as St. Louis-on-the-Lake, became the second abbey in the United States. St. John's Abbey and College (the original name of that monastery was subsequently changed) is doing in Minnesota for the good of religion, what its mother, old St. Vincent's, continues to do in Pennsylvania.

After the happy settlement of his affairs in Rome, Abbot Wimmer at once returned to America, in order to be present at the opening of the second Plenary Council of Baltimore.

Extension of Landed Property

The advantages accruing to a Benedictine house from the possession of extensive lands were, in the mind of Abbot Wimmer, of such paramount importance that he regarded the possession and proper cultivation of land as one of the conditions of prosperity and of an independent existence. "Large tracts of land," he would say, "not only furnish the means of subsistence, but also give healthy and suitable occupation to a large number of able-bodied men who will continue to enter as lay brothers."

The purchase in 1850 of a large tract on the Chestnut Ridge has been mentioned.

A farm of 200 acres, situated two miles west of St. Vincent's and owned by Henry Kuhn, was bought in 1854. The log-house erected by the pioneer settler is still in use. The Kuhn's-farm with its crystal spring and shady grove lives in the memory of all the former students of St. Vincent's. How many merry outings have had for their terminus the charming woods at the Kuhn's-farm!

Some years later the Abbey's territory was increased by the purchase of George Smith's land adjacent to St. Vincent's. The land of Ignatius Elder, north of the abbey, by the provisions of the last will of that devout Christian, became the property of St. Vincent's in 1895.

The Benefactors

If for a moment we look back and take a general survey of what Abbot Wimmer accomplished, it is impossible not to recognize the hand of a kind Providence. For the furtherance of the good work, God inspired scores of generous souls, who on more than one occasion cheerfully and liberally rendered assistance, thus relieving the straits in which the poverty-stricken community found itself so many times in the early days.

The list of the benefactors of St. Vincent's is a large one; space forbids to mention them all by name. But, in order that the future generation of Benedictines at St. Vincent's may retain in grateful memory those noble helpers who in the day of greatest need stretched out a charitable hand to the infant community, we will quote from a report, dated 1856, and sent by Abbot Wimmer to the Louis Mission Society.

"King Louis of Bavaria not only took a lively interest in our undertaking, but also contributed 10,000 florins out of his personal purse in 1851, when we were so sadly in need of help, and in 1855 he was personally instrumental in Rome in having St. Vincent's raised to the dignity of an abbey and placed under the immediate jurisdiction of the Holy See. Archbishop Cardinal Reisach, and with him the Louis Mission Society, also contributed annually 5000 florins and the last two years 7000 florins. The late Bishop Ziegler of Linz also has a claim upon the gratitude of St. Vincent's; he not only sent assistance at different times but also remembered us in has last will.

"Abbot Gregory of Metten and Abbot Rupert of Scheyern are also numbered among the benefactors of our Abbey.

"One of the greatest benefactors of St. Vincent's whose name cannot be passed over in silence is Joseph Ferdinand Mueller, chaplain to King Louis of Bavaria and for some time business-manager of the Louis Mission Society. He has sent us many good men as candidates for the Order. He also supplied us with many things required for the internal equipment of the monastery and seminary. He furnished a great number of books for the library, all the musical instruments, designs for drawing, vestments, chalices, missals, and many other necessary and useful articles. In every possible way he tried to show himself a practical friend of St. Vincent's....."

It is no more than right that the community of St. Vincent's, mindful of its debt of gratitude, should make returns. Every day after the noonday meal, a prayer is offered up for all our benefactors, and once a year there is celebrated a solemn anniversary for the repose of their souls.

Abbot Wimmer at the Vatican Council

Pope Pius IX, seeing the religion of Jesus Christ menaced by an ever increasing conflict with heresy, liberalism, materialism, and false science, decided to apply an extraordinary remedy. He proclaimed a General Council of all bishops of the Catholic Church, which was to open in the Basilica of St. Peter's on December 8th, 1869.

As president of the American Cassinese Congregation, Abbot Wimmer was granted the privilege of a seat and vote in that august assembly; wherefore, in the fall of 1869, he set out on his third visit to Rome.

Abbot Wimmer took a very active part in the deliberations of the Council; he not only participated in all the General Sessions, but also with characteristic energy applied himself to the special work entailed on him as member of the Committee on Regulars.

The political events of 1870 are well known. The city of Rome being occupied by the Piedmontese army, the Council was indefinitely adjourned on October 20, 1870, whereupon the Abbot left Italy. On his way back to America he visited among other places also the abbey of Scheyern to see his old friend Abbot Rupert and also Father Lechner. The latter, as will be remembered, had been at St. Vincent's, where, in 1847 and 1848, he had done great service assisting Father Wimmer to establish and strengthen the true monastic spirit in the young community.

Father Lechner, possessing extraordinary biblical erudition, had written a commentary on the entire Old and New Testament, but could find no publisher for his work. Accordingly, the manuscript was offered to Abbot Wimmer to have it printed and published at St. Vincent's, if such an undertaking was considered practicable.

Not much pecuniary profit could be expected from the publication, in America, of a German commentary on the Bible. However, as the good of religion would be served, and the long and learned labors of the saintly Benedictine not lost altogether, the Abbot concluded to take the manuscript along to America. After a most careful revision by a competent scholar at St. Vincent's, the commentary was printed and appeared in four stately volumes.

Twenty-Fifth Anniversary of the Foundation of St. Vincent's Monastery

In October, 1871, the Benedictine Order in America completed its twenty-fifth year of existence. Wherefore a jubilee festival was arranged for the 24th of that month. It was made the occasion of a joyous reunion of a large number of priests, secular and regular, who, wholly or in part, had received their education at St. Vincent's. With these, a large representation of the lay alumni of the College and the entire St. Vincent's parish united to make the day one of general rejoicing and thanksgiving.

What words could express the sentiments that must have filled the heart of Abbot Boniface, as on that day he chanted the *Gratias agamus* in the Pontifical High Mass! With what fullness of heart could the survivors of the noble band of pioneer Benedictines join in the response: *Dignum et justum est!* Seven of the original eighteen followers of Father Boniface were present in the sanctuary: namely, Fathers Celestine Englbrecht, Benedict Haindl, and Charles Geyerstanger, and the Brothers Andrew Binder, Jacob Reitmayer, Engelbert Nusser, and Conrad Reinbold.

The Right Rev. Bishop Domenec, of Pittsburgh, who honored the occasion with his presence, delivered the sermon, in which he eloquently described the planting of the Order in 1846 amid privations and hardships, its spread over several States, and its flourishing condition after the lapse of a quarter of a century. "Here," said the distinguished speaker, "is truly the hand of God Almighty, and I join to-day with Abbot Wimmer and his community in rendering thanks to God for the innumerable blessings conferred on this holy foundation. I give thanks to the Almighty for the great good done in the cause of religion and education in my diocese by the sons of St. Benedict."

Among the honored guests of the Abbey on this day, was the venerable Father Stillinger, who was pastor of St. Vincent's from 1830 to 1845, and built the old brick church. In response to a toast to him at the banquet, Father Stillinger, in his own hearty and humorous way, related his early experiences at Sportsman's Hall. When speaking of the old block house, he made an eloquent plea for its preservation as a constant reminder for the younger generation of the humble beginnings of St. Vincent's and of the apostolic zeal that filled the founder of the parish, the sainted Father Brouwers.

Alas, the vandal hand of time and the ruthless stride of progress have left no trace of the old building that once stood a few feet from the spot where now rises the north main tower of the new church.

At the time of its silver jubilee, St. Vincent's had already established two branch houses in the West and Northwest: viz., the Abbey of St. Louis-on-the-Lake in Minnesota, of which Right Rev. Rupert Seidenbusch was abbot, and the independent Priory of St. Benedict in Kansas. There belonged to the American Cassinese Congregation one bishop—Right Rev. Louis M. Fink—two abbots, and eighty-five priests. The Fathers conducted four colleges—at St. Vincent's; at Collegeville, Minn.; at Atchison, Ks.; at Newark, N.J.—and exercised the care of souls in eighty-eight places, parishes and missions, distributed over the States of Pennsylvania, New Jersey, Kentucky, Virginia, Illinois, Kansas, and Minnesota.

St. Vincent's numbered, at the time mentioned, fifty-nine priests, twenty clerics, eight novices, ninety-six lay brothers, and seventy-seven scholastics. There were fifteen seminarians in the Ecclesiastical Course, one hundred and forty-five students in the Classical, sixty-nine in the Commercial, and thirty-six in the Preparatory.

It is worthy of note that, at the annual commencement on June 28, 1871, academic degrees were for the first time conferred at St. Vincent's, the College having been incorporated by the State Legislature the year previous. The first recipients of degrees were Michael Bergrath, Westphalia, Mich.; Max Betzel, Staten Island, N.Y.; and William A. Sweeney, Wilbur, N. Y.—the two former taking the degree of Bachelor of Arts and the latter that of Master of Accounts.

During the years immediately following its silver jubilee, St. Vincent's continued to grow and expand. Additions were made to the buildings, by which the old church was entirely enclosed. The picturesque clock tower was erected in 1872, and two years later three large bells installed therein. The big tower clock has been tolling the hours since 1876.

It may be interesting to the lover of old things to know that, shortly after the large bells were swung into position in the tower, the little bell that had hung in the belfry of the old church since 1835 was sent to the Ridge, in exchange for a smaller one doing duty there, and continues by its silvery tones to call together, for divine service, the faithful living on the mountain top.

Missions in the South

In 1875 Abbot Wimmer received several requests to take charge of some missions in North Carolina and Alabama. That the Catholics in those parts were generally poor and forsaken, prompted him the more to come to their aid. Two flourishing abbeys—St. Mary's in North Carolina and St. Bernard's in Alabama—are the fruits of the Abbot's unselfish missionary zeal.

There was one missionary enterprise in the South, however, to which Abbot Wimmer was devoted in an extraordinary degree. It was the agricultural school for colored boys which he established, in 1877, on Skidaway Island, near Savannah. His plan was to bring together a number of poor colored boys; house, clothe, and feed them; instruct them in religion and the common school branches; and teach them agriculture, by giving them every day a few hours of work on the farm of the institution.

The Abbot ever gave unqualified assent to the well-recognized maxim, that the farmers are the conservative element of a nation. "The more independent farmers there are in a country," he would say, "the better for the people of that country." Wherefore he expected from the execution of his plans the greatest benefits, not only for the poor colored boys, but even for the nation at large.

Yet, though great sacrifices were brought to maintain the school, and such earnest and devoted workers as Fathers Oswald Moosmueller and Melchior Reichert were put in charge, it did not prosper and was finally abandoned after almost fifteen years of existence.

Centenary of St. Benedict

On March 21st, 1880, all Benedictine monasteries the world over celebrated the fourteen hundredth anniversary of the birth of St. Benedict, the founder of the Order.

Through the initiative of Abbot Wimmer, the tomb of St. Benedict at Monte Cassino, Italy, was made the center of festivities that, for grandeur and solemnity, were seldom equaled—never surpassed—in that ancient abbey. Already several years before, the Abbot suggested and strongly advocated the propriety of making the fourteenth centenary of St. Benedict's birth a fitting occasion for the Benedictine abbots of the world to assemble at the tomb of their holy founder, in order to celebrate the anniversary with imposing splendor. The proposition met with enthusiastic endorsement on the part of every prelate of the Order, and was heartily commended by Pope Leo XIII in a letter addressed to the abbots of all the monasteries under the Rule of St. Benedict.

With Sunday, May 16, 1880, having been settled upon as the date of the great celebration, Abbot Wimmer, about the middle of April, set out on what was to be his last trip to Europe. At Monte Cassino he was received with marked honors and took a prominent part in the jubilee festivities, consecrating one of the altars in the newly restored *torretta*, the most ancient part of the famous abbey building and once the abode of St. Benedict.

The Abbot's sojourn in Europe was of short duration, for the fifteenth of September found him again, hale and hearty, with this community at St. Vincent's.

Memorable Days

On August 1, 1881, Abbot Wimmer celebrated the golden jubilee of priesthood. Several bishops and abbots, and a large number of priests and laymen, mostly alumni of St. Vincent's, came to take part in the festivities. Sentiments of heartfelt congratulations, profound esteem, and sincere gratitude, joined with expressions of admiration for the grand work accomplished by Abbot Wimmer in his two score and ten years of the sacred ministry, found eloquent utterance. Right Rev. Bishop M. Marty, O.S.B., preached at the Pontifical High Mass celebrated by the venerable jubilarian. It was freely remarked at this occasion that old age and the years of trouble and hardships seemed to have made little impression upon the rugged constitution of the Abbot. Indeed, who that had the good fortune to see the sturdy septuagenarian as celebrant at the altar, does not bear in memory the unusual vigor and sprightliness shown in his every movement and the refreshing heartiness of voice in his chanting of the Preface and the Pater noster?

Yet another day of joy and thanksgiving was vouchsafed Abbot Wimmer; on December 29, 1883, he commemorated the golden jubilee of his solemn profession. It was again a time when all roads led to St. Vincent's: her sons—bishops, abbots, priests, and laymen—from far and near, united to do honor to the "grand old man."

On the eve of the feast, a reception for the jubilarian was held in the College hall. Bishop Rademacher opened the rounds of congratulations by reading a decree, issued by Pope Leo XIII., bestowing the title of Archabbot on Abbot Wimmer, and at the same time granting him the personal prerogative of wearing the *Cappa Magna* at solemn functions. Then and there, midst tumultuous applause, the Archabbot, though protesting, was vested by Bishop Watterson with the stately garment. He did not feel comfortable in the new habiliment and compared himself with David, the shepherd boy, encumbered with the armor of Saul—in the simple garb of St. Benedict, that he had worn and cherished for more than fifty years, he could breathe and move more freely.

It were to deny him human feeling to say that Archabbot Wimmer was not pleased and touched by the sentiments expressed by Father M. J. Decker in his masterly Latin address on the part of the alumni or by the protestations of love and gratitude voiced by Father Prior Michael Hofmayer in behalf of the community; but the happiest moment for the jubilarian, despite all titles and honors bestowed upon him that evening, was when the venerable Brother Andrew Binder, one of his heroic followers in 1846, came forward to congratulate him in the name of the Brothers. The good Brother had not many words; the tears that coursed down his cheeks told more eloquently the feelings of his heart—and the moisture glistening in the Archabbot's eyes in turn spoke plainly the delight of his big heart.

The main celebration naturally centered in the Pontifical High Mass next day, during which the jubilarian renewed the vows, reading in a firm voice the formula of profession from the selfsame manuscript that he had written and signed when pronouncing his vows at Metten fifty years before—Abbot of Metten having graciously presented the document to St. Vincent's as a memorial of the occasion.

A mighty *Te Deum*, in which the vast assemblage joined with heart and soul, concluded the impressive ceremony.

Decline and Death of the Archabbot

For several years after these happy events the Archabbot, now well advanced in the seventies, still continued with unabated energy to perform his duties as monk and superior. With unfailing regularity he made long journeys, seemingly without hardship or fatigue, to visit the distant houses of the Order. However, in the fall of 1886 symptoms of decline began to manifest themselves. An insidious and painful malady set in, which slowly, but irresistably, sapped his vitality. For those that knew Archabbot Wimmer in the prime of life or even in his vigorous old age, it was a painful spectacle now to see him gradually waste away till there was little more than a living shadow of his former powerful frame. Fully a year he continued to suffer with edifying patience and resignation. All that science could suggest was done by the physicians in attendance to relieve his sufferings and prolong his life, but to no avail: he grew steadily weaker, until, on December 8, 1887, the feast of the Immaculate Conception of the Blessed Virgin Mary, just as the *Gloria in Excelsis* was intoned at the Solemn High Mass, he peacefully expired amid the prayers of his spiritual children surrounding the deathbed.

The bereaved community looked upon it as more than a mere coincidence that their beloved father had been called to his reward on the great feast of the Blessed Virgin, whom he had venerated through life with a tender and childlike devotion; and they felt no little consolation in cherishing the hope that the deceased had, through the intercession of our Blessed Lady, found mercy before the Judge of the living and the dead.

The solemn obsequies were held on December 13th in the presence of five bishops, five abbots, over one hundred priests, and a large gathering of the laity. Right Rev. Bishop Phelan, of Pittsburgh, celebrated the Pontifical Mass of Requiem, and Right Rev. Bishop O'Hara, of Scranton, delievered the funeral oration, after which all the bishops in succession pronounced the last absolution.

The remains of Archabbot Wimmer were laid to rest beside those of Father Brouwers in the vault beneath the large stone cross in the cemetery.

Personal Traits of Archabbot Wimmer

In the life of Archabbot Wimmer we find revealed traits of character as beautiful as they were becoming in a man of his mould. Pre-eminently among these stands out his practical and unstinting charity. Many a young man that desired to study for the holy priesthood, but had neither friends nor means, was generously received by the Archabbot and offered the opportunity of reaching the goal of his laudable ambition. Temporal returns in matters of this kind were to him but secondary considerations; the one great motive that influenced his charitable heart was the honor and glory of God — in very close accord with St. Benedict's motto: *Ut in omnibus glorificetur Deus*. Again, he provided and maintained priests in parishes and on the missions where, in the beginning, the people were too poor to support a pastor; and, when these parishes became self-supporting and the Bishop had priests to place in charge, he readily surrendered them to the Ordinary. More than fifty parishes could be named that were thus founded or upheld by Archabbot Wimmer.

In giving to the poor that applied for charity at the monastery, the Archabbot was not wont to inquire as to the worthiness or unworthiness of the needy applicant. All were amply supplied with food, in many cases with clothing and shelter. The historic "Tramps' Hotel," situated in the rear of the former bakery, was built for the purpose of lodging poor wayfarers; and the orders to the brother in charge were to allow each man that behaved himself properly board and lodging for three days. Naturally, such liberality made St. Vincent's the Mecca of the roving "gentlemen of leisure" from all parts, and in consequence called forth expressions of disapproval on the part of those that dreaded the apparent encouragement given to the establishment of a "tramp army" in the immediate neighborhood. The Abbot, however, would not look at it in that light. The tramp nuisance, he declared, must be laid to the charge of existing social and industrial conditions, and not be blamed on the hospitality and charity exercised at the monastery. The monasteries had at all times been the refuge of the poor, whom St. Benedict asks his followers to receive and entertain as they would Christ himself. If a man came here asking for something to eat, he must be hungry and should be given to eat and anything else he needed; should only one in every hundred receiving charity be deserving, it would nevertheless bring upon the community the blessing of God.

Not less striking than his warm-hearted charity were Archabbot Wimmer's tenacity of purpose and his love of prayer, both of which qualities fitted him to accomplish the great work God had laid out for him. *Omnis sanctus pertinax*, was one of his pet sayings in defense of such as seemed overly headstrong. How pertinently these words could be applied to him! Those that had the privilege of knowing Archabbot Wimmer intimately and of associating with him as his spiritual children, recollect many an occasion when his pertinacity, if we may call it so, manifested itself in a marked degree, and, as after events proved, served him and his community a good purpose. Once he had conceived an idea and deliberately weighed it, he put it into execution. Difficulties, that to others might seem disheartening and insurmountable, merely incited him to greater effort and greater trust in God's help. He had an absolute and childlike confidence in the guidance of Divine Providence, and in all the troubles and trials of his long years ever sought consolation and enlightenment in prayer. With edifying regularity, even in his old age, he joined with his community in the reciting and chanting of the Divine Office, and every evening before the hour of retiring he could be found in the chapel in devout adoration before the Blessed Sacrament. His firm belief in the efficacy of prayer showed itself at all times. He associated the *ora* most intimately with the *labora,* and would have his followers do the same. The present writer well remembers often seeing him in springtime walking over the Abbey fields in which crops were growing. To the casual observer it might have seemed that the Archabbot was out merely for a little exercise: such was not the case. Though fond of walking, his visits to the fields at those times were for another purpose. In passing from one field to another he would pause for a few moments, take from his pocket the Ritual and pronounce the blessing of Holy Church over the growing crops. The successful harvest could be attributed to something more than the labor of man's hands!

That the Lord blessed the resolute and persevering labors of Archabbot Wimmer is evidenced by what he accomplished. He had undertaken the task of establishing Benedictine monasteries, centers of culture and learning and of missionary activity, on the plan of those glorious monastic institutions of the Middle Ages, in a land that, at the time, was permeated with anti-Catholic prejudice and, for the most part, knew monks and monastic life only from the distorted views presented in current literature. And what success crowned his efforts! At the time of Archabbot Wimmer's death, five abbeys — each conducting a college — over two hundred Fathers and as many professed Clerics and Brothers belonged to the American Casinese Benedictine Congregation that he had founded. More than two thirds of the Fathers were laboring in the care of souls. Statistics drawn up about the same time show that there were nearly four hundred diocesan priests in the United States who had, either wholly or in part, received their education at St. Vincent's.

Truly the hand of God was with Boniface Wimmer and his undertaking, and well could the aged patriarch, beholding the host of his spiritual children taking up and extending the work his tired hands had relinquished, exclaim with the Psalmist: *A Domino factum est istud: et est mirabile in oculis nostris . . . . .Confitemini Domino quoniam bonus.* (This is the Lord's doing: and it is wonderful in our eyes . . . . . . Give praise to the Lord, for he is good. Ps. 117.)

The Election of a Successor

In conformity with the provisions of Canon Law, arrangements were made, shortly after the burial of Archabbot Wimmer, for the election of a worthy successor. February 8th, 1888, was the day set for the important event.

The day of the election found practically all the Fathers belonging to the community assembled at St. Vincent's; a few who were unable to come were represented by proxies. A Solemn High Mass having been celebrated to implore God's guidance in the momentous proceeding, the electors convened in the choir chapel, where the election was held under the presidency of Abbot Alexius Edelbrock of St. John's, Minnesota. The third ballot resulted in the election of Abbot Innocent Wolf, of St. Benedict's, Kansas, who was at once notified by telegraph; but, while appreciating the honor, he declined to accept. Thereupon another ballot was taken, and the choice of the community fell upon Father Andrew Hintenach. He, too, was loath to accept, but finally yielded to the urgent entreaties of both Abbot Alexius and the community, and took upon himself the responsible and burdensome office.

Father Andrew came to St. Vincent's in September, 1851, when but a little over ten years old. On July 11th, 1861, he pronounced his vows, and was ordained priest on April 12th, 1867. Ever since his ordination, with the exception of one year spent on the missions in Alabama, Father Andrew had lived at St. Vincent's, occupying at various times the positions of Professor of Classics, of Claustral Prior, and of Master of Novices. The community, therefore, looked upon him as worthy, as well as eminently fitted, to walk in the footsteps of Archabbot Boniface Wimmer, under whose eye he had grown from boy to man, and by whose fatherly precepts and worthy example he had profited during his many years of monastic life.

The Holy See having confirmed the election, the impressive ceremony of the benediction and installation of Abbot Andrew was performed on July 5, 1888, by the Right Reverend Bishop Phelan, of Pittsburgh, in the presence of the other abbots of the American Cassinese Congregation, of two abbots of the Swiss American Congregation, and of a large gathering of the clergy and the laity. A month later, there arrived from Rome a document, dated July 4, 1888, in which the Holy Father, Leo XIII, conferred on Abbot Andrew the title of Archabbot.

One of the first acts of the new Archabbot was in fulfillment of a promise made by Archabbot Wimmer to Bishop Schumacher, of Ecuador, to establish a colony of Benedictines in his diocese. Three Fathers who had volunteered were sent on this arduous mission. Not long after their arrival in Ecuador, however, the outbreak of a revolution—the sad heritage of all South American republics—and the death of the Superior, Father Augustine Schneider, put an end to the attempt of founding a monastery in that country.

St. Bede's College

In the early part of 1889, the Fathers of St. Joseph's Priory, Chicago, transmitted a joint letter to the Chapter at Saint Vincent's, in which they urgently advocated the erection of a college in that city or within easy reach of it. The enthusiastic presentation of the bright prospects existing for such an institution in the Middle West gained the day for the new enterprise. When, therefore, Bishop Spalding of Peoria, shortly afterwards addressed a communication to St. Vincent's, wherein he expressed the desire of having the Benedictines establish a college in his diocese, assuring at the same time his hearty cooperation, he met with ready acquiescence on the part of the Archabbot and the Chapter.

After looking over several sites for the future institution, the Archabbot purchased a tract of two hundred acres situated about halfway between the towns of Peru and Spring Valley, and known as the "Webster Farm," having at one time been owned by America's great statesman, Daniel Webster. A high knoll overlooking the Illinois River valley, made famous by the exploits of Father Marquette, Hennepin, and La Salle, was chosen as the site of the proposed buildings. The erection of the buildings was prosecuted with such vigor that by the latter part of August, 1891, the magnificent edifice was ready for occupancy. The College was named after the great English Benedictine, Venerable Bede, and solemnly blessed on October 12 by Bishop Spalding.

Though in the first years of its existence St. Bede's could not boast of an overcrowding attendance, the yearly accessions to its number of students have been such that, for several years past, many applicants could not be received for want of room. A large addition to the buildings, that will in a measure relieve the crowded condition of the flourishing institution, is now nearing completion.

The New Church

The idea of having a church-building at St. Vincent's commensurate with the dignity of the Abbey was not a new one: every great celebration held in the old church emphasized not only the propriety, but the necessity, of such a structure. Thus already in the late 70s, Archabbot Wimmer had plans prepared for a new church; but they came to naught, because the needs of the outlying missions and branches of the Order were at the time more pressing. A fresh impetus to the movement was given by the celebration, on April 16, 1890, of the hundredth anniversary of the day on which Sportsman's Hall was transferred by deed to Father Brouwers. After the Solemn High Mass on that day a meeting was held, at which Archabbot Andrew apprised the parishioners of his conviction that the time had come to begin in earnest the erection of a new church and of his determination to have preparations for the work begun at once. All entered heartily into the project and promised to aid cheerfully toward its accomplishment.

Naturally, the preliminaries for an undertaking of such significance and importance for the present as well as for future generations consumed considerable time; so that actual work on the site of the new church did not begin until December 21, 1891. The ceremony attending the turning of the first sod for the excavation was both unusual and memorable. Father Edward Andelfinger, the pastor, had invited the children of the parochial schools, the future thews and sinews of the parish, to lend the strength of their little arms in removing the first soil on the site of the grand Abbey Church. On the eventful day Solemn High Mass was celebrated to implore God's blessing on the work, after which the children, arrayed in holiday attire, marched in orderly ranks to the scene of action—about one hundred and fifty of them—and enthusiastically fell to work amid the applause of their elders. When they had, in a few moments filled all the available carts, they surrendered the picks and shovels to stronger arms, and work began in earnest.

Digging operations were carried on with such activity that in honor of the twenty-fifth anniversary of Archabbot Andrew's ordination to the priesthood in April of 1892, the first stone of the foundation could be laid. The placing of the stone was an altogether informal and impromptu affair; yet that selfsame Kuhn's-farm sandstone block enjoys an enviable distinction over its fellows in the foundation walls. It was set by other than ordinary masons' hands: Bishop Phelan, Archabbot Andrew, the visiting Abbots, and several other guests at the silver jubilee celebration, each in turn essayed to wield the trowel and hammer, surely with more enthusiasm than expertness, in laying the favored stone which should mark the beginning of the grand structure.

The Resignation of Archabbot Andrew

Affairs were thus happily progressing under a superior whom every one in the community looked upon as a worthy successor of the beloved founder of St. Vincent's, when on June 14, 1892, an announcement to the Chapter was made that was like a thunderbolt from a clear sky. Archabbot Andrew communicated to the Fathers that his resignation had been accepted by the Holy Father, and that he was no longer their superior. At the same time, he stated that already two years previous he had petitioned the Holy See to relieve him of his responsible office, but his first request had met with a refusal.

What was to be done? The first impulse of the community was to beg the Holy Father to withdraw the permission granted Archabbot Andrew to resign; however, subsequent serious reflection caused many to change their view of the matter. In the first place, it began to be realized that the Holy See, having refused the first petition of the Archabbot and granted the second, would hardly rescind its action in a case thus pressed. Again, it appeared to be an ungracious act towards a beloved and respected superior to thrust upon him an office which he had so reluctantly accepted and against which he felt such a settled antipathy. No other course, therefore, seemed open but that provided in Canon Law for such a contingency. Accordingly, Father Vincent Huber, at the time Claustral Prior, was chosen Vicar of the Chapter, and the following 15th of July set for the election of a successor to Archabbot Andrew.

Archabbot Leander Schnerr

On the appointed day the election was held under the presidency of Right Rev. Leo Haid, Vicar Apostolic of North Carolina and then president of the American Cassinese Congregation. The second ballot resulted in the election of Father Leander Schnerr by an almost unanimous vote. In the face of such a pronounced expression of confidence, Father Leander could not reasonably refuse to accept, yet it was with a feeling of relief and satisfaction, accompanied by heartfelt applause, that the Fathers heard him announce with agitated voice his readiness to accept the burden placed on his shoulders.

Father Leander was born on September 27, 1836, in Gommersdorf, Baden, but when quite young came to this country with his parents. In 1850 he entered the Scholasticate, made his solemn profession on January 6, 1857, and was ordained priest on September 20, 1859. Soon after his ordination, he was assigned to parochial duties and continued laboring in the care of souls at various places until his elevation to the abbacy. At the time of his election, he was prior and pastor of St. Mary's Church, Allegheny, which position he had successfully filled for fifteen years. The executive ability displayed in the administration of parish affairs, temporal as well as spiritual, coupled with his engaging qualities of heart and mind, made him the choice of his brethren to rule the community and augured well for the future of St. Vincent's.

A month after the election, the papers of confirmation arrived from Rome together with a decree of the Holy See raising St. Vincent's to the rank of an Archabbey. The title of Archabbot heretofore given by the Holy Father to Abbot Wimmer and Abbot Andrew had been a purely personal distinction; from now forward every abbot of St. Vincent's is *ipso facto* Archabbot.

The solemn blessing and formal installation of the new Archabbot took place on October 5, 1892, the feast of St. Placidus, the protomartyr of the Order. The Right Rev. Bishop Phelan officiated, and Rev. Father M.J. Decker, a classmate of Archabbot Leander in the '50s, delivered the sermon. A very gratifying feature of the celebration was the presence at the ceremonies of over three hundred of the Archabbot's late parishioners, who had come by special train from Allegheny to do honor to their former pastor.

In the afternoon of the same day the cornerstone of the new church was laid by Bishop Phelan. Father Stephen Wall, Vicar General of Pittsburgh, preached an appropriate sermon, the concluding words of which in reference to the new church found a responsive echo in the hearts of his hearers: "May it be God's holy will that what the first Abbot of St. Vincent's so faithfully prepared and the second so resolutely commenced, the third may as happily complete for the Lord's greater honor and glory."

From the day of his installation Archabbot Leander has had little time or leisure for anything outside the sphere of his high office. Besides the government of a large community — in itself an exacting task — the carrying on of the church building and the erection of other necessary structures claimed his attention, and not merely in the way of having existing plans executed, but in wisely apportioning the execution of the work so as to prevent any untoward inroads on the funds at command.

Within the thirteen years that have elapsed of Archabbot Leander's administration there has been unwonted activity in building at St. Vincent's. In the first place comes the completion of the grand church; then, the erection of the fire proof building between the monastery and the church, containing on the first floor the library, on the second the choir-chapel; further, the building of the splendid gymnasium and auditorium; again, the establishment of St. Leander's College at Pueblo, Col., and the erection of a suitable college building at that place; likewise, the putting up of two large shop buildings in place of those that stood in the way of the new church; moreover, the rebuilding of the extensive barn destroyed by fire on the morning of October 11, 1903; and lastly, the construction, now going on, of an addition to the College, made necessary by the increase in the number of students.

During these busy years the Archabbot made two journeys to Rome: the first, in April, 1893, was for the purpose of assisting at the cornerstone laying of St. Anselm's International Benedictine College on the Aventine, founded under the auspices of Pope Leo XIII, and of attending the conference of Benedictine Abbots called together by the Holy Father; the second, undertaken in September, 1900, in response to a very pressing invitation of the Abbot-Primate, the Right Rev. Hildebrand de Hemptinne, to be present at the consecration of the beautiful Basilica of St. Anselm's. The Archabbot had the honor of consecrating one of the altars in the crypt of the Basilica.

The New Church

The several views of the Abbey church presented in this memorial give one a fair idea of its beauty and stateliness. The style of architecture, the Romanesque, has been carried out with almost scrupulous care, even to minor details, in consonance with the plans of the architect, Mr. William Schickel of New York. His plans and specifications covered not merely the building but every piece of interior furnishing, so as to insure an agreeable harmony in the whole structure and its appointments. The execution of the work was intrusted to our master-builder, Brother Wolfgang Traxler, who labored assiduously and successfully with his cosmopolitan force of craftsmen to give concrete form to the architect's designs.

The church is built of brick with stone and terra cotta trimmings. The brick were made in the brickyard at the head of the historic "Cherry Path"; the stone came from the Kuhn's-farm, from Fayette County, Pa., from Ohio and Indiana, and even from far Scotland—the eighteen monoliths of polished granite that carry the clerestory and the galleries are from the Bonnie Land. Very little wood entered into the construction of the building, excepting the timbering of the roof. Whatever there is of it—oak, black walnut, and cherry—was contributed by the Abbey forests of the Ridge.

The church is 230 feet long, from the entrance on the east to the apse on the west. The nave and aisles, as well as the choir and its aisles, are 75 feet wide, while the transept measures 122 feet. The height of the nave and choir ceiling is 62 feet, of the transept 68 feet. The sanctuary and choir occupy almost half of the building, the communion railing being on the meeting line of nave and crossing. This arrangement limits the accommodations for the congregation to a few over eight hundred seats, which number, however, is more than sufficient for the needs of the parish.

The altars, nine in number, were built at Carrara, Italy. They are of pure white marble, with the columns and inlaid work of Sienna and the panels of Pavonazzo, the former a yellow, the latter a purplish marble. The high altar, situated at the meeting of the choir and crossing, is fittingly one of the most beautiful and striking features of the church. Its simplicity of design and faultlessness of proportion are enhanced by the delicate contrasts of color and the richness and artistic excellence of the carving. Six of the minor altars are in the aisles of the choir and two in the ends of the transept.

Among the furnishings of the church, the grand, electrically controlled organ of fifty-two speaking stops, built by the Austin Organ Company of Hartford, Conn., stands forth with well-merited prominence. The great delicacy and characteristic quality of tone in the various stops, the dignified power of the full organ, without a suggestion of harshness, and the perfect blending of the whole into one massive and brilliant tone, — these qualities, joined with ease and accuracy of action and control, put this instrument into the foremost rank of its kind.

The organ consists of eight sections or distinct organs, distributed over four manuals and pedal—one Great Organ, two Swells, one Orchestral, one Choir, one Solo, and two Pedal Organs having a 32 ft. Magnation foundation. Two electric blowers, one of three, the other of ten horsepower, supply wind under three pressures—5 inch, 10 inch, and 15 inch—giving to each family of stops the most favorable conditions of speech. The pipes stand upon the Austin air chests, which mark a radical departure from conventional methods in organ construction. One can enter into these chests as into a room, and find the whole working mechanism within view and easy reach—a valuable arrangement in every case of complicated machinery, such as a large organ must necessarily be.

The four-manual consoles, one placed in the choir, the other—nearly two hundred feet away—in the east gallery, are exact duplicates and so connected electrically that either the gallery organ (38 stops) or the choir organ (14 stops) or both together may be played from either position. This feature is quite unique in organ construction, and called for the highest skill and ingenuity on the part of the builders.

The stained glass windows of the church are fitting specimens of modern art. Those in the nave, choir, transept, and apse, are figure windows and were produced in two of Munich's famous studios; those in the clerestory and the rose windows are filled with decorative glass of American make. The windows in the nave present various scenes of the life of our Lord: the Nativity, the Epiphany, Christ in the midst of the Doctors, the Holy Family, the Baptism of Christ, the Transfiguration, Christ blessing the Children, the Resurrection, the Ascension, the Sending of the Holy Ghost. In the transepts are pictured: the Good Shepherd, the Prodigal Son, the Pharisee and the Publican, the Good Samaritan, the Sacred Heart, St. John the Baptist, St. Martin of Tours, St. Boniface; in the choir: the Guardian Angel, the Meeting of St. Benedict and St. Scholastica, the Death of St. Benedict, St. Vincent de Paul. The founders of the five monastic orders, St. Benedict, St. Romuald, St. Bernard of Clairvaux, St. Dominic, and St. Francis of Assisi, are represented in the apse.

The frescoing of the church, the work of Mr. Joseph Reiter, a Munich artist, is well adapted to bring into relief the architectural beauty of the structure. The color-scheme is subdued and chaste in tone, yet rich and withal in excellent taste. Some of the mural paintings are in place. The ceiling of the crossing is ornamented by heroic size paintings of the four Evangelists, whilst in the apse are pictured the nine choirs of the Angels and the four great Doctors of the Church: St. Augustine, St. Ambrose, St. Jerome and St. Gregory the Great. The large panels on the walls of the clerestory are to be filled, when time and circumstances permit, with paintings representing various memorable events in the history of the Order.

On a par with the fresco work — as well in good taste as in artistic execution — is the stone carving done by Mr. Ladislaus Vitalis, a Polish artist. The finely chiselled capitals throughout the church and the beautiful group above the main entrance, representing Christ giving the keys to St. Peter in presence of the other Apostles, are notable and much admired specimens of artistic work.

The Stations of the Cross are of ivory-tint composition with exquisitely modelled figures in half relief, and come from art-loving Munich. They are set in decorated frames of staff, which may, perhaps, at some future time, be supplanted by such of bronze or marble.

The pulpit, pews, confessionals, and choir stalls—which last are the handiwork of the Brothers—are of oak, solidly and substantially built, and handsome in dark antique finish. There are some traces of ornament and carving, but, on the whole, these appointments are in consistent accord with the chaste and stately simplicity of the entire structure.

The Consecration of the Abbey Church

When the question was raised as to an appropriate day for the consecration of the new church, two dates immediately suggested themselves. One was the 19th of July, 1905, the seventieth anniversary of the dedication of the old church by Bishop Kenrick; the other, the 24th of August of the same year, the fiftieth anniversary of the elevation of St. Vincent's to an abbey. The latter date was selected, mainly with a view of avoiding any hapless and unseemly incompleteness of the church and its appointments. It proved a wise choise; for, even to a few days before the consecration, the church resounded with the din and hum of busy labor, each artisan bent on completing his task.

Already several days previous to the consecration guests began to arrive from far and near, and the old halls of the Abbey and College gradually woke up from the usual quiet of the vacation months. There gathered for the long-hoped-for celebration archbishops and bishops, abbots and monsignori, priests and laymen, — most of them St. Vincent's alumni. The central figure of this grand assembly was His Excellency the Most Reverend Diomede Falconio, the Apostolic Delegate, whose presence on this gala day at St. Vincent's as the representative of the Holy Father, was a source of joy and gratification to the community as well as to the parish.

On the vigil of the consecration, the relics of the holy Martyrs that were to be enclosed in the altars of the new church, were, as prescribed by the rubrics, recognized—that is, examined as to their authenticity—by the Right Rev. Consecrator, Bishop Canevin, of Pittsburgh. Immediately after this ceremony, which took place in the old church where the sacred relics reposed on a throne of honor, matins and lauds of the Martyrs were chanted by the monastic choir.

In the evening the guests assembled in the brilliantly-lighted church to attend the opening recital on the grand organ by Mr. Caspar P. Koch, organist of Carnegie Hall, Allegheny. Several *a cappella* numbers were rendered by the Scholastics' Choir and the St. Vincent's Maennerchor.

Thursday, August 24th, the day that was to witness the consecration to the service of the Almighty of the grand structure started almost fourteen years before, dawned fair and bright. Promptly at seven o'clock, the Right Rev. Bishop Regis Canevin was escorted in procession to the front of the new church and began the ceremony with the blessing of the foundation and walls, whilst the monastic *Schola Cantorum* chanted the liturgy, using the grand and time-honored Benedictine melodies of Solesmes. The lengthy and intricate ceremonial proceeded throughout with that imposing dignity and grandeur rarely to be found outside of cathedrals and large monastic institutions.

It was a brilliant spectacle that presented itself when, amid the chanting of psalms and the joyous peal of the church bells, the sacred relics were borne to the new house of worship, accompanied in solemn procession by the members of the community and all the visiting dignitaries and priests. After the procession had entered the church and the sacred relics had been deposited in the sanctuary, the consecration of the altars took place.

The High Altar, in honor of St. Vincent de Paul, was consecrated by the Right Rev. Bishop Regis Canevin and received the relics of St. Vincent, Martyr, and St. Cyprian. The minor altars were named and consecrated as follows:

The altar in honor of the Blessed Virgin, with the relics of St. Callistus and St. Crispin, by the Most Rev. Sebastian Gebhart Messmer, Archbishop of Milwaukee, Wis.

The altar in honor of St. Joseph, with the relics of St. Melithon and St. Urban, by the Most Rev. Francis Albinus Symon, Archbishop of Attalia — lately appointed to the Metropolitan See of Russia.

The altar in honor of St. Anthony of Padua, with the relics of St. Theopistus and St. Aurelia, by the Right Rev. Henry Joseph Richter, Bishop of Grand Rapids, Mich.

The altar in honor of St. Boniface, with the relics of St. Flavia Domitilla and St. Apollonia, by the Right Rev. Camillus Paul Maes, Bishop of Covington, Ky.

The altar in honor of St. Maurus and St. Placidus, with the relics of St. Dennis and St. Crescentius, by the Right Rev. Leo Haid, O.S.B., Bishop of Messene, Vicar Apostolic of North Carolina and Abbot of Maryhelp Abbey.

The altar in honor of the Guardian Angels, with the relics of St. Candidus and St. Columba, by the Right Rev. John E. Fitzmaurice, Bishop of Erie, Pa.

The altar in honor of St. Benedict, with the relics of St. Victor and St. Donatus, by the Right Rev. Eugene A. Garvey, Bishop of Altoona, Pa.

The altar in honor of St. Scholastica, with the relics of St. Zephyrinus and St. Ignatius, by the Right Rev. John W. Shanahan, Bishop of Harrisburg, Pa.

After the consecration of the altars His Excellency the Apostolic Delegate celebrated Solemn Pontifical High Mass, during which the "Salve Regina" Mass by J.G. Stehle was rendered by the Scholastics' Choir and the St. Benedict's Orchestra. Besides the Most Rev. and Right Rev. Consecrators there assisted in the sanctuary: The Right Rev. Bishops, James A. McFaul, of Trenton, and Patrick J. Donahue, of Wheeling; the Right Rev. Benedictine Abbots Peter Engel, St. John's Abbey, Minnesota, President of the American Cassinese Congregation; Frowin Conrad, Conception Abbey, Missouri, President of the Swiss American Congregation; Archabbots Leander Schnerr and Andrew Hintenach, St. Vincent's; Athanasius Schmitt, St. Meinrad, Indiana; Innocent Wolf, Atchison, Kansas; Hilary Pfraengle, Newark, New Jersey; Nepomucene Jaeger, Chicago, Illinois; Charles Mohr, St. Leo, Florida and Bernard Menges, St. Bernard, Alabama; further the Right Rev. Monsignori, Michael J. Decker, Erie, Pa., and Peter Dauffenbach, Brooklyn, N.Y., and more than two hundred priests, secular and regular.

At the conclusion of the High Mass, the Apostolic Delegate, by virtue of special faculties bestowed by the Holy Father, granted to all the faithful present a plenary indulgence. Then followed the sermon by the Right Rev. James A. McFaul, Bishop of Trenton, an alumnus of St. Vincent's.

After congratulating St. Vincent's and the Benedictines on the success of their missionary and educational activity in the United States, Bishop McFaul took up the subject of his discourse the divine mission of Holy Church and showed in a masterly manner how she is fulfilling her God-given mission in our own country, as she has done in all times and among the other nations of the world.

At one o'clock dinner was served in the College auditorium, which had been transformed into a vast and beautiful banquet hall. Music by St. Benedict's Orchestra added spice and zest to the varied menu that did all honor to the monastic purveyors.

In the evening, Solemn Pontifical Vespers, with the Right Rev. Archabbot as celebrant, concluded the program of the day. It was a source of gratification that the Archabbot, for more than two years afflicted with a painful malady and for a long time almost completely paralyzed, had so far recovered as to be able to take an active part in the memorable celebration. Those present could well conceive what feelings of gratitude to Almighty God filled his heart, as he for the first time intoned the *Deus in adjutorium* in the grand house of worship.

The Saint Vincent Archabbey Church

By Melvin C. Rupprecht, O.S.B.

Written in partial fulfillment of the requirements for the degree Bachelor of Arts
Saint Vincent College Department of History, © 1938
© 2005 Saint Vincent Archabbey Publications
Latrobe, Pennsylvania

Introduction

To most travelers every ancient cathedral is like a book written in a strange language. The lofty spires, delicate architectural lines, majestic statuary figures, and lifelike frescoes can readily be seen with the corporal eyes, but their real meaning is hidden beneath the external appearances. The intelligent traveler wants to know the what, the when, the why, and the how of the whole edifice and all its parts. His curiosity will be partly satisfied by guides and guide books, but usually most of the information of this kind has been lost in the dark mists of the centuries or has been transformed into legend and folklore.

Although it may be fantastical to suppose that Saint Vincent Archabbey Church will at some time be a mecca of sightseers or a favorite shrine of pilgrims, it cannot be denied that a fair number of visitors have admired its beauty and have been inspired by the spirit of soothing devotion which, like an angel of peace, pervades its hallowed interior. And they too have inquired about the why and wherefore of many of its features. It cannot be known how many times they have received confessions of ignorance in answer to their questions, but it is safe to say that such responses were in the majority.

It was primarily to supply the need of a handbook of general information about the Archabbey Church that this treatise was undertaken. It is recognized that since but a few were aware of what was going on behind the scenes while the church was in building, many curious facts are inaccessible to the majority of those who might be interested in them. The author has consulted a number of those who were concerned with the construction of the church and has set down what was thought to be of interest to the general reader. Moreover, it is presupposed that the reader is already acquainted with the building, and for this reason, most of the descriptive material that could have been included and that should be included in a work of this nature if intended for any but local readers, was omitted.

A secondary impetus for the thesis is the desire to preserve in print and save from otherwise inevitable oblivion many facts that have never been written and thus to add to the growing store of Saint Vincent history and tradition.

The first part of the treatise is a history of the construction of the church and a lengthy account of the consecration ceremonies. Most of the material for this section was culled from *Saint Vincent Journals*. The second part contains a general account of the building as a whole and of each of the items that were considered to be of interest to the average visitor. Here, too, it will be noticed that no detailed descriptions are given but only such information as is not readily evident from the appearances of things. It might properly be called a source book, because whenever it was possible to discover who was responsible for the various parts, their names were given. Moreover, wherever criticism, either good or bad, was to be had, it was included with strict impartiality. One of the authoritative critics quoted is the late John T. Comes, the prominent Pittsburgh architect of the firm of Comes and McMullen. In the *Christian Art* magazine of November, 1907, he wrote a descriptive article of Saint Vincent Archabbey Church, in which he let fall choice bits of criticism, which were snatched up and included in this work to give the reader a knowledge of the value of the works of art.

In compliance with a personal request Mr. Leo A. McMullen, R.A., of the same firm consented to give some critical notes, and these too were used whenever an opportunity presented itself. He is an accepted authority on this type of architecture; moreover, to add to his prestige, he has to his credit in the Pittsburgh district, the University of Pittsburgh, the Carnegie Tech group of buildings, and the Schenley Apartments.

The nature of the third part is the same as that of the preceding, but it differs in its content in as much as it is an account of the additions and changes that have been introduced since the consecration of the church in 1905. They could have readily been included in the second section but it was considered preferable to describe the church as it existed at its completion and to add the innovations in a separate chapter.

The author does not lay claim to any new discoveries. Everything in the thesis has been gleaned either from persons who were living at the time of the building of the church or from books or from documents in the Saint Vincent archives. Special acknowledgement is due the Very Rev. Felix Fellner, O.S.B., prior of the archabbey, who has supplied much of the information contained in the following pages. In the capacity of faculty advisor he gave freely and willingly of his time, knowledge, and encouragement, and made possible access to the archives of the Archabbey.

Perhaps the most helpful source, especially for the first part, is the *Saint Vincent College Journal.* From the numerous references scattered through the pages of the first sixteen volumes almost the whole history of the construction can be pieced together. Most of the critical remarks were borrowed from the article of the late John T. Comes, written in the *Christian Art* magazine, and from the booklet *Saint Vincent.* The latter was written as a souvenir of the consecration of the church. Its principal author is the late Rev. Louis Haas, O.S.B. It was not finished in time for the ceremonies and for a while it remained in this condition until the Very Rev. Felix Fellner, O.S.B., undertook its completion. Only a few copies were printed, one of which is in the possession of the second author; several others are in the Archabbey library. Clippings from several Pittsburgh newspapers were borrowed from the archives and quoted as the expression of the public sentiments of the day.

Although only the sources of direct quotations were given, the author lays claim to no original contribution, since all information was derived from sources mentioned above.

Chapter I

A history of the construction of Saint Vincent Archabbey Church.

At the coming of Father Boniface Wimmer to Saint Vincent in 1846 the parishioners were worshipping in a substantial brick structure that had been dedicated to Saint Vincent de Paul just nine years before. This church, 87 x 51 feet, afforded at the time of its completion ample space for the few struggling farmers of the district. Around this building as a nucleus, the archabbey gradually took shape and the monks naturally used it as their chapel. In time, as the monastery grew and became more and more independent of benefactors and more pretentious in appearance, it was recognized that a new church which would properly be called an abbey church was becoming a necessity. "Thus already in the late 70s Archabbot Wimmer had plans prepared for a new church, but they came to naught, because the needs of the outlying missions and branches of the Order were at the time more pressing." (1)

Similar strains of thought were expressed in the *Saint Vincent Journal* in July, 1901:

"It has seemed strange to many all over the country who have known or have heard of Saint Vincent, with its half century of history, that its community and its people should still be worshipping in the old frail building erected in the poverty of more than fifty years ago, while splendid churches have been continually going up everywhere in the city and wilderness. A few words will explain the reason.

"In the first place the congregation of Saint Vincent is a congregation of farmers, who have enough to do to make ends meet, and are entirely out of the path of commercial prosperity; and consequently not much can be expected from that source, although it must be said that they have done what was reasonably expected of them. Again, from the hour of the establishment of the Order in 1846, in the then back woods of Western Pennsylvania, it was an inflexible principle with the late Archabbot Wimmer—maintained by his successors—to extend its labors where most needed, and as soon as it was possible for him to respond to a pressing demand of some poor, hardworking bishop, with a large geographical territory, and with few priests. Over and over again he refused tempting offers of promising parishes in large southern and eastern cities, saying that he did not come to America to settle down in cities; that the radius of Benedictine work and usefulness must extend as little as possible beyond the ambit of the sparse and scattered country populations; and hence Saint Vincent still retains, externally, much of its primitive plainness. But, *si monumentum quaeris, circumspice!* Instead of spending all its progressive activities in local architectural elaboration, Saint Vincent sent out colonies which for some time were a drain, not only upon its academical capacity, but upon its slender pecuniary resources. From the log cabin known in the early geography of Western Pennsylvania as 'Sportsman's Hall' have branched forth the Abbeys of Saint John's in Minnesota, Saint Benedict's in Kansas, Saint Mary's in Newark, Saint

Mary's in North Carolina and Saint Bernard's in Alabama, with their colleges and many small parishes and scattered missions throughout these states. Besides these, within the past ten years has been established the college Saint Bede's in Illinois, a splendid building, but hitherto, as regards Saint Vincent, merely another artery of financial percolation. The same may be said of the Priory of Cluny in the same State—still a poor relation of the mother house. We think these reasons sufficiently explain why Saint Vincent is not the picturesque show place it might be and would be but for the inherited law of expansion towards the desert that began early to operate; and why it is still without as befitting abbey church." (2)

From this quotation it can be seen that the intention of building a large church for the abbey alone had given way to the idea of a combination of monastery and parish building. In the 80s it was becoming more and more evident that the congregation of Saint Vincent was outgrowing the capacity of its old brick church. This fact was emphasized at every important function. But the congregation, too, lacked sufficient funds to erect a new building. As a result the poor decided to help the poor. The outcome was a proposal by the Rt. Rev. Archabbot to build with the assistance of the parishioners a new church proportionate to the needs of both. The first decisive step was taken on April 16, 1890. On that day the present Archabbey Church was born. The occasion was the celebration of the centenary of the transference of the ownership of Sportman's Hall to Father Brouwers, a pre-Saint Vincent event that is mentioned only because of its incidental connection with the beginning of the new church. At the meeting of the parishioners on that day, the Rt. Rev. Archabbot Andrew Hintenach expressed his conviction that the construction of a new church was an immediate necessity. He would delay no longer, he said, but would begin operations at once. Enthusiastic and hearty was the response of the parishioners, who gave their assurance that they would do all in their power toward the erection of the proposed church.

Accordingly, preparations were begun at once and continued over a period of a year and a half. The adoption of a plan, the selection of building material, and the choice of an architect were some of the major problems that called for due deliberation and discussion.

The first public signs of preparation were seen in August 1891 when by the services of former parishioners, the first stones were hauled to the site of the future church. By November 500 perch of stone were piled up ready for the chisel of the stone dresser. At the same time the brick-makers were busy putting out brick at the rate of 1200 a day.

And so, when all the necessary preparations had been completed, actual work on the foundation was begun on December 21, 1891. From the detailed description given in the *Saint Vincent Journal*, the whole scene can be easily reconstructed.

"The formal opening of the excavation for the new Abbey Church took place on Monday December 21 at 10 o'clock A.M. The scene of the occasion was one that will be long and fondly remembered by the parents and children of Saint Vincent's congregation. The morning was all that could be desired. The sun shone brightly, not a cloud floated in the firmament, the air was sharp and bracing whilst the crystal blades of the frost sparkled and glistened in the sunlight.

"Solemn High Mass had been announced for 9 o'clock to implore God's benediction upon the great undertaking. The parish children had been especially invited to be present on the occasion to lend the strength of their tender little arms and be the first in removing the soil for the great Abbey Church. They are the seed in the foundation destined to be the bone and sinew of its future support.

"Early in the morning fathers and mothers came with their little sons and daughters from the surrounding country to be present at the Mass and participate in the formal opening. The boys and girls were attired in holyday apparel; the little heroes wore red and blue topped boots, their hands encased in home-spun mittens, whilst the heroines were robed in wraps and mufflers all wearing a bright and merry countenance.

"After the celebration of the solemn High Mass, the children assembled at the porter's where they were individually presented with a beautiful little picture as a memento of the occasion. They then fell into file, the boys going two by two, followed by the girls in the same order. When arrived at the scene of action, horses and carts were found to be in readiness, picks and shovels were brought into requisition, but at the words "start to work" artificial instruments were rapidly discarded and the natural arms that God had given to those children went into play. For fully an hour the little ones worked as though for life. Earth and stones and fragments of dirt flew through the air as missiles in a sweeping storm. Fathers laughed and shouted their little ones on to greater activity. Mothers holding infants in their arms placed small pieces of ground in their tiny hands and made them deposit it in the standing carts. Frequently the poor cart-horse came in for undue punishment, the result of youthful enthusiasm: in their eagerness to fill the carts some violent throwers overreached the mark and pelted the horse, but even the dumb animals seemed to appreciate the celebration and take their ill-treatment good-naturedly. After several carts had been filled and carried away, Father Edward Andelfinger thanked the children for their earnest labor, urged them to be ever faithful and zealous in this truly great work of God and then dismissed them to return to their homes and cherish the memory of the great day." (3)

Enthusiasm ran high; members of the monastery, students, and parishioners as well as nonparishioners far and near were waiting in pleasant expectation for the erection of an edifice that was to surpass in size and beauty all others of its kind in the diocese. Regardless of the snow and cold, week after week, for four winter months a crew of men dug and scraped a bed for the future house of God. This process necessitated the removal of 7000 cubic yards of earth, which, when translated into more striking and intelligible figures, means that this amount of dirt would cover two and a quarter miles of highway to a depth of one foot. This, however, includes the earth taken from the foundation of the library and chapel, which were built jointly with the church.

The digging of the foundation completed, the laying of the wall was begun. The first stone was laid in April of 1892, in honor of the 25th anniversary of Archabbot Andrew's ordination to the Priesthood.

"The placing of the stone was an altogether informal and impromptu affair: yet the selfsame Kuhn's-farm sandstone block enjoyed an enviable distinction over its fellows in the foundation walls. It was set by other than ordinary masons' hands; Bishop Phelan, Archabbot Andrew, the visiting abbots (of Saint John's, Saint Benedict's, Saint Bernard's, Saint Meinrad's abbeys) and several other guests at the silver jubilee celebration, each in turn essayed to wield the trowel and hammer, surely with more enthusiasm than expertness, in laying the favored stone which should mark the beginning of the grand structure." (4)

In accordance with the wish of the Rt. Reverend Archabbot that the exterior of the library and chapel should be completed before winter, most of the efforts were centered about these two items to the exclusion of the Church. Partly for this reason and partly because of the difficulty in procuring facing stone, the foundation of the Church progressed rather slowly. It was supervised by Mr. Sebastian Wimmer, a nephew of the late Archabbot Boniface Wimmer and "one of the best civil engineers in the country." (5)

On June 14, 1892 in the midst of the hustle and bustle of the building operations, Rt. Rev. Archabbot Andrew announced to the capitulars of the monastery his resignation as Archabbot of Saint Vincent. The man who had been the principle driving force behind the construction of the church, who had nursed it through its tender infancy, and had shouldered its responsibilities with unquestioned ability, suddenly stepped from his guiding position and left the completion of his work to other hands. Sad and disappointed, the community petitioned their spiritual father to reconsider his decision but he stood firm. Accordingly, not much time was lost in selecting a successor, for already on July 15 Father Leander Schnerr was chosen as the third Archabbot of Saint Vincent.

October of the same year saw the celebration of a double solemnity. Amid the pomp and ceremony characteristic of great solemnities, the new chosen Archabbot was officially installed in his office. To joy was added more joy when on the same day the corner stone of the Archabbey Church was laid. About four o'clock in the afternoon the ceremonies began with the Right Rev. Bishop Phelan officiating, assisted by Revs. Vincent Huber O.S.B. and Alexius Grass O.S.B. The Revs. Thomas Wolf O.S.B. and Leo Eichenlaub O.S.B. were masters of ceremonies. Besides a host of friends, there were present Rt. Rev. Archabbot Andrew, the abbots of Saint John's Abbey in Minnesota, of Saint Benedict's in Kansas, and of Saint Mary's in Newark, New Jersey; the Very Revs. Adelhelm Odermath and Nepomucene Jaeger, the priors of Oregon and Chicago respectively. Very Rev. Stephen Wall, Vicar General of Pittsburgh, preached the sermon, the concluding words of which were fitting tribute to the Archabbots of Saint Vincent. "May it be God's holy will that what the first abbot of Saint Vincent so faithfully prepared and the second so resolutely commenced the third may as happily complete for the Lord's great honor and glory." (6)

According to the *Saint Vincent Journal* the following articles were enclosed in a leaden box and deposited in the stone:

"United States coins, *Saint Vincent's Journal,* medals, *Latrobe Clipper, Pittsburgh Dispatch, Pittsburgh Post,* Photograph of the Fathers, Photograph of the first stone, Photograph of the foundation and a document in Latin written by Rev. Michael Hofmeyer of which the following is a copy (translation):

"In the year of the Incarnation of our Lord Jesus Christ, 1892, the fifth day of October, in the festival of Saint Placidus, protomartyr of our Order, Our most Holy Lord Leo XIII occupying the chair of Saint Peter's; Right Rev. Richard Phelan being bishop of Pittsburgh; Right Rev. Leander Schnerr, who on the same day, decorated with the mitre, being Abbot of the monastery of Saint Vincent de Paul; Benjamin J. Harrison being President of the United States, and Melville J. Fuller, Chief Justice; Robert E. Pattison being Governor of this State of Pennsylvania; to the honor and glory of Almighty God and under the invocation of the ever Blessed Virgin Mary, Mother of God; of our Holy Father Saint Benedict; of Saint Vincent de Paul, local patron; and of all the saints; the Corner Stone of this temple was laid according to the Ritual of the Holy Roman Church by the Right Rev. Regis Canevin, Bishop of Pittsburgh, in the presence of many prelates and dignitaries, of the Chapter of the monastery of Saint Vincent, of secular and regular clergy, and a great concourse of the faithful.

"This document was signed by the Rt. Rev. Bishop, by the four Abbots, and many of the Fathers." (7)

Up to this time building operations progressed almost as rapidly as had been expected, but what the future held in store was neither pleasant nor encouraging. Difficulties both numerous and distressing necessitated a complete change in the plans of the Church and caused delays that eventually amounted to nine years; it was the intention of the Rt. Rev. Archabbot that the church should be finished by 1896, the 50th anniversary of the founding of Saint Vincent. As will be seen, however, the Church was not completed until 1905.

From the laying of the corner stone in October 5, 1892, until June of the next year the basement of the Church was completed, and so it rested for nearly two years. A project that had been begun with promising enthusiasm and encouraging auspiciousness was unexpectedly interrupted almost as soon as it began to take form. For two long years it rested in mute expectation and seemed to long in impatient anxiety to be permitted to bear a structure worthy to be dedicated to the hallowed name of God, so that His praises should resound therein for generations to come. Curiosity, too, was aroused, and it soon led to wonder and wonder to inquiries. People sought an explanation of the long delay. Why, they asked, did operations cease so unexpectedly and so completely and for so long a time?

All the reasons may be summed up in the phrase, "lack of funds." The Archabbot, whose policy it was to build no faster than ready cash permitted found the abbey's income adversely affected by the national financial trouble. This condition, coupled with the high price of stone made it necessary to change the original plan, which called for a stone structure, and to build the church of brick as the best substitute. An unfortunate change it was, for the stone church was to be an architectural gem, but under the circumstances nothing else could be done. Moreover, the building operations on the new gymnasium were begun in the spring of 1893, and retarded operations on the church still more.

After what seemed a disheartening silence the click of tools was again heard in the spring of 1895. During the summer of that year the walls were built to a height of about thirty feet with the exception of the front, which was retarded because of the late arrival of the stone required in the three large door-ways. As cold weather set in, a temporary roof was built and work ceased again for the winter.

With the advance of warm weather the next spring the temporary roof and the wall protection were removed and the bricklayers again took up the trowel. Nearly every day of this summer of 1896 saw the walls rise higher and higher, so that at the end of the year all the exterior brickwork was completed except the towers and a small portion of the sides. This done, a crew of carpenters went to work to roof the building before heavy snows made their appearance. During the summer the stately columns were also hoisted into position and added considerably in giving a more definite outlook to the interior.

Thus the year 1896, which was to see the completion of the stone church, saw only a hollow skeleton of brick. There was consolation, however, in the thought that everything possible was being done to hasten its completion and that those in charge were both determined and competent to finish what had been so happily begun.

Unlike the previous winters, that of 1896-1897 fairly teemed with activity. During the time when the cold and snow prevented work on the exterior, the interior was webbed with a labyrinth of scaffolding. About the middle of April 1897, work on the front towers and the exterior rotundas was resumed. Although bricklayers worked intermittently on this portion of the building for the next six months, winter set in before the front towers were entirely completed.

This winter season was employed in making preparations for more interior work. How much was accomplished in this regard during the next year can be only roughly estimated, because the only source of date information in these matters, the *Saint Vincent's Journal,* which had up to this time kept its readers informed on the progress of the church, is silent on the subject from September, 1897 until July, 1899. From the following remarks, however, one can estimate approximately the amount of progress that was made during this period.

"The plastering is nearing completion, but the stucco work will run into the beginning of next winter. The carving of the stone capitals is a masterpiece of workmanship and is nearly complete. In two months the frescoing of the ceiling will begin." (8)

By the end of July, 1901 all interior construction of the church was finished. The scaffolding had been removed, and although the lack of so many essentials like the altars, pews, lights and stations of the cross, produced an unmistakable sense of emptiness and incompleteness, a spirit of beauty and symmetry pervaded the whole. Here the beholder could see a true example of that ancient Benedictine tradition which has lavished the best of art and beauty on so many world-famous cathedrals and basilicas.

As for the windows, all those in the clerestory and five of those in the apse had been put into position. Wooden boards took the place of the other windows and served the one good purpose of keeping out the destructive elements. There is no doubt that the gaps in the wall looked large both literally and figuratively, too large, in fact, to be filled by funds that were on hand at the time. The difficulty was so pressing that the Archabbot thought it necessary for Saint Vincent to make its first appeal to the public.

Through the medium of the *Journal* a request was made to the friends of Saint Vincent to assist in the building of the church by donating a window. In the same request was explained the condition of the parishioners, who were for the most part farmers struggling for existence and consequently unable, without great sacrifice, to live up to the custom of paying for the windows of their parish church. The appeal resulted in 13 full donations and 2 part contributions. Eventually all 17 windows in the nave and transepts were donated. The names of the donors will be given in the second part of this treatise.

The contract for the windows, therefore, was let and little time was lost in having them placed in position. Already in November, 1902 nine of these were occupying their coveted place of honor in the house of God. The rest were finished within the next six months. By the middle of the summer of 1903 the church showed a completed exterior. Inside, however, there was yet much to be done. Practically no furnishings were yet to be seen but during the next month the altars were erected, and in the latter part of 1904 the mosaic floor was laid.

Since practically all the major parts of the church had been completed, it was only natural that plans should be begun for the grand finale of fifteen years of labor and worry. After it had been tentatively decided that the church should be consecrated during the summer of 1905, the Rev. Frs. Germain Ball, Louis Haas, and Edward Andelfinger were appointed to act as a committee on invitations, and the Revs. Louis and Valerian Winter were placed in charge of the musical arrangements. Later another committee, consisting of the Rt. Rev. Archabbot, Very Rev. Fr. Edgar Zuercher, prior; Rev. Fr. Baldwin Ambros, Master of Novices; Rev. Frs. Louis Haas, Germain Ball, Ernest Gensheimer, Aurelius Stehle, and Felix Fellner, was appointed for the arrangements of the consecration ceremonies.

There were, however, some important items yet to be completed, and because of unforseen difficulties no definite date was set. General plans, however, gradually shaped themselves, while the finishing touches were applied now to one part, now to the next part of the church.

Although work was continued during the spring, it was not until early and middle summer that the interior presented anything like a finished appearance. The pulpit, stations of the cross, confessionals, pews, communion rail, and organ were all completed during July and August. So close did the consecration follow the completion of the church that the din of workers' tools did not cease until a very few days before the guests began to arrive.

When the question arose about the exact time of consecration, two dates naturally suggested themselves. One was July 19, the day of the consecration of the old Saint Vincent Church, the present college chapel; the other, August 24, the 50th anniversary of the elevation of Saint Vincent to the dignity of an abbey. Taught, perhaps, by experience that difficulties often arise at the most inopportune times, those in charge of the affair chose the latter date to avoid any embarrassing postponements.

The events of the day itself are fully described in the *Saint Vincent Journal.* Since they were probably written by an eye witness, the writer takes the privilege to quote copiously from that source to give the reader the benefit of that original freshness and interesting description of details that can only come from one who has seen them.

"...there is little doubt that the twenty-fourth of August will remain a day ever memorable in the annals of Saint Vincent Abbey. Fourteen years have elapsed since the foundation stone of the Church was laid, years of patient labor, and, as a consequence, the day of consecration assumed greater importance in the eyes of all interested. Besides, the celebration was—we say it unblushingly—grand, and the church—we reiterate it beamingly—worthy of the celebration. Moreover, that fact that the fiftieth milestone in the existence of Saint Vincent as an Abbey had been passed, with energy undiminished and feet unflagging, entered largely into the spirit of the day...

"There had been steadily fostered the determination that the occasion should mark a day of glory in the annals of the institution. Great interest had been manifested by our old students and friends, and the unanimous resolve that something approaching the magnificent should be aimed at did not result in disappointment. August 23rd saw fore-gather Archbishops and Bishops, Abbots and Monsignors, and hundreds of priests who followed the scriptural injunction and hied them from the East and West, for they had heard and heeded the call that came from the mountains of Westmoreland. His Excellency, the Apostolic Delegate, The Most Rev. Diomede Falconio, D.D., was the central figure of this grand sacerdotal assembly.

"On the vigil of the Consecration the Rt. Rev. Bishop Canevin arrived at the monastery to recognize—we use the word in its technical liturgical sense—according to rite, the relics of the Holy Martyrs. At 5:00 P.M. this ceremony took place in the old Abbey Church where the sacred relics were exposed and the Divine Office was recited.

"In the evening, at 7:30, the guests were entertained by a recital on the grand organ of the new Abbey Church. All the power and sweetness of the instrument was evoked by Professor Caspar P. Koch, Organist of Carnegie Hall, Allegheny, Pa.

"...The morning of Thursday, August 24th, dawned fair and bright. At 7:00 A.M. all was in readiness, and the services commenced. Rising majestically into the air the grand structure seemed to await a special consecration to dedicate it forever, from foundation to pinnacle, from altar-stone to clerestory to the service of the Almighty. Three times the procession moved around the church, and Bishop Canevin blessed the foundation, walls and door, whilst a schola composed of monks chanted the liturgy, using the pure time-honored melodies of Solesmes. It was a memorable scene, begun in the sunshine without and ended in the more mystic glow within, all proceeding in stately order through a ceremonial, whose very intricacy of detail told of the ages through which it had passed and in which it had accumulated the wealth of symbolism so characteristic of the Church.

"In the meantime the clergy assembled in the library of the monastery, where the line of march was to be formed. At 8:30 the stately procession, marshalled by the master of ceremonies, emerged. It was an inspiring sight that met the eye, and amid the joyous and vigorous peal of the bells the sacred relics were borne around the new Church, while the grand swell of the Gregorian chant broke exultant on the expectant ears of the crowd.

"The great oaken doors were now swung wide open, and the consecration of altars commenced. The Rt. Rev. Regis Canevin, Bishop of Pittsburgh, consecrated the main altar. The following is a full list of the Prelates who consecrated the side altars:

Altar in honor of the Blessed Virgin. Relics: Saint Callistus and Saint Crispinus: by the Most Rev. Sebastian Gebhart Messmer, D.D. D.C.L., Archbishop of Milwaukee.

Altar in honor of Saint Joseph. Most Rev. Francescus Albinus Symon, D.D., Archbishop of Attalia. Relics: Saint Melithon and Saint Urban.

Altar in honor of Saint Anthony of Padua. Relics: Saint Theopistus and Saint Aurelia: by the Rt. Rev. Henry Richter, D.D., Bishop of Grand Rapids, Mich.

Altar in honor of Saint Boniface. Relics: Saint Flavia Domitilla and Saint Apollonia: by the Rt. Rev. Camillus Paul Maes, D.D., Bishop of Covington, Ky.

Altar in honor of Saint Benedict. Relics: Saint Victor and Saint Donatus: by the Rt. Rev. Eugene A. Garvey, D.D., Biship of Altoona, Pa.

Altar in honor of Saint Scholastica. Relics: Saint Zephyrinus and Saint Ignatius: by the Rt. Rev. John W. Shanahan, D.D., Bishop of Harrisburg, Pa.

Altar in honor of Saint Maurus and Placidus. Relics: Saint Dennis and Saint Crescentius: by the Rt. Rev. Leo Haid, O.S.B. D.D., Titular Bishop of Messene and Vicar Apostolic of North Carolina.

Altar in honor of the Guardian Angels. Relics: Saint Columba and Saint Candidus: by the Rt. Rev. John E. Fitzmaurice D.D., Bishop of Erie, Pa.

"In the meantime the work of admitting and seating the congregation and lay guests had been accomplished with ease and precision by a corps of ushers, under the direction of the committee of arrangements. The scene within was now a brilliant one. In the sanctuary had assembled prelates and dignitaries, priests of the secular and regular clergy, in number sufficient to give it almost the appearance and dignity of a Minor Council of the Church. Besides the Bishops mentioned, there were in the Sanctuary:

Rt. Rev. James A. McFaul, D.D., Bishop of Trenton; Rt. Rev. Patrick J. Donahue, D.D., Bishop of Wheeling; Rt. Rev. Monsignors M. J. Decker of Erie and Peter Dauffenbach of Brooklyn. The following Benedictine Abbots occupied the Epistle side in the sanctuary; Rt. Rev. Peter Engel of Saint John's Abbey, Minnesota, Praeses of the American Cassinese Congregation; Rt. Rev. Leander Schnerr, of Saint Vincent Archabbey; Rt. Rev. Athanasius Schmitt, D.D., of Saint Meinrad's Abbey, Ind.; Rt. Rev. Frowin Conrad of Conception Abbey, Missouri; Rt. Rev. Demetrius Juenemann, Washington State, of the Swiss American Benedictines; Rt. Rev. Innocent Wolf, D.D., of Saint Benedict's Abbey, Kansas; Rt. Rev. Hilary Pfraengle, D.D., of Saint Mary's Abbey, Newark, N.J.; Rt. Rev. Nepomucene Jaeger, of Saint Procopius Abbey, Chicago; Rt. Rev. Charles Mohr, of Saint Leo's Abbey, Florida; Rt. Rev. Bernard Menges of Saint Bernard's Abbey, Alabama.

"After the solemn consecration of the main altar the Rt. Rev. Regis Canevin once more passed down the right aisle, and blessed and anointed the mural crosses. The Most Rev. Diomede Falconio then began a Solemn Pontifical High Mass, and at its conclusion bestowed the Papal benediction............." (9)

From the *Pittsburgh Post*, which gave much space and praise to an account of the consecration, the following excerpt is taken:

"The solemn strains of the Gregorian chants echoed through the church for nearly two hours, while the Most Rev. Diomede Falconio, D.D., apostolic delegate to the United States, celebrated the mass. The right and impressive tones of the magnificent new organ could not have been heard to better effect than they were in the rendition of the "Preis Messe" and "Ecce Sacerdos". Father Louis Haas is leader of the monastery choir, and Father Valerian Winter is organist.

"Assisting the apostolic delegate in the mass were the following: Very Rev. Anthony Scheidler, arch priest; Vicar General John Boyle and Very Rev. Joseph Schrembs, deacons of honor; Rev. Henry Ganss, Deacon; Rev. George Winkler, subdeacon; Father Aurelius, Master of Ceremonies, and Brother Lawrence, assistant master of ceremonies. The clerics of the monastery assisted in the mass.

"There were at least 400 clergymen in attendance at the celebration of the mass. On the epistle side of the high altar were the...Benedictine Abbots, heads of houses throughout the United States...On the gospel side of the high altar were the...Archbishops and Bishops...

"Behind these prelates, within the communion rail, were more than 150 priests from all parts of the United States, the greater number of them being graduates of Saint Vincent College...

"It was nearly one o'clock when mass was over and prelates, clergy and invited guests wended their way toward the dining rooms which were numerous enough to feed thousands of people. The invited guests and members of the surrounding parishes who attended the ceremonies dined at the monastery and in the college gymnasium while the guests of honor partook of a banquet given by the college alumni in the auditorium." (10)

Other papers published in the same city likewise speak in glowing terms of the never-to-be-forgotten event. The following account is taken from the *"Pittsburgh Observer"*:

"Not soon will the vast throng who were present on Thursday, August 24 at the solemn and most impressive ceremonies connected with the consecration of the magnificent new church of Saint Vincent Archabbey near Beatty, Pa., forget that historic event—for historic, indeed, it was, in every sense of the word, forming as it unquestionably did, a brilliant page in the absorbingly interesting history of this great Benedictine institution.

The very atmosphere inside and outside the new church and the archabbey with which it is connected seemed pervaded with the spirit of true religion. The solemn "rites that sanctified the pile", the gorgeous vestments of the distinguished prelates who participated in the ceremonies, the indelible impressiveness of these sacred ceremonies, made up a composite mental image that will never fade from the memories of very many of those who were present." (11)

Indeed, the testimony of eyewitnesses who are still living in this, the thirty-third year after the consecration, has proved that the scribe who penned the above prediction was not a false prophet.

Chapter I Notes

(1) *Saint Vincent*, p. 46.
(2) *Saint Vincent Journal*, Vol. X, pp. 463-464.
(3) *Saint Vincent Journal*, Vol. I, pp. 236-237.
(4) *Saint Vincent*, p. 47.
(5) *Saint Vincent Journal*, Vol. I, p. 179.
(6) *Saint Vincent*, p. 50.
(7) *Saint Vincent Journal*, Vol. II, pp. 55, 56.
(8) *Saint Vincent Journal*, Vol. VIII, p. 423.
(9) *Saint Vincent Journal* Vol. XV, pp. 17-24.
(10) *Pittsburgh Post*, Aug. 24, 1905.
(11) *The Pittsburgh Observer*, Aug. 24, 1905.

Chapter II

A general description of the Archabbey Church, a short account of the sources of the various details of the building, and a critical account of the works of art.

Saint Vincent Archabbey Church is a modification and adaptation of the Rhenish Romanesque architecture, that traditional style of the Benedictine Order, fostered by them through all its early stages of development in the fifth century to its fullest expression as a distinct style in the eleventh and twelfth centuries. Saint Vincent Archabbey Church may be said to be a continuation of this Benedictine work that has been in progress for more than a dozen centuries. "It is not a little curious", wrote the late John T. Comes, prominent Pittsburgh architect, "to find in the twentieth century, and in this country a place in which the traditions of an older day are still operative, and to discover that the sons of Saint Benedict today are not altogether unworthy of their forerunners of the ages of faith." (1)

Giving his opinions of the Archabbey Church he continued:

"It is something to gladden the heart of the church architect, grown weary with the tricks of the commercial and ecclesiastical decorator and furnisher...I recall distinctly my own sensations on first seeing the new church, in the days when the talk of reform in church building was confined to a few enthusiasts and when a truly consistent church edifice was hard to find. Through a vista of trees and against a background of deep purple with which the autumn clothes the slopes of the Blue Ridge I saw this dignified and well-proportioned church. I was almost afraid to venture within. I thought I knew the class of church to which it belonged, and the sensation of agreeable surprise with which I surveyed the interior from the doorway is one of the pleasant recollections of my professional life. There was an atmosphere of honesty and beauty about it that was a refreshing to the spirit of the architect as the brisk morning air among the hills was to the man from the pent-up city. The interior was long and well proportioned....the decoration, restrained and quiet, in excellent taste; especially pleasing was the color scheme of the apse, variegated old gold and green, with an effective and everchanging play of light and shade." (2)

The most pertinent remarks of Mr. McMullen are these:

"The floor plan of the church follows the Romanesque type as developed in the northern part of France....A prototype of this plan (excepting the location of sacristies) is found in the Church of Saint Etienne (Abbaye aux Hommes) Caen, France, to which prototype the Abbey Church holds closely in smaller and simplified form.

"The elemental form of the exterior may also be found in the Abbaye aux Hommes. The great western towers with entrances at the base, along with a central entrance as used at Saint Vincent, may be seen at Caen. With this much established, however, the teutonic taste of the designer comes into play. The great German Romanesque churches had an apse at each end, with entrances in the aisles; but this plan was evidently not acceptable; so he adopted the French floor plan along with its structural forms, and dressed it in the garb of the Romanesque of the Rhine provinces.

"As to the detail of the exterior, it is in character with that style, but is executed in an extremely simplified form. The wall arcading at the top of the small apsidal structures attached to the western towers recall the eave arcading of the German churches. One feature that might have been used with telling effect is the lantern over the Crossing, a most striking detail of German Romanesque.

"The interior is noble and devotional in character and possesses a flavor that is distinctly German although I am unable to designate any particular building as the source of inspiration.

"To sum up the whole, we may have a French scheme, carried out in German idiom resulting in an edifice in which mistakes were made in certain features (mostly replaceable) on account of a low standard of taste existing among artists of the Period; but in the building we discern an honesty of purpose that distinguishes it as an Architectural Monument a building worthy to the extent that is humanly possible, of dedication to the Honor and Glory of God."

The church is 230 feet long and 75 feet wide at the nave and choir. The transepts are 112 feet in length and 40 feet in width. From the floor to the ceiling there is a distance of 62 feet, except in the sanctuary, the dome of which is six feet higher.

It has a volume of 820,000 cubic feet. Its seating capacity is only 800 persons. For such a large church this number seems extraordinarily small. The explanation is found in the fact that the church also serves the needs of the archabbey; the monks' choir behind the high altar and the spacious sanctuary occupy nearly half the space of the building.

The church was intended to be slightly longer than it actually is, and by some is considered to be somewhat out of proportion. Another window was to be added, but the presence of a large carpenter shop which stood at right angle with the church precluded the possibility of adding the sixth window. It could have been dismantled, but, since it was so near the church (it was only a few yards away) it was very convenient for fashioning the wood to be used in the construction of the church. Nevertheless, it was removed shortly after the completion of the edifice and replaced by the present carpenter shop several hundred feet to the southeast.

It is likewise evident that the front towers have not yet reached their proper height. They are only 120 feet high, just 130 shorter than the plans specified. The tips of the rear towers are 150 feet from the ground and are completed according to the original plans. The same circumstance that necessitated other changes treated in the first part of this treatise, namely the lack of funds, also made it impossible to extend the towers to their full 250 feet. The extraordinary thickness of the lower walls shows plainly that they were built to support a much heavier weight. Only time will tell whether they will ever be completed. It is probably the common opinion that this work, which can have no practical value, should not be pushed in preference to more urgent needs which are constantly presenting themselves and which are using up all the ready resources. From the standpoint of art and beauty, there is no doubt that the stub towers are a noticeable defect on the exterior of the church.

A strange fact it is that many of the most common objects of observation are the least known and the least noticed. There are some people who do not know the color of the rooms in which they have been living for years; others do not know how many sides of the same room are provided with windows. And so it is that one of the features of the Archabbey Church which has been seen by thousands has not been noticed except by a few. Reference is made to the slab of grey marble that has been inserted in the floor of the corridor that leads from the monastery to the right transept of the church. It is interesting to speculate what purpose the archaeologists of the year 3000 A.D. would assign to this apparently useless piece of marble. They would probably conjecture that it served as a convenient passage for the transference of the coffins of the dead monks to the crypts beneath. They might be disappointed, though, when they found no crypts nor any signs of burial places. Yet their guess would not be wrong. The thick stone plate is removable and was actually intended as an opening through which the coffins of the monks could be lowered to the basement for burial. Two considerations, however, militated against the carrying out of this plan. In the first place, Rt. Rev. Leander

Schnerr, in the true Benedictine family spirit, thought it proper that all the monks be buried in the community cemetery together with their brethren who had preceded them. Moreover, the preservation of ideal sanitation seemed to demand the same procedure, because it was feared that the steam pipes which pass through the basement would heat the air to such an extent as to endanger a proper decomposition of the bodies. Consequently, today the marble slab is but a sign of what was to be but never has been.

Yet another unused and almost unseen passageway is that leading from the choir chapel to the sacristy of the Archabbey church. It was originally intended as a convenient doorway between these two houses of God, but it has never been utilized, and today it is altogether hidden on the chapel side by a large cupboard while on the sacristy side it is so near the ceiling as to escape the notice of all but the scrutinizing observer.

Architect

The one most responsible for the plans of the church, both general and particular, is probably the architect, Mr. Wm. Schickel of New York City. His designs covered not only the general outlines but every piece of interior furnishings; even the candle sticks were made according to his specifications to help to insure an agreeable harmony throughout the building. He had a sense of utility and of architectural beauty, and he combined the two qualities as harmoniously as he was able. From his correspondence with the Rt. Rev. Archabbot it is evident that he put the best of his talents and efforts into the various plans. In reference to the altars he wrote in 1902: "I have made the plans for the third time, because they didn't suit me, and I wanted to give you something of a high artistic merit and still not too elaborate." That he succeeded in his purpose has been attested by many able critics.

Of Mr. Schickel's reputation as an architect little is known except that he built several churches in New York. One thing, however, is certain. His good name suffered no injury because of his work on the Archabbey Church. There is a remark in the *Saint Vincent Journal* that this building is considered one of his best creations. (3) Mr. McMullen has said that it is a good example of Romanesque architecture and that if Mr. Schickel's other creations are on a par with this edifice, he is an architect of outstanding ability.

Brothers' Contribution

The development of architecture owes much to the monks. Not only monasteries, those bulwarks of learning, culture, and civilization, but also their necessary complement, the Abbey churches, many of whose spires still lift their slender arms to heaven, owe their existence to the prayerful toil of dark-robed religious. For these consecrated souls, to whom "we owe the magnificent churches of Canterbury, Lincoln, Rochester, Durham, and Gloucester", work was its own reward. (4) They labored not for the deceitful pleasures of earthly wealth or for the thin bubbles of earthly fame; their work was a work of love and obedience; they breathed from their souls into their creations and God blessed them. The results are still admired today as rare specimens of Architectural achievement.

"When we say that the numberless monastic churches scattered throughout the whole of Europe were built by the monks, the assertion must be taken in its literal sense. They were, in fact, not only the architects, but masons; after having arranged their plans, the noble and skillful designs which still excite our admiration, they executed them with their own hands, and generally without the aid of stranger workmen. They sang psalms while they laboured, and quitted their tools only to go to the altar or the choir."(5)

Perhaps it is this same spirit of prayer and love that gives Saint Vincent Archabbey Church its strange air of awe-inspiring beauty that seems to grip the beholder. Perhaps this it is that prompted one of its recent visitors to express his surprise at finding here what he had traveled all the way to Europe to see.

True, not all the construction work was done by the monks of Saint Vincent, but the prayers of the whole community were poured out upon it and what the monks could not do with their hands, they asked God to bless by their prayers. Of the monks who did actual work on the church the most outstanding is Brother Wolfgang Traxler, O.S.B. This skilled craftsman, who spent nearly all of the 77 years of his life at Saint Vincent, supervised with skillful and diligent eye all the construction of the building which, doubtless, owes much of its practicality and sturdiness to the directive genius of this humble monk.

Besides Brother Wolfgang, more of the 75 Brothers that were at Saint Vincent at that time put their labor into the church. Some worked in the brickyard where all the bricks used in the church were formed. Others gave their services in the blacksmith shop and still others applied the skill of a carpenter while fashioning the wooden parts of the building.

Sculptor

The sculpture work was done by a Polish Artist named Ladislaus Vitalis. Perched on a platform erected around the marble pillars, he chiselled, in true artistic fashion, intricate designs on the rough Indiana sandstone. His carving has been acclaimed by some as "notable and much admired specimens of artistic work". (6) On the other hand John T. Comes made the following comment: "The capitals of the columns carved in stone, while of excellent design, lack variety and freedom and are somewhat monotonous in their similarity." (7) A close examination of the work will bear out the truth of this statement: all the capitals are actually of the same design. We suspect that the writer could have used more censorious language had he commented on the fact that the capitals of all the half-columns that are inserted in the walls for a decorative purpose only, are not of stone, but of plaster molds! In all truth it should be mentioned that only the carving of the supporting columns is genuine.

The finely wrought groups above the main entrances were executed by the same artist. These he himself rated among his greatest creations. It has been said that even on his deathbed he remarked that this work had always proved a source of consolation and pardonable pride.

Painter

One familiar with the interior of the Congressional library might notice a marked resemblance between the fresco pattern of that building and of the Archabbey Church. Neither is the similarity an accidental one. While Mr. Joseph Reiter, an immigrant Munich artist, was plying his brush on the walls of the largest library in the world he was asked to decorate the walls of the new buildings at Saint Vincent. Accordingly, he arrived at the Archabbey during the early part of 1899 and painted the walls and ceiling of the library and choir chapel. The results were so satisfactory that he was given the contract for the decoration of the Archabbey Church, which he completed in 1904.

Paintings

The frescoes, all painted by Mr. Reiter in oil flat colors, are chaste yet rich in tone and compare very favorably with the artistic character of the Church. On the sanctuary ceiling he painted life-size pictures of the four Evangelists with the characteristic symbols of their offices. On the wall of the apse, he executed paintings of four great doctors of the Catholic Church: Sts. Augustine, Ambrose, Gregory, and Jerome. Here are also pictured the nine choirs of angels according to the conception of the same artist. Several other smaller paintings are found here and there, all in good taste and excellent harmony with the general color scheme.

It has often been asked why the large panels on the walls of the church have never been filled with mural paintings. It must be admitted that these bare spaces, like empty picture frames, look odd and incomplete. That the panels were intended to contain paintings cannot be doubted. From what has been said about the financial status of the monastery, it is not difficult to guess why the work was not done at the same time as the other paintings, but another more cogent reason was the dearth of competent artists. The completion of a project of such proportion would require a life time if done in a highly artistic style.

Whether the brush of an artist will ever decorate the walls that have been bare for nearly forty years is merely a matter of conjecture. It would be very desirable for some talented members of the community of Saint Vincent to practice their art in the Archabbey Church and enliven the walls thereof with scenes from the life of Saint Benedict or of the history of his order and thereby make the church more truly a Benedictine edifice. At various times steps have been taken in this direction, but the plans have never materialized.

In 1923 Rev. Fr. Raphael Pfisterer O.S.B., founder of the Catholic Art Association, who is at present a member of Saint Anselm's Abbey, sketched various pictures for this purpose and made a miniature replica of the church with elaborate interior decorations to show how the pictures would appear in actuality. He himself, a competent artist, with the assistance of several other monks was supposed to ply the brush. For some unknown reason, however, nothing further was accomplished although the paintings are still preserved. Since that time nothing has been done, but it is the fond desire of the community that a day will some time dawn that will see the walls of Saint Vincent Archabbey Church fittingly and artistically decorated.

Windows

During the Middle Ages, when the making of stained glass windows was practiced as a recognized art, the price of stained glass was so forbidding that only the wealthiest churches could afford to buy them. In the last centuries, however, probably to lower the cost of the glass and to increase its popularity, there has been developed another kind of stained glass, at first sight similar to the old type, yet in makeup entirely different. The first stained glass windows were composed of a mosaic of varicoloured glass, each piece of which was colored while in a molten state so that the entire substance was permeated with the pigment. Most of the modern glass, on the other hand, is made by painting the color on clear glass and baking it into the surface. This paint is composed of metallic oxides, and sulphides of iron, magnesium, cobalt or copper and is heated to a temperature of from 1150 to 1250 degrees Fahrenheit. The pigment, the melting point of which is at least 500 degrees lower than that of the glass, penetrates the surface and fuses with the glass. This last process is much more simple and inexpensive and has made stained glass windows a possibility for every large church.

It must not be imagined, however, that the making of stained glass is a lost art. On the contrary, America and Europe both produce today by the ancient process a type of glass that according to connoisseurs compares very well with the best examples produced in the Middle Ages. The present day artists, however, use the painting process also to retouch their windows, to add flesh tints, and emphasize various details that the colored glass does not make sufficiently distinct. It may be remarked, too, that the price of modern glass is very forbidding—$45 to $75 per square foot.

The difference between the windows made of colored glass and those whose tints are baked in is described as the difference between dancing vitality and motionless severity. The modern or quasi-stained glass windows, even though they be rich and delicate in tone color, do not produce the sudden change of light that greets the beholder every time the angle of vision is changed. At every movement of the eye the light transmitted by the window changes with such pleasing variety and such rich blending of colors, that the spectator is simply fascinated. This quality, however, is lacking in the other type of glass.

The foregoing digression may at first seem unwarranted, but it was included for the purpose of giving the reader a more exact conception of the type of window in the Archabbey Church. They are of the more modern type, the coloring having been produced by the process of painting and baking.

The windows in the apse, representing from left to right, Saint Romuald, Saint Dominic, Saint Benedict, Saint Bernard of Clairvaux, and Saint Francis of Assisi, were made by the Mayer Co. of Munich, a firm whose artists have done work for the Vatican and for many European churches and cathedrals. These windows were ordered several years before the others and were intended to serve as a basis for deciding what windows would be used for the rest of the church. Because of their subdued tone color, they proved unsatisfactory to Archabbot Leander and his committee of four: Frs. Ernest Gensheimer, Callistus Stehle, Aurelius Stehle, and Anthony Wirtner. It was the intention of the Rt. Rev. Archabbot that the windows should admit sufficient light to preclude the necessity of artificial illumination by day. Since it was judged that windows like the ones already in place would not fulfill this requirement, the contract for the other figure-windows, in the nave as well as in the transepts and choir, was given to the Stoltzenberg Co., also of Munich.

Following is a list of the windows and their donators:

Transepts	*Donor*
Good Shepherd	Philip & Elizabeth Thomas
Saint John the Baptist	Mrs. Boehm & Family
Prodigal Son	Wolfgang & Mary Winters
Saint Martin of Tours	Rev. E. E. Gellhof
Good Samaritan	Mrs. Anna Rocks
Sacred Heart	Mr. & Mrs. W. A. Showalter Sr.
Pharisee and Publican	Mr. James Rock
Saint Boniface	Adalbert Hune
Nave	**Donor**
Nativity	Joseph & Mary Stratman
Epiphany	Mr. & Mrs. John F. Kintz
Christ in the Midst of the Doctors	Mr. & Mrs. And. Strittmatter
Holy Family	James and Grace Rodgers
Baptism of Christ	Thomas Barrett & wife Bridgett Barrett

Transfiguration	Mr. & Mrs. Francis J. Stader
Christ Blessing the Children	Michael & Catherine Goodman
Resurrection	James and Ann Toner
Ascension	John Kintz, Sr.
Coming of the Holy Ghost	Slovak Society of Whitney

In the choir, the windows, undonated, represent the Guardian Angel, the Meeting of Saint Benedict and Saint Scholastica, Saint Vincent de Paul, and the Death of Saint Benedict. The windows of the clerestory and the three rose windows are of decorative glass, the former made by the Riordan Co. of Cincinnati, the latter by the Kinsella Co. of Chicago.

As to the quality of the windows, they are generally considered excellent examples of that art, and an art it is, just as truly as is the painting of a picture on a canvas. *The Saint Vincent Journal* has called them "magnificent specimens of the artist's work." (8) The authors of Saint Vincent have said that they are "fitting specimens of modern art." (9) A more competent critic, however, the late John T. Comes has sounded a less enthusiastic note. "The inevitable Munich window does what it can to disturb the general harmony." (10) This pronouncement, however, was directed against the Munich windows in general and not against those in the Archabbey Church in particular. The same critic realized, too, the favorable reputation that this same type of windows enjoys, for he adds: "To criticize Munich windows is, in some quarters, to be anathema, but *entre nous* one may say these things without incurring a suspicion of heresy." (11) Still, Mr. McMullen's criticism seems to bear out the testimony of his former partner: "The stained glass was executed at an unfortunate period in the history of this noble art; when its traditional principles had been set aside, and windows given the character of easel painting."

Altars

The altars, nine in number, are made of pure white marble, and may be said to signify the immaculate purity of the Christ. Secured through the Fucigna Brothers of New York, they were built in Carrara, Italy, a town that has given its name to the stone taken from its quarries. The side altars in the choir are inlaid with yellow Siena marble and panelled with purple Pavanozzo, both quarried in Italy. This arrangement is reversed in the right transept altar, where the inlaid work is of Pavanozzo and the panels of Siena. As a result the dark lines are more evident, and if the altar is compared with the other side altars it appears slightly darker as a whole, a condition emphasized also by the two columns of African black marble that seem to support the mensa. This same altar is further distinguished by a white statuary marble figure of our Lord in the tomb, which is carved in half relief under the mensa.

The platforms of the six side altars are made of grey Tennessee marble which also forms a wide belt of wainscoting around the nave of the church. To offset the close shades of color between the latter and the wall, a narrow strip of reddish Numidian marble was added to the grey Tennessee stone.

The high altar is "a thing of beauty." "Its simplicity of design and faultlessness of proportion are enhanced by the delicate contrasts of color and richness and artistic excellence of the carving." (12) Surmounted by a columned cupola the top of which is 25 feet from the floor, it rightly occupies the most commanding position in the church. For years the dome was further enhanced by a brilliant flood of light emanating through the openwork of its highly polished surface, a custom which was discontinued because it was considered unliturgical.

It is true that the main altar, considered in itself, possesses a high artistic value, but it is a regrettable fact that it is wholly unsuitable for its present location. Both from a practical and a liturgical point of view it is blameworthy. Liturgical use would require an altar in such a place to have no part higher than the mensa and to be overshadowed by a baldachino. Practically considered, also, this latter arrangement would be more satisfactory because both the monks in choir and the congregation in the church would have a full view of the functions at the altar, whereas the celebrant cannot be seen from the choir as it now stands.

The cause of this unsatisfactory state of affairs is easily explained. The original plans specified that the altar be placed in the apse where the console for the choir organ now rests. The special stone reinforcement intended for its support still stands under this spot in the foundation. In the latter part of the last century, however, the Rt. Rev. Archabbot visited Rome, where he noticed that the altars in many Roman cathedrals, like Saint Peter's, Saint Paul's outside the Walls, Saint Mary Major, to mention but a few, are located in the body of the church. This arrangement appealed to the Rt. Rev. Archabbot as being very practical. The thought naturally occurred to him that an altar located at one extreme of the Archabbey church would be out of the convenient vision of the majority of the congregation. Moreover, this defect would be emphasized by the presence of choir stall and monks between the altar and congregation.

It was therefore decided, and correctly so, to place the altar in its present position. The objection might still be raised that the altar should have been built to suit that position. It must be remembered, however, that the liturgical movement, which has revived the spirit of a proper liturgy, and has more or less established a definite propriety for church furnishings, was not yet known at that time. There was no thought in the minds of the builders about a liturgically correct altar. For many years the altar received unstinted praise for its beauty and its high artistic value and it was not until the laity and clergy were made liturgically conscious by the praiseworthy efforts of the liturgists that its intrinsic merit was questioned.

Whether these qualities should be sacrificed to liturgically correctness by the replacement of another altar has evidently been decided in the negative, although the time may yet come when this decision will be reversed.

Organ

One of the proudest features of the church at the time of its completion was its grand organ. The original design and specifications are the work of Mr. Robert Hope-Jones, an English organ-builder of international reputation, but later some changes were made by Rev. Fr. Louis Haas, the head of the music department at that time; he also negotiated the purchase of the organ and to him is due most of the credit for having given such a fine instrument to Saint Vincent.

Pages could and have been filled in a detailed description of this instrument, but realizing both the average reader's disgust for details and the writer's own inability to give an exact account of such a complicated and unfamiliar affair, a short quotation has been borrowed from the booklet *Saint Vincent* which probably contains all the information that may interest the casual observer.

"Among the furnishings of the church, the grand, electrically controlled organ of fifty-two speaking stops built by the Austin Organ Company, of Hartford, Conn., stands forth with well-merited prominence. The great delicacy and characteristic quality of tone in the various stops, the dignified power of the full organ, without a suggestion of harshness, and the perfect blending of the whole into one massive and brilliant tone...these qualities, joined with ease and accuracy of action and control, put this instrument into the foremost rank of its kind.

"The organ consists of eight sections, or distinct organs, distributed over four manuals and pedal...one Great Organ, two Swells, one Orchestral, one Choir, one Solo, and two Pedal Organs having a 32 ft. Magnation foundation. Two electric blowers, one of three, the other of ten horsepower, supply wind under three pressures—5 inch, 10 inch, and 15 inch—giving to each family of stops the most favorable conditions of a speech. The pipes stand upon the Austin air chests, which mark a radical departure from conventional methods in organ construction. One can enter into these chests as into a room, and find the whole working mechanism within view and easy reach—a valuable arrangement in every case of complicated machinery, such as a large organ must necessarily be.

"The four-manual consoles, one placed in the choir, the other—nearly two hundred feet away—in the east gallery, are exact duplicates and so connected electrically that either the gallery organ (38 stops) or the choir organ (14 stops) or both together may be played from either position. This feature is quite unique in organ construction, and called for the highest skill and ingenuity on the part of the builders." (13)

Unfortunately this same description cannot truthfully be applied to the organ today. Since 1935 the large section in the gallery has been completely silenced. Up to that time the thunderous and majestic recitals given every Sunday after Vespers had maintained its longstanding reputation as an extraordinary instrument. Since then, however, its claim to fame consists solely in its imposing appearance.

The cause of the organ's short-lived career can be attributed chiefly to unfavorable atmospheric conditions. In the first place, the quick changes of temperature and excessive humidity to which its delicate parts have been subjected has caused untold damage. Then, too, the many beehive coke ovens in the district charged the air with dust and smoke that did much to deteriorate the air passages. Under the present ideal conditions of pure and fresh air it is difficult to imagine that there was a time when clear visibility in this district was limited to a few hundred yards. Yet such was the case, and delicate musical instruments are no match for dust laden air.

Even the smaller sanctuary organ had become so deteriorated that it required a complete renovation, which it received in 1937, but it too has lost all indications of its former greatness.

Stations of the Cross

The stations of the Cross, eight feet high and four feet wide, "are of ivory-tint composition with exquisitely modelled figures in half relief, and come from the art-loving Munich (Bavarian Art Co.). They are set in decorated frames of staff, which may, perhaps, at some future time, be supplanted by such of bronze or marble."

Communion Rail

Like the altars, the Communion rail is made of Carrara or architectural statuary marble inlaid with yellow sienna. Its high polish and refreshing whiteness blend harmoniously with the light background of marble floor and altars, yet it seems to stand out as something that has its own claim to beauty. The three gates, a double one in the center and two single ones in the sides, are made of an intricate pattern of bronze, which according to V. A. Fucigna of New York City, the contractor, are "the best that could be obtained as far as execution and workmanship."

Mosaic Floor

Despite 35 years of wear of shuffling feet, the marble floors still present a very clean and artistic appearance. The small cube-like blocks are set in mosaic fashion in such a way that the predominant gray field is checkered at regular intervals by block-like formations of light brown marble. The same kind of stone of various colors also forms a border around the whole. Every part of free floor space is composed of these mosaics, all of which were imported from Italy by the contractors, Pellarin and Co. of New York City.

Pews, Choir Stalls, Confessionals

In keeping with the general idea of a fireproof building, but little wood went into the construction of the Archabbey Church. What was used—mostly as roof-supporting rafters—is of solid oak, grown on Saint Vincent's own land on the Chestnut Ridge and prepared in her own workshops by her own lay brothers.

In the furnishings, however, wood was used in abundance, and most appropriately so. Most of this, too, is of oak, but not all grown on the lands of Saint Vincent. Only the choir stalls behind the main altar and the pews of the basement chapel came from that source. These incidentally, were also carved by the lay brothers in the monastery carpenter shop.

The pews for the congregation were furnished by H. J. Engbet of New Baltimore, Pa. Charles E. McKenry of Pittsburgh, Pa., furnished the red oak confessionals and executed all the carving by hand.

Pulpit, Acoustics

The pulpit "of quartered white oak stained semi-antique of color to match the other furniture in the church;....built up in the very best and most workmanlike manner" was made by R. Geissler of 56 West 8th Saint, New York City. (14) The carving "done in the most artistic manner" is rather elaborate. Of special interest are the carved brackets over the capitals which appropriately represent the symbols of the four Evangelists, the composers of the words that are to be proclaimed from the pulpit. The emblems have their origin in the description of the vision of the prophet Ezechiel as related in the first chapter of his prophecy, and in the vision of Saint John which is contained in the Apocalypse.

And as for the likeness of their faces: there was the face of a man in front, and the face of a lion on the right side of all the four: and the face of an ox, on the left side of all the four: and the face of an eagle at the back.

And their wings were stretched upward: two wings of every one were joined, and two covered their bodies. (Ezechiel, I, 10-11)

The human head represents Saint Matthew, because he opens his Gospel with Christ's human ancestry. Saint Mark opens his narrative with the mission of Saint John the Baptist, who was the "voice of one crying in the wilderness." Symbolically the lion, as king of the animal kingdom in the wilderness, is taken to represent Saint Mark. Because the first chapter of Saint Luke's Gospel is concerned with an account of the priest, Zachary, whose duty it was to offer sacrifice, the winged ox was selected as the most suitable symbol for Saint Luke. "In the beginning was the Word, and the Word was with God, and the Word was God." Thus begins the Gospel of Saint John, who carries us to heaven itself. Appropriately then, was the eagle, the denizen of the skies, chosen as the emblem of the fourth Evangelist.

The oval shaped sounding board, with its representation of a white dove in a sky of blue, is the work of J. J. Holwell & Son of Brooklyn, New York. Although it is mounted so that it can be swung freely in any direction, the primary purpose of this free action—to enable "the preacher to be heard evenly and distinctly in all parts of the church" has not at all been realized. (15) It is agreed by all who have listened to the confused reverberation of sounds in the Archabbey Church that its acoustical properties are by no means satisfactory. The prolonged clashing of echoes that follows every sound often proves disastrous to sermons and musical renditions and always grates on the ears of the congregation. Although it has always been realized that this defect should be remedied, yet nothing has been done in actual improvement. It is evident, however, that at least once corrective plans were considered because there is extant a letter in which W. R. C. Rowan, an acoustical engineer in Pittsburgh, wrote to the Rt. Rev. Archabbot that "the adjustment of the acoustical properties of the Church involves a by no means simple problem....However it is entirely possible to correct the trouble."

Bricks, Stones

As mentioned before, all the bricks used in the church were kilned at Saint Vincent within a stone's throw from the scene of construction. This brickyard, with a daily capacity of 15,000 bricks, was located on the site of the Saint Vincent stadium. Several brothers were employed there, but most of the work was done by outside help. As a point of special interest it may be well to note that all the buildings at Saint Vincent except the college, the northeast wing of the Archabbey, the Seminary and the Sisters' Convent, were built of bricks made in its own brickyards, located at various times on four different spots on the campus.

The stone for the foundation of the church was quarried at the Kuhn farm and at Donahoe Station, both several miles west of Saint Vincent. The indentation made in the landscape by the removal of the stones is still noticeable at these places today. The red sandstone that forms part of the foundation above ground was taken from a quarry in Ohio. According to the original plans the whole structure was to be of this type of stone but, as mentioned in the first part of this work, its high cost forbade such a procedure. The window sills are made of a white sandstone from Fayette County. To qualify it as white would seem today to apply a misnomer, but such was its original color. The excessive smoke referred to above in the description of the organ has left its traces on the stones too. Their damp surfaces easily absorbed black particles from the air. The terra cotta, which forms some of the exterior trimmings has retained most of its freshness because its inability to absorb moisture has rendered it impervious to the attacks of smoke. Consequently, for the sake of brevity, it can be said that all the exterior trimmings which are conspicuous by their light color are made of terra cotta. It was furnished by the Perth Amboy Terra Cotta Co. of New Jersey. Berean sandstone from Indiana was used for the bases and capitals within the church.

One of the most outstanding features of the Archabbey Church from the viewpoint of beauty is the double row of highly polished columns of dark red granite. There are 18 of these mammoth monoliths, eight of which are required for the support of the nave. These are fourteen feet five inches high, two feet and two inches in diameter, and weigh four and a half tons each. Six others, twelve feet and seven inches in height and one and a half feet in diameter bear the weight of the two balconies in the transepts and the choir loft. The other four, each having the same height as the last mentioned and the same diameter as the first mentioned, are used in the choir.

Other types of granite and stone were considered for the pillars, but these Peterhead granite shafts were chosen as the most suitable both for beauty and for practicality. They were procured through the firm of Batterson and Eisele of New York City and came direct from Aberdeen, Scotland.

The sanctuary roof is supported by four trefoil columns of solid stone blocks. Their 12 1/2 foot circumference produce an unmistakable sense of massiveness and give the impression that they were built to stand until the end of time.

As mentioned before, the half columns on the walls of the church as well as those at the four corners of the sanctuary, having no weight to support, are built of brick covered with plaster in an imitation stone effect. As sin-ning against true art they are reprehensible, but economically they were more satisfactory than stone pillars. The same fault can be imputed to the wooden railings of the three galleries which are painted to give the appearance of stone; likewise to all the arches, which are painted to represent stone vaussoirs.

Electric Lights

Five hundred and fifty electric lights for one church seem like a large order. Yet such was the contract given to the Wester Gas Fixture Co. of Toledo, Ohio, and such was the extent of the lighting system in the Archabbey Church. In view of the modern high-voltage lights, the above figure would seem unintelligible. It must be realized, however, that thirty years ago the power of ordinary electric bulbs did not exceed 60 watts. To supply a large church with sufficient light would require a larger number of lamps than at present. With the advent of more brilliant lights the number of bulbs was reduced without the sacrifice of illumination. On the contrary, because of the fact that one 200-watt bulb will furnish more light than five 40-watt bulbs, the efficiency of the lighting system could be very effectively and economically increased. Accordingly, the large chandelier in the sanctuary dome, which formerly contained 100 lamps, gave less light than the sixteen 200-watt bulbs which it now contains. Similarly the 50 lights in the chandeliers of the nave and choir were replaced by twelve 200-watt lights.

All the larger chandeliers are fitted with windlasses to enable them to be lowered to the church floor with a minimum of effort. The electric power is generated by Saint Vincent's own power house located about 500 feet southeast of the church.

Chapter II Notes

(1) *Christian Art,* Nov. 1907, p. 82.
(2) *Christian Art,* Nov. 1907, pp. 84-85.
(3) *Saint Vincent Journal,* Vol. XIV, p. 468.
(4) *The Monks of the West,* Vol. V, p. 175. Count de Montalembert.
(5) *The Monks of the West,* Vol. V, p. 176, Count de Montalembert.
(6) *Saint Vincent,* p. 54.
(7) *Christian Art,* Nov. 1907, p. 86.
(8) *Saint Vincent Journal,* Vol. XIII, p. 380.
(9) *Saint Vincent,* p. 53.
(10) *Christian Art,* Nov. 1907, p. 86.
(11) *Christian Art,* Nov. 1907, p. 86.
(12) *Saint Vincent,* p. 52.
(13) *Saint Vincent,* p. 52
(14) Quotation from contract.
(15) Quoted from letter written by the contractor to the pastor of the Archabbey Church.

Chapter III

An account of the additions and improvements made upon the Archabbey Church since its consecration.

Statues

The most outstanding addition to the church since its completion is the heroic-size statue of the founder of Saint Vincent Archabbey, Archabbot Boniface Wimmer, which was unveiled September 1, 1931.

It was only fitting that Saint Vincent should pay high honors to a man of such moral and intellectual worth, who, in the true pioneer spirit, left behind him home, confreres, and friends to bring the consolations of religion to the scattered settlers of woody Western Pennsylvania. He nursed the tender, uncertain, and starving little community in its infancy; he encouraged and nourished it till it could stand alone, and when it was sufficiently developed to shift for itself, his guiding hand still shaped its ways and brought it to its full stature as a flourishing Benedictine Community.

"After so many days of waiting the event which so many of us had hoped to see enacted was consummated under a beaming September sky and to the fanfare of trumpets when the linen cloth veiling the statue of the late Boniface Wimmer, O.S.B., first Archabbot of Saint Vincent Archabbey and the pioneer Benedictine of the New World was pulled away by the Rt. Rev. Abbot Ernest Helmstetter, O.S.B., president of the American Cassinese Congregation." (1)

The Rt. Rev. Hugh C. Boyle, D.D., bishop of Pittsburgh, celebrated the solemn Pontifical Mass at 9:00. He was assisted by the Very Rev. Felix Fellner, prior, as Archpriest; the Rev. Frs. Ernest Gensheimer and Nepomucene Hruza as Deacons of Honor; by Rev. Fr. Gregory McAtee as deacon of the Mass and by Rev. Fr. Edward Wenstrup as subdeacon. The following dignitaries were seated in the sanctuary:

Rt. Rev. Joseph Schrembs, Bishop of Cleveland; Rt. Rev. Philip McDevitt, Bishop of Harrisburg; Rt. Rev. Ernest Helmstetter, O.S.B., Abbot of Saint Mary's Abbey, Newark, N.J., Praeses of the American Cassinese Congregation; Rt. Rev. Alfred Koch, O.S.B., Archabbot of Saint Vincent; Rt. Rev. Bernard Menges, O.S.B., Abbot of Saint Bernard Abbey, Saint Bernard, Alabama; Rt. Rev. Vincent Huber, O.S.B., Abbot of Saint Bede's Abbey, Peru, Ill.; Rt. Rev. Valentine Kohlbeck, O.S.B., Abbot of Saint Procopius Abbey, Lisle, Ill.; Rt. Rev. Martin Veth, O.S.B., Abbot of Saint Benedict's Abbey, Atchison, Kansas; Rt. Rev. Alcuin Deutsch, O.S.B., Abbot of Saint John's Abbey, Collegeville, Minn.; Rt. Rev. Vincent Taylor, O.S.B., Abbot Ordinary of Belmont Abbey, Belmont, N.C.; Rt. Rev. Bertrand Dolan, O.S.B., Abbot of Saint Anselm's Abbey, Manchester, N.H.

"The Rt. Rev. Joseph J. Schrembs, D.D., delivered the address at the unveiling and whole passages of his inspired words will outlive their speaker. The Latrobe American Legion Bugle and Drum Corps and the Latrobe American Legion Band were present and played for the procession, attended Mass, and played before and after the unveiling." (2)

The statue is the work of Ferdinand Seeboeck, an Austrian by birth, who practiced his art in Rome. He and his work are well known and highly praised in the Eternal City and in many places of Europe. He was a close friend of the late Pope Pius X, of whom he executed a bust which is preserved in the Vatican Picture Gallery.

The statue was ordered by the late Rt. Rev. Archabbot Aurelius during his visit to Rome in 1929. The contract called for a six foot statue, but when the sculptor placed his plaster model in a miniature replica of its intended surroundings, he realized that it would be out of proportion. Accordingly, he wrote to the Very Rev. Felix Fellner, prior, who since the death of the Archabbot several months before, had charge of the affair, and strongly urged the making of a larger statue. Having received the consent of the Chapter, the Very Rev. Prior ordered the present twelve foot, hollow two ton statue.

Ferdinand Seeboeck made the clay and plaster model, but the bronze was poured in the foundry of Signor Bruno, situated a short distance from the famous church of Saint Lawrence. As a curious bit of information, it may be stated that the surplice Archabbot Boniface is represented as wearing was once used by the late Pope Pius X. The clay model, namely, from which the statue was copied, was dressed by the sculptor in this precious garment.

On the reredos of four of the side altars are the statues of Sts. Benedict, Scholastica, Maurus, and Placidus, which were erected a short time after the bronze statue of Archabbot Boniface Wimmer. They are the work of the same artist and the cost was partly paid by a bequest of the Geeck family of Saint Marys, Pa.

The two Carrara marble statues that adorn either side of the sanctuary were solemnly blessed March 22, 1914. The ceremony was performed by Rt. Rev. Archabbot Leander; Rev. Daniel Kaib, O.S.B. preached an eloquent sermon on the veneration of images. The statues were donated by the Peter Straub Family of Saint Marys and the Eichenlaub Family of Erie, Pa.

The making of these latter statues was negotiated by the late Rev. Ambrose Kohlbeck, O.S.B., who at the time was professor of dogmatic theology at the international Benedictine College of Saint Anselm's in Rome. They were carved by an Italian artist, Giovanni Sugari.

Reliquaries

One of the least noticed and noticeable additions to the furnishing is the set of new reliquaries acquired in 1931. They are a special gift of the various parishes under the care of Saint Vincent priests given to the Rt. Rev. Archabbot Alfred in memory of his solemn blessing. Later part of the expenses was also defrayed by an inheritance of Ven. Brother Anselm Spitz, O.S.B. Designed by Rev. Malachy Brawley, O.S.B., they were made by the Herren Co. of Pittsburgh. In harmony with the architecture of the church they are Romanesque in style; moreover the four larger ones are especially adapted to the high altar in as much as they have the same design as the tabernacle. Since gold had already been used extensively for the furnishings of the altars, copper was preferred for the material of the reliquaries for the purpose of constraint. They are nevertheless valuable because they are made of solid copper of the same pure quality throughout.

There are 20 reliquaries in all, four large ones for the high altar and two smaller ones for each of the side altars. They contain about 175 documented relics, the names of which are appended at the end of this treatise.

Grotto Basement Chapel

For many visitors the most favored spot in the Archabbey Church is probably the Grotto of Lourdes in the basement chapel. It is truly a devotional nook, where the troubles and distractions of the world fade away and yield to a feeling of peace and contentment. Many newly ordained priests choose this hallowed place for the celebration of their first Holy Mass, and many husbands and wives betroth eternal love kneeling at the feet of the Lady of Lourdes.

The whole grotto was built by Mr. Francis Aretz, a well known Pittsburgh sculptor. He carved the statue of the Blessed Virgin out of Carrara marble. All the other carving, including the six angels on the walls, the intervening ornaments and decorative frieze was also executed by his hand. With the exception of the statue of the Blessed Virgin all the work, including the altar and figure of Saint Bernadette, was done in cement stone, harmoniously shaded to produce a proper blending of colors. The altar and candelabra are much admired for their artistic value and liturgical correctness. The pews were designed by John T. Comes and fashioned in Saint Vincent's carpenter shop.

The shrine was constructed in thanksgiving for favors bestowed upon the monastery by the Mother of God. It was blessed by Rt. Rev. Leander Schnerr on Sunday, May 23, 1920.

"A church within a church," is an epithet that aptly characterizes the basement chapel of the Archabbey Church. It was not originally intended to serve its present purpose, for until 1907 it was but an unused apartment. In that year it was furnished with pews that were made by Saint Vincent carpenters. Four altars were also installed, the largest of which is the handiwork of Ven. Brother Cosmas Wolf. The chapel was fitted up to serve the needs of the Slovak parishioners, who were then rapidly increasing. Since many of them could not understand the sermons given in the Archabbey Church, they were provided with a special curate who would tend to their spiritual wants, hold services for them, and preach to them in their native tongue.

Interior Renovation

This work can be appropriately concluded with an improvement that was all-embracing in its effects. In August, 1933 the church was invaded by a crew of men under the supervision of A. H. Rodkey of Erie, Pa., bent on the renovation of the interior walls. In short order a scaffolding of pipes was fitted together, and the first clean spots were soon seen contrasting with the soiled ceiling. With marvelous dexterity the scaffold was reduced or extended to any shape or size and rolled over the pews or floor from one end of the building to the other. Like the shapeless amoeba it glided over altars, confessionals, and pews and around pillars and arches and assumed a hundred shapes to fit every nook and corner in the edifice. For three and a half months the troop of cleaners rubbed away the 35 years of accumulated dust and left the interior of the house of God as fresh, as brilliant, and as clean as it was when on August 24, 1905, it was dedicated to the service of the Spotless Lamb.

Chapter III Notes

(1) *Saint Vincent Journal*, Vol. XLI, p. 3.
(2) *Saint Vincent Journal*, Vol. XLI, p. 4.

Appendix

A list of the Saints whose relics are enclosed in the new copper reliquaries of Saint Vincent Archabbey Church.

List of Saints whose relics are in the large reliquaries.
Aloysius, C. (tomb)*
Alpherius, first abbot and founder of the monastery of Cava.
Ambrose, Ep. C. D. (2)**
Anselm, Ep. C. D. (2)
Anthony, Abb. C.
Athanasius, Ep. C. D.
Augustine, Ep. C. D.
Barbara, V. M.
Basil, Ep. C. D.
Beatrix II of Este
Benedict, founder of Benedictines (2)
Benedict, founder of Benedictines (tomb)
Bernard, Abb. C. D. (veil in which his bones were wrapped.)
Boneventure, Ep. C.
Bruno, Abb. C.
Candidus, M.
Cecilia, V. M.
Charles Borromeo
Clare of Montefalco
Cletus, M.
Constabilis, fourth abbot of Cava
Cyril, Ep. D.

Dominic, (clothing)
Felix, M.
Francis de Sales
Francis Xavier (tomb)
Gregory the Great (2)
Gregory Nazienzen (veil in which his bones were wrapped)
Gregory of Nyssa (veil in which his bones were wrapped)
Hilary, Ep. C. D.
James, Ap. M. (2)
Jane de Chantal
John Chrysostom, Ep. C. D.
John Nepomucene, M.
Justin, M.
Leo I, P. (2)
Leo, second abbot of Cava
Lucia, V. M.
Lucius, M. (2)
Marcellinus, M.
Maurus, Abb. C.
Pancratius, M.
Paul of the Cross
Paul, Ap.
Perpetua, M.
Peter, Ap.
Peter Chrysologus, Ep. C. D.
Peter, third abbot of Cava
Philip, Ap.
Placidus, (relics of his companions)
Rose of Lima
Scholastica, V.
Sebastian, M.
Severus, M.
Stephen, protomartyr
Theodore, M.
Theresa of the Child Jesus
Thomas Aquinas (3)
Timothy, Ep. M.
Ubald (clothing)
Vitalis, M.
Vincent de Paul
Zeno (relics of his companions)

    Besides these, there are also particles said to be of the manger and tomb of Christ, from the table on which the Last Supper was eaten, and two particles of the home of the Blessed Virgin.

List of Saints whose relics are in the small reliquaries:
Agatho, M.
Agnes, V.
Albert the Great
Alexius
Aloysius Gonzaga (2)
Ambrose, Ep. C. D. (2)
Ananias, Disciple of our Lord (2)
Anselm, Ep. C. D.
Antoninus, Ep.
Athanasius, Ep. C. D. (2)
Augustine, Ep. C. D. (cotton in which his bones were wrapped)
Balbina, V. M.
Barbara, V. M. (3)
Barnaba, V.
Basil, Ep. C. D. (2)
Basil, M. (2)
Beatrix II of Este (hair)
Benedict, Abb.
Benedict, M.
Benedict Joseph Labre (clothing)
Bibiana, V. M.
Bonaventure, Ep. C. D.
Boniface, Ep. M. (2)
Candida, V. M.
Catherine, V. M.
Chrysanthus, M. (2)
Clara, V. (2)
Clarida, M.
Cletus, M.
Conrad of Parzham, C.
Constabilis
Cure of Ars
Dionysius the Areopagite (2)
Fortunatus, M.
Francis of Assisi (tunic)
Gertrude, V.
Gordian, M. (2)
Gregory the Great, (3)
Gregory VII
Gregory Nazienzen
Ignatius Loyola (tomb)
Irenaeus, M.
Jerome, Priest C. D.
John the Baptist (2)

John Berchmans (ashes of his bones)
John Bosco
John Damascene
Joseph, Spouse of B.V.M. (tomb and home)
Justin, M. (2)
Justina, V.
Leo I, P. (2)
Leonard of Port Maurice (handkerchief)
Lucidus, M.
Magnus, M.
Marcellinus
Marcellus, M.
Margaret of Cortona
Margaret, V.
Martin, Ep.
Mary, Blessed Virgin (tomb)
Matthias, Ap.
Pancratius, M. (2)
Paul, Ap.
Paul of the Cross
Perpetua, M. (3)
Peter, Ap.
Peter, Ep.
Philip Neri (clothing)
Philomena, V. M.
Pius V, P.
Probus, M. (2)
Scholastica, V.
Sebastian, M. (2)
Sevatus, M.
Severus, M. (2)
Stanislaus Kostka
Sylvester, P.
Thaddeus, Ap. (2)
Theodore, M. (2)
Theresa of the Child Jesus (shirt)
Trier (Martyrs of)
Thomas Aquinas
Urban, M.
Ursula, V.
Utto, Abb.
Valerian, M.
Vitalis, M.
Vincent, M. (3)
Walburga, V.
Xystus, P. M. (2)

*The relics are particles of the body unless otherwise specified.

** **If there are more than one, the number of relics will be given in this manner.**

Apostolic Brief N. 136/1955
Declaring the Saint Vincent Archabbey Church a Minor Basilica
Pope Pius XII
In Perpetual Memory of the Event—(The Centenary Celebration)

As a fountain of light, radiating the surrounding region, a Holy Temple in honor of St. Vincent de Paul was joined to the Benedictine monastery, or as it is called, an archabbey with the same name (St. Vincent Archabbey) in Latrobe of the United States of North America. From here then the Catholic Faith was propagated everywhere; from here the monks went forth to found new monasteries, schools and minor seminaries (centers of Christian training). This very temple indeed is of ample magnitude, venerable and the very structure of the stone and walls was built in what they call a 'Baroque-Romanesque' style.

There (in the Temple) for veneration are statues and images depicted in elegant colors; altars that shine in varying colors of marble; and sacred furnishings which are adorned with precious metals. Moreover there are lofty towers which are attached to this venerable house of God and underneath the main Church there is a spacious Crypt suitable for carrying out divine functions. (H) When this abbey of St. Vincent and at the same time the American Cassinese Monastic Congregation completed the centenary of its founding, our Beloved Son Denis Strittmatter, President of the Congregation and Archabbot of St. Vincent, which we mentioned above, humbly petitioned us, that for augmenting the joy of this celebration, to grant the honor and title of 'Minor Basilica' to that Temple (Church). Viewing the request in so worthy a matter and as a favor to our Venerable Brethren, Hamleto John Cicognoni, Titular Archbishop of Laodicea in Phrygia and Apostolic Delegate of the United States of North America, and Hugh Aloysius Lamb, Bishop of the diocese of Greensburg in whose territory that Holy Temple is situated, we have decided to comply willingly with the request.

Therefore, from this decree of the Sacred Congregation of Rites, with certain knowledge and mature deliberation, and from the fullness of our Apostolic Authority, in virtue of the request, once and for always, we elevate the Sacred Temple of St. Vincent de Paul in Latrobe, within the see of the diocese of Greensburg, to the honor and dignity of a Minor Basilica with all the rights and privileges attached to it and which properly accompany this title.

Withstanding everything to the contrary,

We declare, establish and decide that the present letters of request continually stand forth and remain firm, valid and efficacious and that the effects of the request have the nature of being complete and integral, we most fully favor and support the request for those to whom it pertains or can pertain now and in the future, therefore, we rightly judge and define the request as such. If it should happen that anyone tries to change any part of the request from any other authority whatsoever, knowingly or unknowingly, it becomes null and void instantly.

Given from Castle de Gandolfo, under the seal of the fisherman's ring, on this the 22nd day of the month of August, in the year 1955, the seventeenth year of our Pontificate.

From a special mandate of His Holiness
Gildo Cardinal Brugnola
In charge of public affairs of the church
Apostolic Brief

Many of the early photographs of the Basilica construction were made using dry plate photographic techniques, resulting in delicate glass plate negatives.

Early cameras were large and boxy, with a focusing glass on the back of the camera which required the photographer to drape a dark cloth over his head and shoulders in order to capture the image.

Pre-coated dry plates could be stored and processed when convenient, unlike the earlier wet plate technique, in which the photographer only had three to five minutes from the time the photo was taken to develop the image. (If he waited too long, the light sensitivity of the original coating would dry out, which is why the process was called 'wet plate'). In the 1870s, a gelatin-silver bromide was developed which increased sensitivity to light, and allowed for creation of dry plates with less exposure time. Dry plate techniques allowed photographers to leave heavy chests filled with chemicals and their darkroom tents at home, and just concentrate on making images while afield. These glass plate negatives were easily broken, and an uneven application of chemicals frequently caused flaws in the final product. The plates also experience deterioration with the passage of time.

Many times prints were made from these negatives, from which a good, recoverable image was possible. Other times, only the glass plates themselves remained. Fortunately, modern technology makes it possible to recover images from these fragile plates. Images from these glass plates were reproduced by scanning and retouching using Adobe Photoshop ® software on an Apple G4® computer. Some were in excellent condition and only required minimal retouching. Others were in poor condition and even with today's technology it was difficult to bring out the details and airbrush flaws out of the photos. An example is the photo on the left, which is shown exactly as it was scanned from the glass plate. The best efforts at recovery included cropping the foreground, replacing the sky with a neutral gray, and attempting to bring out as much detail as possible (see top photo). No prints from this particular glass plate negative have been found.

Bibliography

Anderson, Kenneth and Agnes Schickel Anderson, with additions by Kenneth Anderson, Jr. *The Architecture of William Schickel.*

Girard, Andre. "Illustrating the Canticles," *Liturgical Arts,* August 1950. Volume 18, Number 4. Pages 85-86, 94-95. N.Y., N.Y.

Haas, Louis G., O.S.B. *St. Vincent's. Souvenir of the Consecration of the New Abbey Church, August 24, 1905, on the Fiftieth Anniversary of the Elevation of St. Vincent's to an Abbey.* St. Vincent's Print, 1905. © Saint Vincent Archabbey.

Kline, Omer U., O.S.B. *The Sportsman's Hall Parish, Later Named Saint Vincent, 1790-1846.* Originally published by Saint Vincent Archabbey Press, Latrobe, Pennsylvania, in 1990. © Saint Vincent Archabbey.

Oetgen, Jerome. *An American Abbot: Boniface Wimmer, O.S.B., 1809-1887.* Washington, D.C.: The Catholic University of America Press. First edition, 1976. Second edition, 1997.

Oetgen, Jerome. *Mission to America: A History of Saint Vincent Archabbey, The First Benedictine Monastery in the United States.* Washington, D.C.: The Catholic University of America Press. First edition, 2000.

Raila, Donald, O.S.B. "The Enigma of Archabbot Andrew: A Man Who Knew His Limits," *Saint Vincent Magazine,* Summer 1988, Pages 6-7.

Rupprecht, Melvin C., O.S.B., *Saint Vincent Archabbey Church,* Originally written in partial fulfillment of the requirements for the degree Bachelor of Arts, Saint Vincent College, Department of History, June 3, 1938. © Saint Vincent Archabbey.

Schaut, Quentin, O.S.B. *The Crypt,* Saint Vincent Archabbey Press, 1949. © Saint Vincent Archabbey.

Selle, Paulinus J., O.S.B. *Building Construction at Saint Vincent, An Historical Treatise.* Originally written in partial fulfillment of the requirements for the degree Bachelor of Arts, Saint Vincent College, Department of History, Latrobe, Pennsylvania, June, 1936. © Saint Vincent Archabbey.

Various authors. *The Saint Vincent Journal.* Volumes 1892-1905.

Illustration and Photo Credits

Kenneth Anderson, Jr.: 12

Emil Kuhar: 14, 111-117, 119-120, 122-128, 130-137

L'Osservatore Romano: 5, 6

Bill Malloy: 152

Rita Malloy: back cover

Julia Marous Straut: 153

Chuck Martin and Bill Metzger: Cover, 10-11, 14, 36, 56, 58-78, 80-91, 117-118, 121, 129, 155, 157-206, 208, 210, 212, 214-251, 257, 293-294, 315, 340

Jonathan Nakles: 13, 52, 53, 93-94, 283, 286

Kimberley A. Opatka-Metzgar: 8, 50, 54, 127, 138-149, 150, 154, 156, 252-253, 263, 265, 275-276, 284

Ronald Raimondo: 151

Fred M. Rogers: 110

Father Noel Rothrauff, O.S.B., 221

Saint Vincent Archabbey Archives: 13, 15-35, 37-53, 55, 92-107, 109, 254-255, 258-261, 264, 266-268, 270-274, 277-278, 281, 283, 286, 290-291, 341